AF573856

ANCIENT CHINESE BRONZE ART

CASTING THE PRECIOUS SACRAL VESSEL

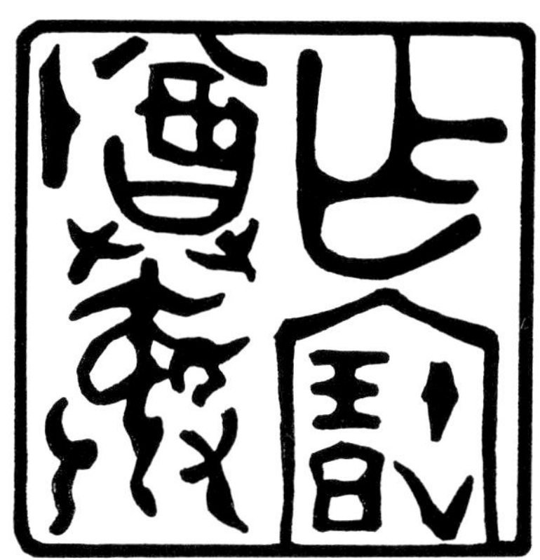

"zuo bao zun yi"

ANCIENT CHINESE BRONZE ART

CASTING THE PRECIOUS SACRAL VESSEL

W. THOMAS CHASE
Catalogue with the assistance of Jung May Lee

Introduction by K. C. Chang

CHINA HOUSE GALLERY
CHINA INSTITUTE IN AMERICA
New York City
1991

Front Cover Illustration (Cat. no. 16):
ZUN
Bronze
Early Western Zhou dynasty
11th-10th century B.C.
The Art Museum, Princeton University, Museum Purchase,
Carl Otto von Kienbusch, Jr., Memorial Collection (y1952-58)

Back Cover Illustration (Cat. no. 60):
MOLD ASSEMBLY FOR A *ZHI* VESSEL
Modern reconstruction
The Shanghai Museum

Chinese is romanized in the *pinyin* system throughout the text and bibliography except for the names of Chinese authors writing in Western languages. Chinese terms cited in Western-language titles remain in their original form and have not been converted.

Copyright © 1991 China Institute in America
Library of Congress Catalog Card Number: 91-70801

China House Gallery, New York City
Exhibition: April 20-June 15, 1991

China Institute in America is a nonpolitical, nonpartisan, bicultural organization founded in 1926 to promote better understanding between the American and Chinese peoples and to assist Chinese in the United States.

This exhibition is made possible, in part, with public funds from the New York State Council on the Arts. Major support for the exhibition and related programs is provided by: The Henry Luce Foundation, The Starr Foundation; Asian Cultural Council; Christie, Manson & Woods International, Inc.; Corning Foundation; and Grumman International, Inc.

The printing of this catalogue is made possible through the generosity of Charlotte C. and John C. Weber

Book design and production by Peter Lukic, New York
Frontispiece illustration by Hai Weilan
Produced in Hong Kong by Techpearl Printing/*Orientations*

ISBN 0-295-97126-6

Distributed by the China Institute in America, New York, and the University of Washington Press, Seattle and London.

CONTENTS

LENDERS TO THE EXHIBITION

Albright-Knox Art Gallery, Buffalo, New York

The Art Institute of Chicago

The Art Museum, Princeton University

Center for Conservation and Technical Studies, Harvard University Art Museums, Cambridge, Massachusetts

Robert H. Ellsworth

Mr. and Mrs. Myron S. Falk, Jr.

Freer Gallery of Art, Smithsonian Institution, Washington, D.C.

D. H. Graham, Jr.

Hermitage Foundation Museum, Norfolk, Virginia

Ho Shih-k'un

The Metropolitan Museum of Art, New York

Dr. and Mrs. David Morowitz, Bethesda, Maryland

The Royal Ontario Museum, Toronto

Arthur M. Sackler Gallery, Smithsonian Institution, Washington, D.C.

Richard J. Salisbury

The Seattle Art Museum

Shanghai Museum

Dr. Paul Singer

The University Museum, University of Pennsylvania, Philadelphia

Worcester Art Museum, Worcester, Massachusetts

Yale University Art Gallery

MESSAGE FROM CHINA INSTITUTE IN AMERICA

This is China Institute's first major collaboration with the Shanghai Museum. In the past, the Shanghai Museum and its director, Ma Chengyuan, have generously shared their incredible expertise and collection with New York institutions. We should be reminded and thankful for their kindness in making possible the *Great Bronze Age of China* exhibition at The Metropolitan Museum of Art in 1980, *The Chinese Scholar's Studio* at the Asia Society in 1987, their annual loan to the Ancient Chinese Galleries at The Metropolitan Museum, and now expanding further on this relationship, working with The China Institute in America to present this unique exhibition, thereby enriching and engendering the bonds of mutual personal and institutional respect and affection.

China's ancient bronze art is nothing less than a milestone in the history of human achievement. On first encountering a Chinese bronze vessel in a museum, the visitor is probably overwhelmed by its sculptural form and the powerful imagery of its decoration. It is unlike anything created in the West. We are compelled to ask, "What kind of society produced such wonderful art forms, and what did it mean to that society?" For the Chinese people, answers to these questions would unlock the early history of their civilization.

For the collector and connoisseur of these ancient Chinese bronzes, there is also delight in the subtle beauty of the various colors and textures of the vessel surface. In handling the objects — feeling their weight and their finely finished decoration — one can only admire the skill of the ancient bronze caster. Our appreciation of the object, on one hand, and our understanding of the birth of Chinese civilization, on the other, are enhanced by knowledge of how the ancient bronzes were produced.

China Institute in America and the Shanghai Museum have joined together to produce an exhibition that educates, while being visually exciting. This cooperative effort also includes the participation of various museums and private collectors. The fruits of our exchange are to be found in this catalogue, which will in turn stimulate an appreciation of a fascinating art form and a great culture.

Charlotte C. Weber
Trustee
China Institute in America

MESSAGE FROM THE SHANGHAI MUSEUM

Chinese bronzes of the Shang and Zhou dynasties are important products of the ceremonial system of a rigidly stratified aristocratic society. Bronzes were used when worshipping gods or ancestors, when embarking on punitive expeditions, and for diplomatic protocol and banquets. An important function of ceremonial bronze vessels was to record for posterity the great events of the state and the different clans in the form of inscriptions. Some of these inscriptions report historical facts of the greatest importance. Bronze vessels of this type in the collection of the Shanghai Museum serve as material witnesses of ancient Chinese history.

The Bronze Age in China ranged from the twenty-first century B.C. to the fifth century B.C. Even in the early Iron Age (5th to 3rd centuries B.C.) continued development was made in the technique of bronze casting. Over this long period of time, technical development and the quantity of production reached incredible levels.

During the past thirty years discoveries have been made in outlying border regions of bronzes of various nationalities distinct from the Shang and Zhou cultural system. These bronzes, with their unique modeling and distinctive local style, are precious material artifacts in the understanding of cultures and the intermingling of nationalities in ancient China.

As an art museum, the Shanghai Museum attaches great importance to collecting every variety of bronze with elegant modeling and decoration. These various forms and artistic styles from different periods document the glorious artistic achievements of the Shang and Zhou dynasties. The Shanghai Museum, possessing over 6,800 pieces, is both a major repository and collector of bronzes as well as a center of research.

Ma Chengyuan
Director
Shanghai Museum

FOREWORD

The technology of China's bronze production is unique in the ancient world and some of the most beautiful and historically important bronzes are represented in the halls of the Shanghai Museum. This great museum is not only a treasury of art but also a research and educational institution. In order to spread knowledge of the cultural and technological achievements of the Chinese people, the Shanghai Museum has lent us facsimiles of well-known bronzes from its collection as well as a complete set of models demonstrating the technique of piece-mold casting. In this unique exhibition, the curator has chosen Chinese bronzes from important American collections as well, not only for their great beauty but also for their instructive value.

We sincerely thank W. Thomas Chase for sharing his rare expertise in the field of bronze technology. Mr. Chase, along with J. May Lee, worked countless hours to produce the invaluable text of this catalogue. Also, we are privileged to have Professor K. C. Chang of Harvard University, one of the foremost authorities on Chinese archaeology, write the informative introduction.

This exhibition could not have been possible without our dedicated Gallery staff. J. May Lee, as Director of China House Gallery, Marsha Beitchman, as registrar, and Hai Weilan, as project assistant, all performed the colossal task of planning, organizing, corresponding, translating, and handling the myriad details necessary for a show of this complexity. Institute staff members, Aime Greene, Helena Yee, Claire Hsiang and Michael Bless, generously helped with assembling and editing the front and back matter of the catalogue. Our book designer, Peter Lukic, paced us through the production process with saintly patience. China Institute also thanks Carl Nardiello who continually develops innovative design concepts for our Gallery; and LeMar Terry who has generously given his time to advise and to light our exhibitions throughout the years.

For their part in developing the concept and goals of this exhibition, we thank the Art Committee, chaired by Dr. Annette Juliano, and the Gallery Committee, chaired by Phyllis D. Collins. Richard and Angela King provided us with working photographs and a videotape of the Shanghai material, so necessary at the planning stage of this project.

We are most grateful to The Henry Luce Foundation and The Starr Foundation for their continuous, generous support. Special sponsors of the exhibition include Christie, Manson & Woods International, Inc.; Corning Foundation; Grumman International; the Asian Cultural Council; Mr. and Mrs. Myron S. Falk, James J. Lally, and Mr. and Mrs. Richard J. Salisbury. We are also ever-indebted to our trustees, patrons, sponsors, and general membership for their support.

China Institute in America extends its gratitude and appreciation to Director Ma Chengyuan, of the Shanghai Museum, and the other lenders to this exhibition for their generosity and their part in promoting understanding between the American and Chinese people.

Finally, the Institute would like to extend a very special thank-you to Charlotte C. and John C. Weber for their generous gift of underwriting the production of this catalogue.

Charles Pei Wang
President
China Institute in America

PREFACE

The writing of this catalogue and the choice of objects for the exhibition have been complicated, not by any lack of material or ideas, but because there is simply too much to put into one exhibition. Scholars are learning more about ancient Chinese metal technology at an ever-increasing rate. In China, archaeologists continue to find bronzes showing new aspects and techniques of metal-working not known before. A stunning example is the 1989 excavation, near Taiyuan in Shanxi Province, of a group of late Zhou bronzes with inlays made from colored paste (see Zhu Qixin, "Bronze Vessels from a Spring and Autumn Period Tomb," *Orientations*, December, 1989, pp. 54-57). Researchers all over the world are also approaching the resolution of many long-standing questions, such as the exact nature of the corrosion-resistant black coatings on Chinese bronze mirrors, with work at present going forward at the British Museum in London, at the Beijing University of Iron and Steel Technology, at the University of Science and Technology, in Hefei, at the Shanghai Museum, and at the Arthur M. Sackler Gallery and Freer Gallery of Art in Washington, D.C. Because of this wealth of material, it is nearly impossible to cover this subject in the detail that one would like.

But the idea behind this complex exhibition is itself quite simple — to show how Chinese bronzes were made. Reproduction molds from the Shanghai Museum, reproduction bronzes made in similar molds, and photographs showing bronze metalworking techniques form the core of the exhibition. The other objects are intended to illustrate aspects of Chinese bronze production and to inspire the viewer with the beauty and power of the finest ancient Chinese bronzes.

In addition to educating the viewer, we sincerely hope that this exhibition will convey the idea that the ancient Chinese metalworker was a master of his craft! About 1500 years of bronze casting is represented here, from its tentative beginnings (Cat. no. 1) through the highly developed casting of the Shang (Cat. nos. 6 and 7), the vigorous art of the Western Zhou bronzes (Cat. no. 13), the sumptuous inlay of the Eastern Zhou (Cat. no. 30), to the dazzling gilding and surface coloration of the Han (Cat. nos. 37 and 38). This is the art of a high and noble craft. Of even more interest to the historian of technology, however, is mold construction, demonstrated by a series of *jue* and their molds (Cat. nos. 41 and 46-48) and the stack mold casting of the early Han dynasty (Cat. nos. 43 and 44).

Through this exhibition, we hope that the visitor will learn about ancient Chinese metal-working techniques and gain some appreciation of the achievements and problems of the ancient foundryman. To the researcher studying the technology of Chinese bronzes, nothing is more thrilling than to gain insight into what the ancient craftsman did and how he did it. We hope that the viewer will share this excitement through both the catalogue and the exhibition.

I would like to acknowledge especially the help of J. May Lee in preparing the catalogue, and to thank Annette Juliano, Chairman of the Art Committee, and the hardworking staff of China Institute in America for making this exhibition possible. I am most thankful to the Shanghai Museum and its Director, Ma Chengyuan, for making available to us their extraordinary reproduction molds, reproduction bronzes, and photographs. Most of the bronze vessels in this exhibition have been drawn from collections in the Eastern United States; I wish to acknowledge with gratitude the assistance of all the collectors and museum curators who have so generously lent their objects and their expertise in assembling this exhibition. Particular thanks also go to Dr. Paul Singer, whose primary interest is not in the technical area, but who is nonetheless willing to lend his collection and let it be viewed by those of us who delight in technological puzzles.

I owe a special debt of thanks to K. C. Chang whose introductory essay lends a much-needed historical perspective to this catalogue.

This exhibition has been made possible by

technical studies done by a great number of people, notably Lynda Zycherman and Barbara Keyser in the Freer Gallery of Art; Tony Frantz and Dick Stone in the Metropolitan Museum of Art; Stuart Fleming of the University Museum, Philadelphia; Pieter Meyers and Steve Weintraub; Robert W. Bagley of Princeton University; Noel Barnard of the Australian National University; Henry Lie of the Center for Conservation and Technical Studies, Harvard University Art Museums; and Elizabeth Childs-Johnson of New York. The assistance rendered by various staff members of the Arthur M. Sackler Gallery and the Freer Gallery of Art has been invaluable; I particularly want to thank Thomas Lawton and Lily Kecskes, for their assistance with the title; Kim Nielsen and Laveta Emory for help with photographs; the entire staff of the Department of Conservation and Scientific Research for their patience while this catalogue was being produced, and especially Elisabeth West FitzHugh for assistance with the bibliography; Jenny So for much assistance and advice; and the Director, Milo Beach for allowing me to work on this project. The catalogue went through a laborious process of refinement at the skillful hands of Elizabeth Powers, who edited the text, with valuable editorial suggestions made by Joe Geneve and Michael Bless. Finally, it could not have been done without the aid and understanding of my family, especially my wife Linda.

W. Thomas Chase
Washington, D.C.

CHRONOLOGY

Xia dynasty	21st-16th century B.C.
Erlitou period	19th-16th century B.C.
Shang dynasty	16th-11th century B.C.
Zhengzhou (Erligang) period	16th-14th century B.C.
Anyang (Yinxu) period	13th-11th century B.C.
Zhou dynasty	11th century-256 B.C.
Western Zhou	11th century-771 B.C.
Eastern Zhou	771-256 B.C.
Spring and Autumn period	(771-476 B.C.)
Warring States period	(475-206 B.C.)
Qin dynasty	221-206 B.C.
Han dynasty	206 B.C.-A.D. 220
Western Han	206 B.C.-A.D. 9
Eastern Han	25-220
Three Kingdom	221-265
Six dynasties	265-589
Sui dynasty	581-618
Tang dynasty	618-906
Five dynasties	907-960
Liao dynasty	907-1125
Song dynasty	960-1279
Northern Song	960-1127
Southern Song	1127-1279
Jin dynasty	1115-1234
Yuan dynasty	1280-1368
Ming dynasty	1368-1644
Qing dynasty	1644-1912

INTRODUCTION: THE IMPORTANCE OF BRONZES IN ANCIENT CHINA

K. C. Chang

Although small objects of copper and other metals have been encountered at Neolithic sites, the significant appearance of bronzes (alloys of copper and tin/lead) in ancient China was concurrent with the emergence of urbanism, writing, and state society associated with the earliest civilizations known in textual history as the Three Dynasties. Indeed, the material culture of the Three Dynasties period is most conspicuously distinguished by its bronzes. This period, comprised of the Xia, Shang, and Zhou dynasties, began toward the end of the third millennium B.C. and ended with the unification of China under the Qin empire in 221 B.C., a time frame almost exactly coinciding with the Chinese Bronze Age, which ended abruptly during the last phase of the Zhou dynasty, when iron came into extensive use (around the sixth century B.C.) and brought about revolutionary changes in every aspect of ancient Chinese culture and society.

Ancient Chinese bronzes became collectors' items long before modern archaeology began to substantiate the traditional textual accounts of the Three Dynasties. Admired for their artistic beauty and attributed with religious power, the bronze relics brought to light by farmers and looters found their way into imperial and private collections of antiquities just a few centuries after the end of the Bronze Age. The earliest scholarly study of these ancient bronzes still extant is the *Kaogutu*, or *Illustrated Study of Antiquities*, a catalogue of bronze and jade objects in the imperial and private collections of the Song dynasty, written in 1092 by the antiquarian Lü Dalin. Many similar studies and catalogues followed in ensuing centuries. Most of the bronzes illustrated in these books were vessels for food and drink, cast with inscriptions and decorated with designs of fantastic-looking animals and birds. On the basis of these inscriptions, which contained names and titles similar to those found in textual accounts, the antiquarian authors of these books attributed many of the illustrated bronzes to a date during the Three Dynasties.

On the question of the significance of these bronzes in Three Dynasties culture, the antiquarians mainly made two points. First, since terms in many inscriptions on the vessels were those which in ancient texts referred to the food and drink vessels used in religious ceremonies, the bronze vessels that were being catalogued were believed to be ritual vessels. Second, the antiquarians made occasional attempts to identify some of the decorative motifs on the bronzes as legendary heroes or villains described in ancient texts, and went on to make moralistic interpretations of the decoration according to such identifications. One example is the so-called *taotie* motif. The fantastic animal masks that were often seen on the decorated vessels were identified with the *taotie*, a legendary ogre in ancient texts known for its voracious greed. Bronze makers of the Three Dynasties, it was speculated, used the motif to remind their descendants of the *taotie* story and to caution them against this vice.

The Three Dynasties and bronzes became firmly linked together by modern archaeology. Beginning in the 1920s, the Western technique of excavating ancient sites and studying ancient remains in their archaeological context was introduced into China. Since then, the archaeological study of each of the Three Dynasties has not only in essence substantiated what the textual history had to say about it, but has also vastly expanded our knowledge of its cultural and social content. The Xia dynasty, many scholars believe, has as its archaeological manifestation the Erlitou Culture, discovered for the first time in 1959 at Erlitou in Yanshi County, Henan Province. With its remains now found in a number of sites in northwestern Henan and southwestern Shanxi, the Erlitou Culture had a geographical area and chronological position (ca. 2200-1500 B.C., according to radiocarbon determinations) consistent with the distribution of the Xia in space and time according to textual history. However, as yet no written record has been found to make the identification certain. Shang dynasty sites have been found by the dozens in Henan, southern Shanxi and southern Hebei, eastern Shandong, and northern Hubei. They can be grouped into two phases, characterized, respectively, by the Shang city in Zhengshou in central Henan (ca. 1500-1350 B.C.), discovered in 1950, and by Yinxu, the last Shang dynasty capital, near Anyang in northern Henan (ca. 1350-1050 B.C.), the excavation of which was begun in 1928. The latter site, Yinxu or the Ruins of Yin, has yielded the famed oracle bone inscriptions, which reveal a full-fledged writing system and contain more than enough information to enable a firm identification of the archaeological culture at the site with the latter segment of the Shang dynasty as described in the textual record. As for the Zhou dynasty, numerous archaeological sites found and excavated since the 1920s point to a predynastic phase in Shaanxi and environs and a dynastic history of development throughout a large part of North China.

At all Three Dynasties sites bronzes are invariably a conspicuous part of the archaeological inventory, which may be unique to the Chinese Bronze Age. Some civilizations did not make bronze artifacts at all, and many that did failed to reach the level of artistry and craftsmanship achieved in China; their bronzes were not the pinnacle of their material culture, and often pale when placed alongside their monumental art objects made of other materials, such as stone, lapis, marble, gold, and the like. In China, bronzes predominate in the archaeological inventory both in quantity and in sophistication when compared with art objects made of other materials. Found exclusively in burials and hoards, bronze objects are found in practically all elite burials, and their numbers, always significant, dramatically increase in proportion to the buried person's social status.

In the lineage cemeteries in the western part of Yinxu, 939 burials were excavated during the years 1969-1977. Eight hundred of the 939 tombs were furnished with mortuary objects. Among the 800, 67 contained bronze ritual vessels and 160 contained bronze weapons; these are presumably the tombs of the elite members of the lineages (Yang and Yang, p. 49). At the top of the Yinxu elite were the kings and their consorts; they were buried in the Royal Cemetery in the northern part of Yinxu. Eleven large tombs have been excavated in the Royal Cemetery, but unfortunately all had been repeatedly looted long before they were opened by archaeologists. There is, however, one tomb of a royal consort, in another part of the Yinxu site, that had remained intact prior to its scientific excavation in 1976, and its richness may give an indication of the scale of royal furnishings in bronze. This was a typical Shang dynasty elite tomb: at the bottom of a vertical earthen pit a wooden chamber had been built, and the coffined body, together with the mortuary furnishings, lay inside the chamber. The pit of this particular tomb was of middling size, only 5.6 by 4 meters at the mouth; but it contained, among other furnished goods, 468 bronze objects, including ritual vessels (some as large as three quarters of a meter tall), musical instruments, weapons, and other items. In addition to all these, there was also a cluster of 109 bronze buttons/discs (Institute of Archaeology, p. 15). From the inscriptions on some of the bronzes we know this to be the tomb of Fu Hao, a royal consort of King Wuding, who reigned near the beginning of the Yinxu period. If the looted tombs in the Royal Cemetery are indeed those of the kings, we can surely surmise that their bronze inventories must have been many times larger. The tomb pit of Fu Hao was only about 22 square meters in size at the top, whereas Liang and Gao have reported measurements of the pits of the published tombs in the Royal Cemetery ranging from 107 to 192 square meters. One can reasonably postulate that the bronze objects originally buried with the eleven Shang kings numbered in the thousands or tens of thousands. Add to this the number of bronzes buried with the dozens or hundreds of lesser nobility, and we can begin to have an idea of the truly enormous quantity of bronze objects that were buried within the confines of this single Shang city during its approximately three hundred years of existence. The same story is repeated at many other archaeological sites of the Chinese Bronze Age.

The quantity alone demands a compelling explanation of the significance of bronzes in ancient China, particularly the extreme preoccupation of ancient Chinese rulers with bronzes. As the following essay by Thomas Chase makes clear, the casting of some of the large and complicated bronze vessels by the section-mold (or piece-mold) technique was a difficult undertaking that required ample labor, precise organization, and complex management. Furthermore, before bronzes could be cast at the foundries in the cities, copper and tin ore had to be mined and smelted at the sources, and ingots had to be transported to the cities through territories that may or may not have been occupied by friendly neighbors. Thus, mining/smelting and transporting the raw materials required vast manpower and military protection. To make the enterprise even more taxing, North China was not a copper- and tin-rich country, and ancient deposits of the metals were few, thin, and easily exhausted (Shi, p. 102). It has been suggested that the reason the Three Dynasties all shifted their capital cities several times was to be near new exploitable fields from which adequate supplies of the pertinent metals could be acquired (Chang, "The system of multiple capitals...").

In view of these difficulties, the significance of the bronzes must be even greater than their numbers would suggest, and the single-minded preoccupation with bronzes on the part of the Three Dynasties rulers leads us to conclude that bronze-making was deadly serious business, that it was not just for aesthetic enjoyment or art-for-art's-sake, and that there must be compelling motives behind this vast enterprise. What could these motives be?

One answer to that question is furnished by the ancient Chinese themselves, in the legend of the Nine Bronze Tripods. In the *Zuozhuan*, a fourth-century commentary on the archival annals of the state of Lu, under the entry for 605 B.C., we read:

> In the past, when the Xia dynasty was distinguished for its virtue, . . . the nine pastors sent in the metal of their provinces. The *ding*-tripods were cast. . . . When the virtue of Jie [last king of Xia] was all-obscured, the tripods were transferred to Shang, for six hundred years. Zhou [last king of Shang] proved cruel and oppressive, and they were transferred to Zhou [dynasty].

Clearly stating that the bronze vessels of the Three Dynasties were symbols of dynastic legitimacy, the story of the Nine Tripods points to political authority and power as the motives behind the great bronze enterprise. The use of ancient Chinese bronzes points in the same direction. In the above-mentioned *Zuozhuan*, under the entry for 577 B.C., we find that a statesman made the pronouncement that "the principal affairs of the state are ritual and war." Almost all of the Three Dynasties bronzes belonged in two categories, ritual paraphernalia (mainly food and drink vessels and musical instruments) and weapons. In other words, in ancient China bronze was cast to serve the principal "affairs of the state," ritual and war.

The political purpose of war is self-evident, but ritual, too, was a crucial factor in the rulers' drive toward political preeminence during the Chinese Bronze Age. In *Art, Myth, and Ritual* (Chang 1983, p. 95), I profile those in ancient China who possessed great political authority and who wielded its power as follows:

> They were born into the right clans and (especially) lineages, married the right partners, sat at the central places, were associated with the right myths, behaved in ways deserving popular support, and last but not least had access — at best, exclusive access — to the ancestral wisdom and foresight derived from ritual, art, and writing. All these factors were requisite, of course, but the last was decisive — the determining factor that tipped the balance. The crucial question for aspirants to power in ancient China was: How do I gain access to that access? The answer was: By controlling a few key resources — above all, bronzes — and by amassing the means to control them.

The control of bronze objects meant not only control of the instruments of war and oppressive power but also control of the access to heaven (where ancestors, deities, ghosts, and their wisdom and foreknowledge could be found), because bronze was the principal material for ritual paraphernalia. Food and drink vessels, musical instruments, and such weapons as the beheading ax for human sacrifice, all for use during ritual ceremonies, were cast in bronze. These vessels, instruments, and weapons were often decorated with symbols of animals and birds, which (notwithstanding the moralistic interpretations of the antiquarians) are believed to have served in ancient Chinese rituals as intermediaries between the deities in heaven and the shamans as the representatives of the living people on earth. Thus, these bronze artifacts were essential to the Bronze Age rulers of the many contending states competing among one another for political preeminence or even political survival. Indeed, they were so essential that the Great Bronze Enterprise became the focus and the core of ancient Chinese civilization.

REFERENCES CITED

Chang, K. C. *Art, Myth, and Ritual: The Path to Political Authority in Ancient China.* Cambridge: Harvard University Press, 1983.

_______. "The System of Multiple Capitals in the Three Dynasties" (in Chinese). *Bulletin of the Institute of History and Philology, Academia Sinica* 55 (1984): 51-71.

_______. *The Archaeology of Ancient China.* New Haven: Yale University Press, 1986.

Institute of Archaeology (Chinese Academy of Social Sciences). *The Tomb of Fu Hao at Yinxu* (in Chinese). Beijing: Wenwu Press, 1980.

Liang Siyong, and Gao Quxun. *Houjiazhuang Royal Tombs* (in Chinese). Taipei: Academia Sinica, 1962-1976.

Shi Zhangru. "Bronze Metallurgy of the Yin Dynasty" (in Chinese). *Bulletin of the Institute of History and Philology, Academia Sinica* 26 (1955): 95-129.

Yang Baocheng, and Yang Xizhang. "Report of the Excavations of Human Burials in the Western District of Yinxu during 1969-77" (in Chinese). *Kaogu Xuebao* (1979) no. 1: 27-146.

ANCIENT CHINESE BRONZE ART: CASTING THE PRECIOUS SACRAL VESSEL

W. Thomas Chase

WHAT ARE CHINESE BRONZES?

The term "Chinese bronzes," as used in the catalogue, refers to Chinese ceremonial vessels cast in bronze during the Three Dynasties (Xia, Shang, and Zhou), traditionally dated from 2205 to 256 B.C. These bronzes were made in ceramic piece molds. Production of bronzes in piece molds in China extends into the Han dynasty as well, although a change to lost-wax casting takes place near the end of the Han.[1] Less is known about later Chinese bronzes, the study of which is only beginning to mature.[2]

The bronzes of the Xia, Shang, and Zhou range from small and delicate vessels up to the monumental *Si mu wu fang ding*, which weighs 875 kgs., or 1,925 pounds—almost a ton![3] Casting a vessel of this size would be a major undertaking even today. Certainly, to make castings nearly a ton in weight during the late second millennium B.C. required a scale of organization in locating ore sources, in metal extraction, and in foundry practice that is truly monumental.[4] It is also clear, as K. C. Chang points out in his Introduction, that the production of bronzes was a noble or royal prerogative. Ritual bronze vessels, identified with the ancient rulers, were both symbols and results of their power.

Other items were produced in bronze as well. These include weapons, preeminent among which is the Shang dynasty *ge* dagger-ax, and later the bronze sword. Bronze mirrors were initially produced in small numbers, but came to be a major production type in the late Zhou and Han dynasties.[5] Except for the early bronze and precious metal ornaments from sites in Gansu, jewelry does not seem to have been used at all by the ancient Chinese. One particular item of personal adornment, the belt hook, is an import from the West, along with specialized dress adopted for mounted cavalry.[6] While chariot fittings and architectural pieces were produced throughout the Shang, Zhou, and Han dynasties, other items, such as crossbow bolt mechanisms, furniture handles, and coins, increase during the Eastern Zhou and Han dynasties.

BRONZE — THE MATERIAL

From what material are these objects, generically called bronzes, made? Bronze is an alloy, a mixture of copper and tin. From the very earliest times, Chinese bronze alloys contained lead as well.[7] The alloys vary widely, from a copper content of about 95 percent with equal parts of lead and tin down to about 65 percent copper with 15 percent tin and 20 percent lead; an average composition for Shang vessels is 80 percent copper, 13 percent tin, and 7 percent lead.[8] Alloys for special uses were made as well; bronze mirrors are normally an alloy of approximately 70 percent copper, 25 percent tin, and 4 percent lead. This is an extremely hard and brittle alloy, but it has a nice silvery-white color and takes a very good polish, ideal for a mirror. Weapons, which required maximum tensile strength, usually contained very little lead, whereas Chinese coinage of the late Zhou, Qin, and Han dynasties sometimes contains 50 percent lead or more, illustrating a conscious manipulation of the lead content to produce the least-expensive alloy possible (Cat. nos. 43 and 44).

The natural color of the bronze alloy in its uncorroded state can often be seen on feet or rims where the metal has been constantly polished by handling. Some other bronzes have simply not corroded or at least have uncorroded spots, so that the original color of the bronze shows through as a warm, almost golden yellow. This is visible on the cylindrical *you* borrowed from The Metropolitan Museum of Art (Cat. no. 15). Uncorroded bronze often shows on the inside of larger pieces, especially covered vessels. In these cases the bronze has almost a "Florentine" finish, slightly rough and not shiny at all. Bronze mirrors, needless to say, were shiny, being made from harder, higher-tin alloys, capable of taking a high polish. Normally, however, bronzes are patinated, either with naturally occurring copper greens (usually malachite or copper-stained tin oxide) (Cat. no. 3) or black or dark brown as the result of surface treatment at the hands of an antiquary or dealer in China, where the dark, shiny patinas were preferred (Cat. no. 31). Techniques that we do not yet completely understand have also been used to color some bronze mirrors (Cat. no. 37).

PROPERTIES OF BRONZE ALLOYS

Properties of bronze alloys vary with the amounts of the different components. Pure copper is soft and quite reddish in color. It is difficult to cast, since it absorbs gases, especially oxygen, while it is molten in the crucible. After the metal is poured into the mold, it cools and gas bubbles form, resulting in a very porous casting. The addition of tin, which acts as a deoxidizer, helps prevent porosity. It is much easier to make sound, non-porous, castings with tin bronzes than with pure copper. The amount of tin also has an effect on the color and hardness of the final alloy: as the tin content is increased, the hue changes from reddish through yellow to white, and the hardness likewise increases.

Lead acts very differently; it does not change the hue of the cast bronze, but it does decrease the intensity or "strength" of the color. Lead, up to about 13 percent, also makes the molten alloy more fluid; above this amount fluidity decreases. This optimum percentage is used in the bronze drums common in southwestern China.[9] Lead strongly affects the mechanical properties of the cast alloy,[10] diminishing tensile strength.

Leaded bronzes have one great problem; they are impossible to form by hammering. Bronzes of a pure tin and copper alloy are malleable, and the higher-tin (approx. 22%) members of the series are especially so. These are the alloys used to make gongs and cymbals,[11] although these objects seem not to have been made in China prior to the Han dynasty. With the addition of lead (more than 0.1%), these alloys break with even moderate hammer blows. The high-tin alloys require special care during melting. Even today, metallurgists exercise particular caution to separate bell-metal production from areas in which leaded bronzes are being made out of concern for accidental contamination of the alloy with lead.

ANCIENT CHINESE KNOWLEDGE OF ALLOYS

It is clear that the ancient Chinese understood bronze formulations and knew how to manipulate the formulas in making bronzes for different uses. This knowledge is reflected in the "Six Formulas" section of the *Rites of Zhou* (Zhou Li, Kao gong qi).[12] While there is still some difficulty in interpreting these formulas, and while the formulas do not mention lead as an alloying element, it is clear that the basic principle of increasing hardness and brittleness by increasing the tin content was known at the time the *Zhou Li* was written.

The early founders, or metal casters, must have controlled alloys not only by manipulating the composition of metals in the crucible, but also by assessing the color and hardness of the finished product. The variation of color from the salmon pink or copper red of pure copper through a reddish yellow orange and orange yellow, or yellow-gray white to silver white, as one brings the tin content up from zero to about 30 percent, can be clearly seen. It is more difficult to determine the lead content by color, but scratching can reveal the increased softness, and the way the cast metal breaks when subjected to a hammer-blow can be quite definitive.

One reason for the Chinese predilection for casting over hammering metal could be that the founders were generally working with leaded alloys. These are ideal alloys for casting, but not for forging or hammering.

ZINC IN CHINESE BRONZES

The role of zinc in Chinese bronzes is still under study. When zinc is used as the alloying element instead of tin, the resulting alloy is called brass. In fact, the term "brass" is reserved for alloys that have the particular greenish-yellow cast that comes from a zinc content of 5 percent or more. Brass is extremely rare in early China.

To date, there are no examples of brasses among undoubtedly authentic bronzes from the Shang, Zhou, and early Han periods.[13] A few very early brass fragments have been discovered in reliable archaeological excavations from the late Neolithic period,[14] which may have resulted from the accidental smelting of copper ores containing zinc. Normally quite volatile when the copper is brought up to casting temperature, the zinc may have been retained in primitive casting practices in which the molten metal was kept at a high temperature for a shorter period of time. Later, when the scale of casting increased and the copper was kept at a high heat in the crucible for a longer period, any "accidental" zinc would have volatilized, resulting in a low zinc content. While one does find zinc occasionally in excavated Chinese bronzes, it is usually below one-half of one percent (0.5%). True brass in China seems to come into currency in the early sixteenth century,[15] although brasses may have come into use earlier in the Tibetan area.

HOW WERE CHINESE BRONZES MADE?

Pre-Han metal technology was based on casting and abrasive finishing. The ancient Chinese founders seem to have thought of metal as a mobile liquid. Quite simply, the metal was melted and poured into a mold where it assumed the shape of the casting space. After cooling, the metal was removed by breaking the mold; then it was rubbed with abrasives to make it shiny and beautiful. The combination of piece-mold casting followed by abrasive finishing is what gives the vessels their characteristic sharp detail on a smooth, even surface.

Piece-Mold Casting: The Basic Process

To understand casting, one must consider carefully the relationship of the model, the mold, and the finished product, and think in terms of negatives and positives. Because of the difficulty of visualizing the process without actually seeing what the molds and models look like, many of them have been included in this exhibition.

The actual casting of the bronze takes an infinitesimal amount of time compared with the steps that precede and follow. A small, thin bronze might take a few seconds to cast, and cooling can be almost instantaneous. Mold design and preparation, on the other hand, require an immense amount of time and skill. The abrasive finishing of the cast bronze also takes many days, especially without modern tools. Like the ancient craftsman, we will put our emphasis, first, on mold construction; and, second, on finishing.

Casting a *Zhi*

It is easiest to explain the basic piece-mold casting technique with the set of reproduction molds from the Shanghai Museum (Cat. no. 60) reproduced here as Color plates VIII, A-G. Color plate VIII, A, displays the original model together with the finished bronze, which is slightly smaller than the model, because as the bronze cools it shrinks an expected 4-7 percent. The model itself could be made of any material against which one could place the mold clay and remove it cleanly. Leather with a water-resistant coating, such as oil or lacquer, wood, metal, or fired and even dried clay could all be used.

Next, a clay impression is taken of the model, as seen in Color plate VIII, B. The clay impression is sectioned where it separates most easily from the model, and keys are then made in the edges of the sectioned pieces, so as to fit them back together again for eventual pouring. Color plate VIII, C, illustrates the four individual pieces that make up the casting mold. Normally, one would call this a two-piece mold because two main mold pieces are used to make up the outside surface, and two mold joints are visible on the side of the vessel. The outer mold pieces are fired to a high temperature to render them dimensionally stable. Any decoration on the outer mold would be done before the firing.

The fired mold pieces can be used to produce the ceramic casting core, which is done by inserting clay into the reassembled mold pieces. When the piece molds are removed from the core, it has the same shape and surface decoration as the finished bronze (see Color plate VIII, C). Since this is a simple and small vessel, the individual mold pieces do not need to be divided further. From left to right and back to front they are one main mold piece, the core, the other main mold piece, and, in front, the foot core.

Finally, the casting space, the empty space into which the molten metal will flow, is established by shaving material from the main core piece and the foot core piece (Color plate VIII, D). At any time, the core can be reassembled with one of the main mold pieces to view the casting space. The founder can control the amount of material removed so that the thickness of the cast metal will be exactly what he wants. As can be seen on the sectioned *ding* from the Freer Gallery of Art (Cat. no. 49), the bronzes can be extremely thin!

The foot core would be made next by the same method. It might have lines or a design engraved in its top, which would come out as positive lines called "Karlbeck lines" (see Cat. no. 19; Fig. 7) in the casting. The sprue (pouring duct) and riser (escape vent) are cut into the foot-core piece at this time. The whole assembly is then dried by heating with a low fire. A full refiring is not carried out, so that the core remains friable (easily crumbled) and able to break under contraction pressure from the cooling bronze. After drying, the mold is reassembled, with chaplets or casting spacers, handles, or any adjuncts to the casting in place. It is covered with a further layer of clay, and possibly dried again. Color plate VIII, E, shows what the mold looks like when it is ready for pouring. Probably a number of these were poured at the same time.

The casting space is shown in a cross section of the assembly in which the thin space for the metal can be clearly seen (Color plate VIII, F). The sprue is at the right top; the riser is at the left top.

The question of mold temperature during pouring is still open, but, to simplify this discussion, let us assume that these molds were poured cold. A number of molds would be prepared, then perhaps buried in the casting floor, with the sprues and vents upward. The metal is heated in the crucible or in a tappable furnace; it is then poured, either from the crucible, or from a ladle, or carried by gravity through a trough into the sprue, thereby filling the mold.

After pouring, there is a cooling period, usually under an hour; but the larger the bronze, the longer it takes to cool. The mold is usually broken off by hitting it with a hammer or stone to reveal the cast vessel (Color plate VIII, G). A slightly rough, black appearance is typical of vessels in the as-cast state. The vessel also has mold flash, metal running into the joints where the mold sections meet. At this point, the vessel requires finishing, as described below.

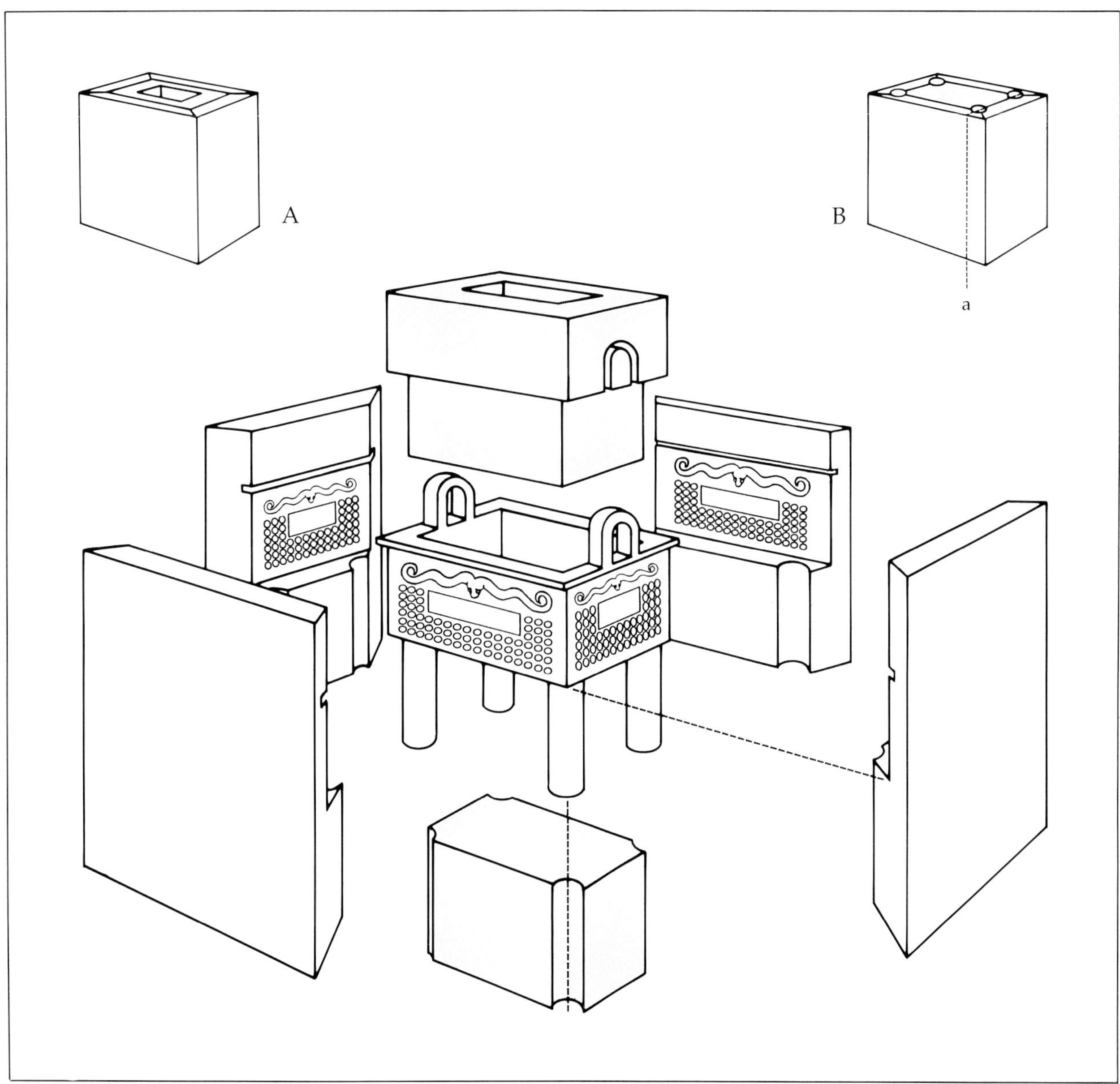

Fig. 1. Mold assembly for casting the *Zuo ce fang ding* (Cat. No. 13). The four outer mold pieces surround the model, shown with the inner core above and the interleg core piece below. The outer mold pieces with the decoration in reverse could have been pulled from the model; or they could simply have been made and decorated without the help of a model. Details in the outer mold pieces would be touched up and refined before firing. The inner core could have been made by shaving down the model; but in this case, it is more likely that the inner core piece was made by inserting a fairly coarse clay mixture into the fired and reassembled mold sections. When the mold sections are removed, the core is shaved down to make the casting space. The process would be repeated with the interleg core piece. The reassembled molds are shown in the inset (A). When then molten metal is ready to pour, this assembly is inverted, with legs up, as illustrated in inset (B).

Casting of *Ding*

The exhibition also includes a mold assembly (Cat. no. 61) for a three-legged *ding* vessel (not illustrated). This is slightly more complicated because the feet have to be cast with an interleg core piece. With a larger vessel, it is more likely that the core and mold will move relative to each other and chaplets would then be required to hold the core and mold in their correct relationship. The same construction was used for the rectangular version of this vessel, the *fang ding*.

Drawings, originally done for a Time-Life publication, *The Metalsmiths*, and based on an examination of all four of the *fang ding* in the *Zuo ce fang ding* set (Cat. no. 13), show the process conceptually (Figs. 1 and 2). Here the main mold sections extend all the way from the top to the bottom of the vessel and include the legs. In some cases, there might have been horizontal or vertical joints as well. The joints in the main mold section would have been made carefully with clay slip and

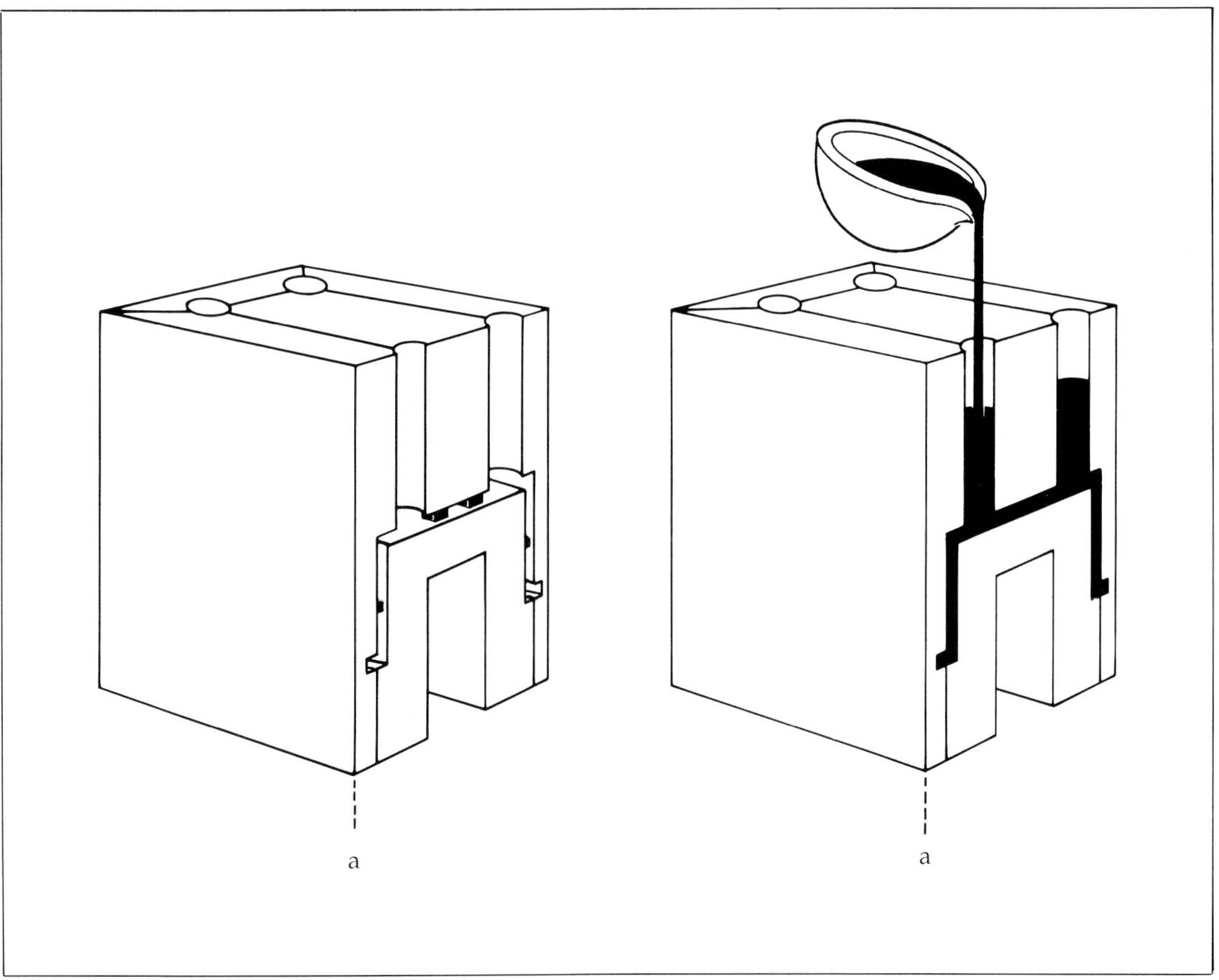

Fig. 2. Casting the *Zuo ce fang ding* (Cat. no. 13). This vessel is cast with the mold assembly inverted, or legs up. The cross section along the dotted line (marked "a") reveals the interior of the assembly with its casting space. Black pegs indicate the bronze chaplets (or spacers) which hold the core and mold apart during casting. The chaplets in the bottom are larger than those in the sides. Metal is melted in a crucible and poured into one leg which functions as the sprue. Displaced air rushes out through the other three legs, which function as the risers. The metal surrounds the chaplets, which are incorporated into the finished bronze vessel. Drawings by Peter Lukic, after illustration in P. Knauth, *The Metalsmiths* (New York: Time-Life Books, 1974).

probably tooled on the inside when the final assembly was being completed for casting. The core piece holds the inside surfaces of the handles and the holes in the handles. The interleg core piece forms the inside of the legs and much of the bottom of the vessel. Mold marks are present on the vessel at the four corners, on the rim and handles, on the back of the legs, and where the interleg core piece meets the main mold pieces.

Many Chinese bronzes look very heavy, a result of the thickening of such visible parts as the rim. On many *gu* vessels, for instance, the upper rim is about 1/4 inch thick at the edge. Although the rim may taper downward to about 1/16 inch of bronze in the body, one would overestimate the body's thickness from the rim edge. Thickening of the visible edge is also clearly demonstrated in the sectioned *ding* from the Study Collection of the Freer Gallery of Art (Cat. no. 49). This thickening is a stylistic peculiarity of many bronze types, due perhaps to the desire to create an impression of greater value. Indeed, bronze was expensive! The belief that bronzes should be heavy is evident in the famous legend about the Nine Tripods, which stresses the weight of the *ding*.

Models or Not?

The above discussion, and many other discussions about Chinese bronze casting techniques, assumes the existence of an initial model from which the mold is made. As with all assertions about ancient techniques, this premise must be examined very carefully. For example, in the Morokome casting process as traditionally practiced in Japan, no model is used.[16] Instead, stone flasks or containers serve as the outside of the molds. Templates are used to apply the clay to the inside of the mold, in a number of layers, working from coarse to fine. After the finest clay is applied to the inside of the mold, it is stamped with designs and hand tooled as necessary. The completed molds are fired quite hard. Then a casting is made by putting clay, in this case reinforced with iron stripping, on the inside. The piece molds are then disassembled from around the clay, leaving a casting that looks exactly like the finished bronze. This is allowed to dry, then filed down to establish the casting space, after which casting proceeds. No model is employed in the process.

Casting Direction: Which Way Is Up?

The question of the direction of casting Chinese bronze ceremonial vessels often arises. The earliest bronzes, especially *jue* and *jia,* were usually cast in an upright position and the posts may come from sprues and risers. Slightly later, *ding* and vessels with ring feet seem to have been cast upside down, foot or legs upward, which can be determined from rising porosity in the legs of *ding*. As an alternative, a mold for a *li ding* in the Museum of Chinese History, Beijing, has a large sprue running into the side of the vessel, showing that the vessel was cast on its side. Casting direction as well as casting temperatures are two promising areas for further study.

Chaplets

Metal chaplets, which are incorporated into the finished casting, were commonly used. This device maintained the casting space and separated the mold from the core. It is sometimes called a "spacer" or "casting spacer." Originally broken pieces of bronze were put between the mold and the core, so that the casting space would not close up while the metal was being poured in. This traditional technique goes back to the beginning of Chinese casting. Regularly spaced chaplets are visible on many Anyang vessels and in later vessels as well. They frequently occur in areas without surface decoration, often clear areas between decoration, as on certain *zun* vessels (Cat. nos. 16 and 17), or in clear bands, as on a *dou* in The Metropolitan Museum of Art (Cat. no. 22). Chaplets became much more frequent in the Han dynasty, although Han chaplets seem to be placed in an irregular fashion.[17]

Rutherford J. Gettens first recognized chaplets on a *zun* in the Freer Gallery of Art that is similar to the two *zun* in this exhibition (Cat. nos. 16 and 17). In all three, chaplets can be seen in the clear areas between the rising blade motifs in the upper part of the vessel. Prior to this discovery, Gettens had thought that these square pieces of different bronze were repairs to casting flaws. In the Freer *zun,* it is clear that the chaplets are arranged in a regular pattern between the rising blades and that they had to have been placed there before the vessel was cast.

Chaplets of this sort are still used in traditional iron casting in Japan. A demonstration of casting iron tea kettles by Keinosuke Totsu of the Tokyo University of Arts, given at the Birmingham Iron Casting Conference in 1987, showed how chaplets are used. The vessel being cast was a round, almost globe-shaped, iron tea kettle with a round foot rim. The mold was composed of three pieces: the core piece, a lower piece, and an upper piece. The mold joint ran around the vessel like an equator. The vessel was cast inverted (with foot rim up). The core piece and mold for the upper section registered well at the mouth, whereas the mold for the lower section (on top when the vessel was cast) had to be supported and registered by three iron chaplets. These were placed on the core on piles of fine sand and the upper part of the mold then closed down on them. With mold contact, most of the sand was pushed out of the joint between the chaplet and core. The mold was then opened and the chaplets were examined. Since they had pushed out almost all of the sand, it was clear that the mold casting space was correct. The loose sand was blown off, with the chaplets left in place, and the mold then closed again. Heavy weights were put on top, and the cast iron was poured in. Chaplet placement and examination required less than a minute in the final mold assembly.

Casting of *Gu*

Precise registration of the foot core and interior core of the vessel is even more difficult with long, thin vessels like the *gu* beaker. With these vessels, two methods were used simultaneously to hold the molds and core in their correct position. The first was to place a chaplet within the septum, or raised bottom, of the *gu*. This served to force the vessel core and the foot core apart, so that there would be room for the metal to flow in. The cross section of a *gu* vessel in the Freer Gallery of Art Study Collection clearly shows the chaplet, which has not fused with the incoming molten metal (Figs. 3a and b).

The other method is more complicated. The foot cores of *gu* often had protruding crosses (or, occasionally, single raised lines) tapering outward. These core-extensions sat in contact with the outer mold and formed cross-shaped holes in the metal.[18] Sometimes, when the contact was not good, the crosses were filled in, as shown in Fig. 4 (Cat. no. 10), or partly filled in (Cat. no. 9). Inside

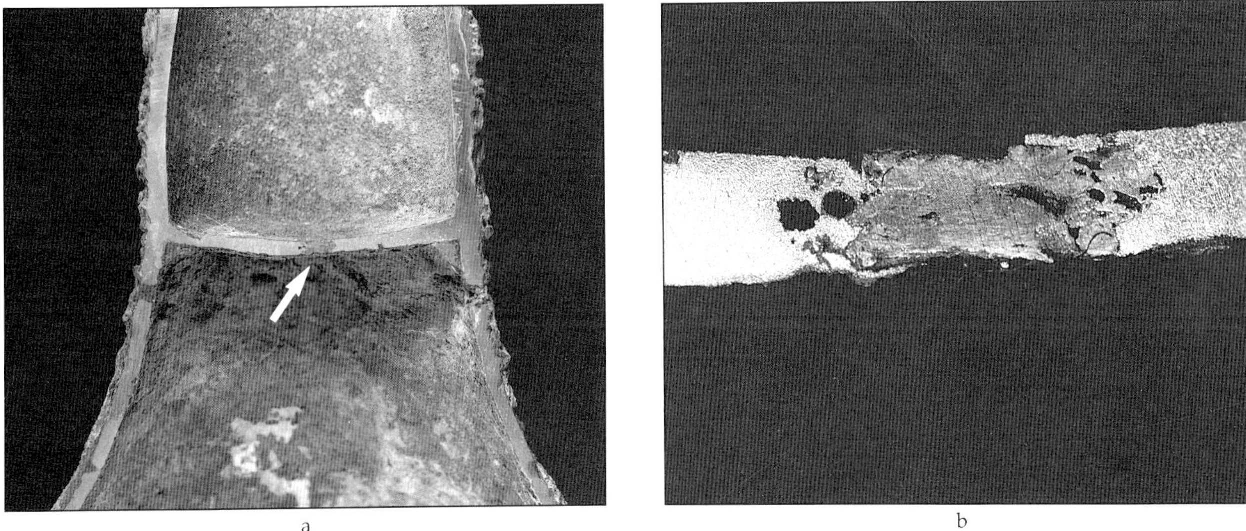

a b

Fig. 3. Cross section (a) of a *gu* from the Freer Gallery of Art Study Collection (SC-B-1) and a macrograph (b), of about seven-fold magnification, reveal the chaplet with the vessel metal cast around it. Photographs courtesy of the Freer Gallery of Art, Smithsonian Institution, Washington, D.C.

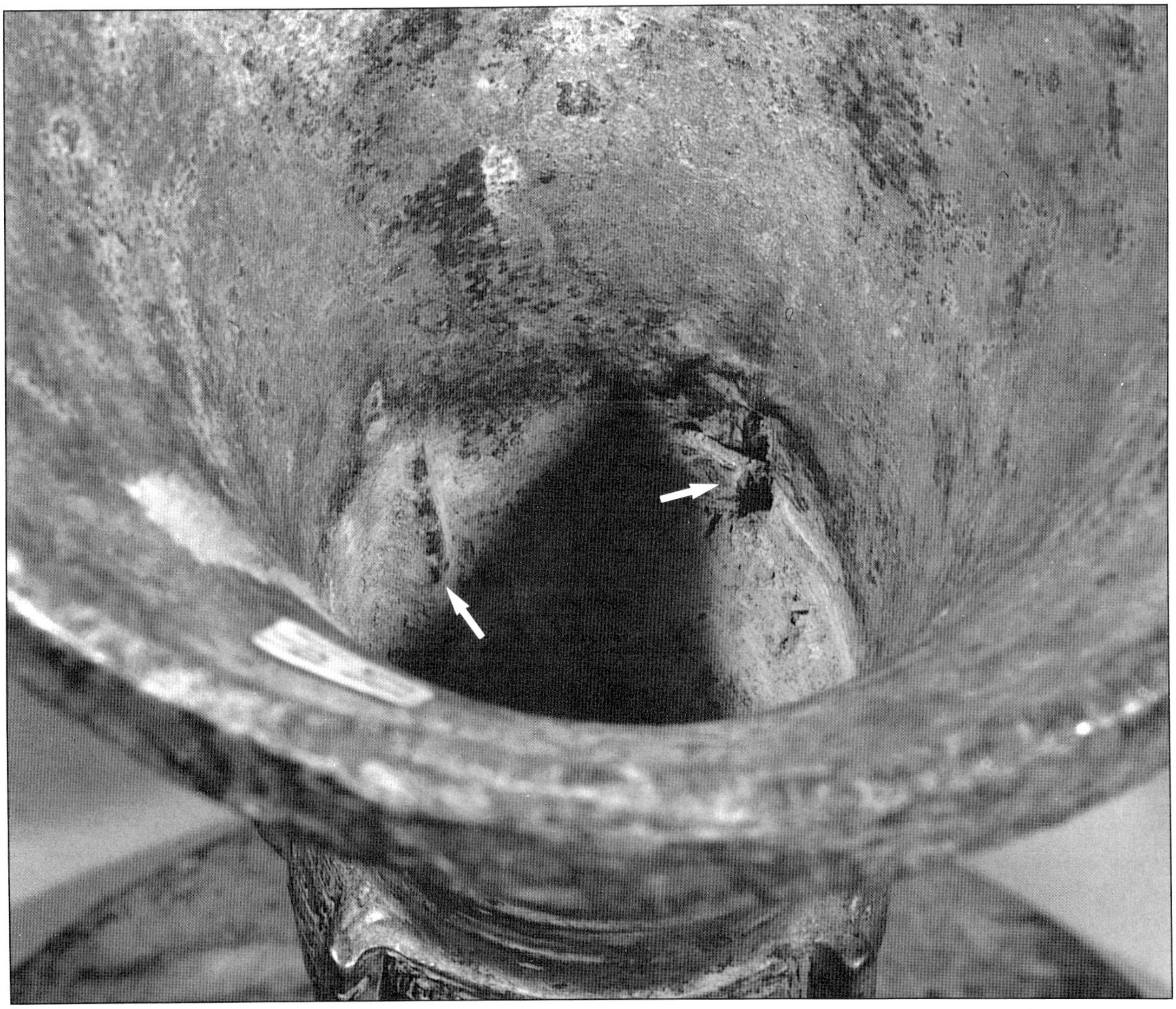

Fig. 4. Interior view of the foot of this *gu* (Cat. no. 10) shows one of the buttresses and a cross-shaped perforation that has been closed over with metal.

these vessels, the tapered shape of the core-extensions is clearly evident.

There are also buttresses in the bottom of *gu* (Fig. 4). These run upward below the septum and were probably included to prevent "hot tearing" of the metal.[19] The stresses in cooling at the center of these exceptionally long and thin *gu* would have been great, and the founders may have discovered that including a little more metal at these points served to prevent the metal from tearing and cracking, which would have rendered the vessel unusable.

Added Parts: Casting-on, Joining, Handles

The piece-mold casting method is eminently suitable for casting shapes like the *gu* and *zhi*, simple vessels with no protruding parts and no included voids, such as handles on *gui* (Cat. no. 18) or re-entrant angles, like the protruding florettes on the openwork ornament (Cat. no. 33). When one adds protruding parts, such as those with included voids, the problems of mold construction become more difficult. One option was to make some parts before the final casting and incorporate them in the mold, so that the vessel metal could run onto them and hold them in place, either by partial fusion or by an interlock. The latter was most commonly used and is seen very clearly in the sectioned *ding* from the Freer Gallery of Art Study Collection (Cat. no. 49; Fig. 5). The legs were cast first, and then the tops of the inner core pieces for the legs were slightly hollowed out so that the metal would be able to run in and lock the legs in place. Next, the legs were incorporated into the mold for the rest of the vessel and set so that their tops just protruded into the casting space. When the molten metal ran into the mold, it enveloped the tops of the legs and locked them in place. The handles here, and those on a *dou* from The Metropolitan Museum of Art (Cat. no. 22), were made in the same way.

The sectioned *ding* shows another type of construction, one in which parts have been cast onto the vessel. Here the replacement legs have been poured over the broken stubs of the old legs (Fig. 5). The metal flowed from the leg onto the vessel, not the other way around, which is more common. Added pieces on other vessels, such as the tiger-shaped feet on the large Sackler *hu* (Cat. no. 30), are also cast onto the vessel, with three separate mold constructions and pours.

Pieces can also be joined by allowing molten metal to flow between them. This sort of construction is seen on the large *fang jia* from the Albright-Knox Art Gallery (Cat. no. 6), where the capped posts have a construction similar to those on a *fang jia* in the Freer Gallery of Art (35.2).[20] The mold marks on the post caps, the vessel, and the metal between them do not agree. The caps and the vessel were made separately, a mold was built to hold the cap and vessel in correct alignment, and a third pour of metal

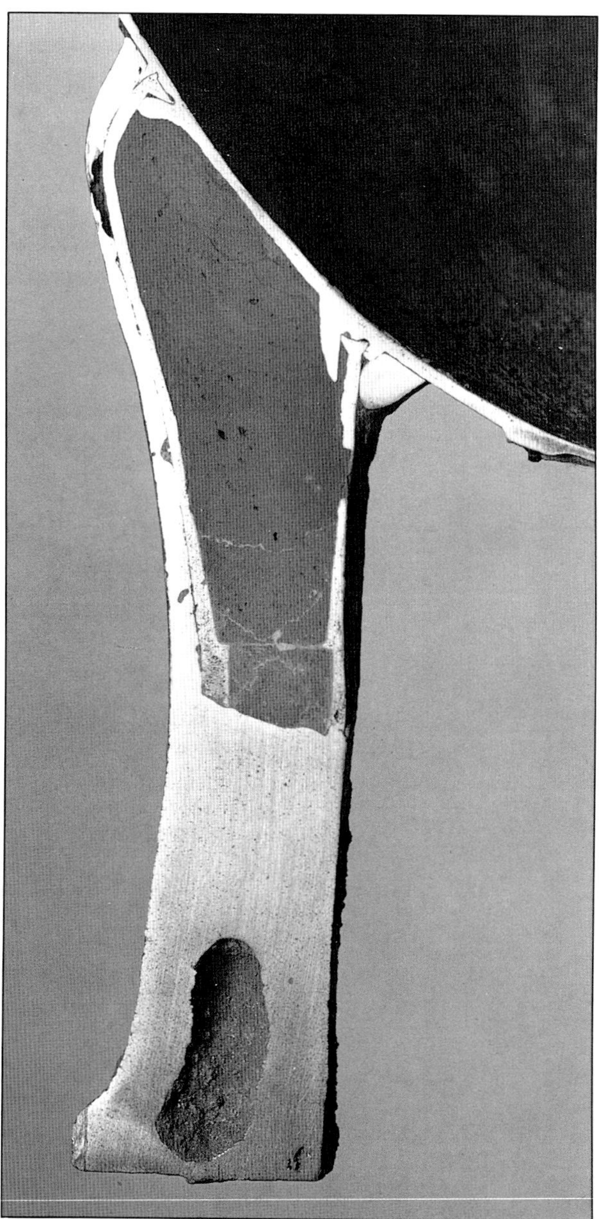

Fig. 5. Close up view of the leg of a sectioned *ding* from the Freer Gallery of Art Study Collection (Cat. no. 49), showing three stages of casting. First, the original leg was cast around a two-piece ceramic core. A dislocation between the two core pieces can be seen at the center. The core was hollowed out at the top and the leg placed into the mold for the vessel. Next, the vessel metal was cast to the leg, thereby interlocking the leg with the vessel. Finally, the leg was broken, and a new leg cast back over the old stub. The metal of the new leg, since it was so thick at the bottom, shrank excessively leaving the large hole. Photograph courtesy of the Freer Gallery of Art.

between the two parts locked them in place.

Swing handles, joined to the vessel by interlocked loops, are made in a similar manner. A common type is seen on the *you* from the Metropolitan Museum of Art (Cat. no. 15), where the handle is cast separately with an incomplete loop, or U-shaped prong, at each end. This prong is looped through a ring on the vessel body and a specially constructed mold is fitted around the opening. Bronze is then poured into the mold to close up the opening and complete the loop. An alternate type of swing handle rotated around projecting pins. The handle was cast first and set into the mold for the vessel body. The pins were cast with the vessel. A real tour de force of interlock casting are the chain handles on later vessels, such as the *hu* belonging to Richard J. Salisbury (Cat. no. 26). They are made with an extremely complicated mold construction and cast in a number of steps (Fig. 6).

Pieces could also be added by brazing (running hot bronze between the two parts until fusion was achieved) or by soft soldering, using a molten mixture of lead and tin to wet the two surfaces and hold them together upon cooling of the mixture. The temperature required by soft soldering is much lower than that required by brazing or casting on. On some vessels, such as the famous *pan-zun* set from the tomb of Zeng Hou Yi, both brazing and soft soldering were used.[21] Since parts attached by brazing will not come loose when soft solder is applied at a lower temperature, the founder exercised good control in assembling these extremely complicated vessels.

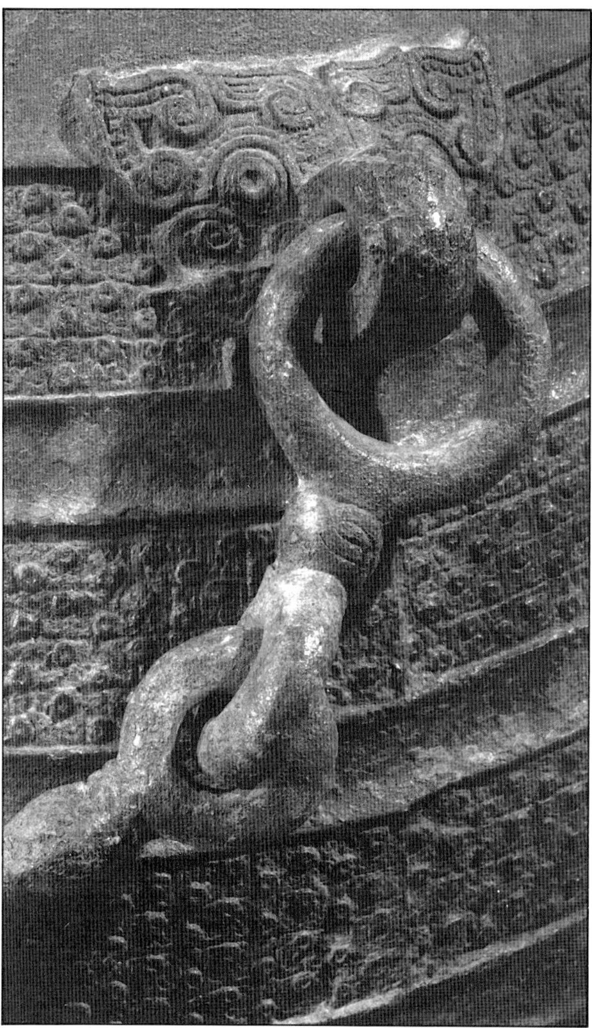

Fig. 6. Detail of animal mask and chain links of an Eastern Zhou *hu* (Cat. no. 26).

Finishing

Most of the bronzes in this show were produced to a high degree of finish, with great care taken all through the casting and finishing process. For contrast, several lead vessels (Cat. nos. 46-48) with which less care was taken in the finishing show what the vessels looked like when they came out of the mold. The steps of the casting process are still open to debate,[22] and finishing renders conclusions even more difficult since it removes some of the evidence of mold construction from the finished vessel.

Finishing was done by abrasion, probably using stones and abrasive powders. Modern abrasive finishing starts with coarse abrasives about the size of fine sand, which leave very visible scratches. As finer and finer abrasives are used, each application obliterates the scratches produced by the previous abrasive. By the end, all scratches disappear. The appearance of the bronze surface proceeds from scratched through a "Florentine" or diffusely reflecting surface to a shiny surface and eventually to mirror brightness. In ancient Chinese practice, buffing (the use of rouge or some fine abrasive on a rapidly rotating felt buff — a common practice in the West today) does not seem to have been used, although in the author's experience buffing is necessary to obtain a high shine on reproduction castings of Chinese mirrors.

Finishing marks are visible on most vessels, usually in less-conspicuous areas. A good example is the *fang ding* from the Hermitage Foundation in Norfolk, Virginia (Cat. no. 13) where the finishing scratches from a fairly coarse abrasive are visible on the underside of the vessel. The other three vessels of this *Zuo ce fang ding* set also have coarse finishing marks on the bottom; the scratches run in different directions on all four vessels, suggesting that the finishing method was somewhat casual. The upper portions of the vessels are finished much more carefully, and any evidence of mold marks is totally erased from handles and upper lips.

General Remarks on Ancient Chinese Casting

During the Shang, Zhou, and Han periods, casting was the pre-eminent technique for working with metal. Hammering vessels from sheet, or joining sheets of metal to make a larger vessel, was not done in China. Even the cutting edges of weapons were not hammered to increase their hardness, as was the practice in other cultures,[23] but were simply finished by abrasion. Hardness was imparted by the tin content. In contrast to hammering, abrasive finishing leaves the metal crystals undisturbed on the surface. The crystalline structure of the metal in edged weapons from the Shang and Zhou dynasties can be seen to proceed right up to the cutting edge.

The ancient Chinese also repaired vessels by casting. This is evident in the early *jue* from the collection of Dr. Paul Singer (Cat. no. 1) to which a repaired leg has been cast. Good examples of other cast repairs are the inlaid decagonal *hu* from the Arthur M. Sackler Gallery (Cat. no. 31) and the owl *zun* (Cat. no. 12). In the latter, the design on the repair can be seen to be a continuation of the original cast design on the vessel. The founders must have opened or begun breaking off the mold and found an area into which the molten metal had not flowed. They simply reclosed this part of the mold and cast metal into the area, leaving the design slightly off-register with the rest of the *zun*. Only in the Han dynasty did riveted metal repairs appear. The earliest repair made with metal sheet and rivets is on a basin from the Western Han tomb of Liu Sheng.[24]

The ancient Chinese were so expert at turning out whatever shapes they wanted with casting methods that they seemed to feel no need to work metal by hammering. The interaction between the piece-mold casting method and the shapes and decoration that can be produced by it has been well told by Robert Bagley.[25] When lost-wax casting appeared it was first used to produce ornaments to be attached to vessels produced in the traditional manner (Cat. no. 33) or to produce more elaborate variations of shapes already being made by the piece-mold method (Cat. nos. 34 and 35). Only in Dian (exemplified by the finds at the Shijaishan site, near Kunming, Yunnan), where bronze serves a different culture with great emphasis on animal hunts and sacrifices and where a clear interest in naturalistic forms is evident, do the potentialities of lost-wax casting really come into their own (Cat. no. 52).

Even gold, which occurs in some Western Zhou tombs in sheet form, was worked by casting, as is seen in the gold vessels from the tomb of the Marquis of Yi at Suixian.[26] The gold is not cast as successfully as bronze would have been for the same shapes. For instance, some of the decoration has been retouched by engraving, and there are large areas of porosity. Perhaps the founders did not have as much experience working with gold as with bronze, and used the wrong casting conditions or temperature.

The reasons for the dominance of ceramic piece-mold casting are many. First, the ancient Chinese had a developed ceramic technology (pyrotechnology) that was already functioning well: they had experience with refractories (heat-resistant materials), the use of clays and loess to produce kilns, and the manipulation of fire, especially in reducing (oxygen-removing) atmospheres. This technology and the molding and, perhaps, stamping process for decoration were the ceramic legacy to the bronze production process. Second, the alloys with which they worked, the leaded tin bronzes, lent themselves to casting and not to hammering or cold-working. Third, and probably most important, the ancient Chinese method of piece-mold casting served well to make the kinds of objects that the Chinese wanted to make. When the demand for bronzes with more baroque, convoluted surfaces increased, the ancient Chinese turned to the lost-wax process; with a shift from vessel production to statuettes and more naturalistic forms, the lost-wax process superseded the piece-mold process entirely.

Lost-wax casting is also called "investment casting" because a burnable model is "invested" (i.e., covered) with the refractory (i.e., non-burnable) mold material. First, a model with the shape of the desired casting is made in a material that will melt or burn out when the mold is heated. Second, the model is invested, or covered, with a refractory mold material. Third, the mold containing the model is heated and the material forming the model is melted out, vaporized, or burned so that none of it remains. If the model was made of wax, the wax is lost during this stage; hence, the name. Finally, the mold, usually still hot, is set with the sprue or ingate upward and the metal is poured in.

This is a simplified description. There are complications, such as when objects must be made with a core, keeping the core in place, choosing a mold material, eliminating bubbles in the investment, and so on. Still, the lost-wax method is ideal for statues that need to be lifelike in volume and plasticity, with projecting limbs. It is also a very good method for repetitive industrial production of small machine parts, a process I witnessed at the East Is Red Tractor Factory in Zhengzhou in 1973.[27]

The similarities between Western casting and

ancient Chinese ceramic piece-mold casting are worth noting. The latter seems to be closest to modern Western casting methods using dies and produces similar fineness of detail. Some of this stems from the direct tooling of the mold surface, present in both processes.

Modern Western lost-wax casting requires the extensive use of sprues and risers to direct the flow of metal. The Chinese, using porous ceramic piece molds, were able to avoid this. Spruing, as far as we can tell, was done with one down-sprue into the mold cavity; occasionally risers would be added. In the case of legged vessels, often cast with the legs up, one leg served as the sprue and the other legs as risers so that gas could escape. For other shapes, the molds seem to have had enough openings, especially around the foot, to prevent gas entrainment. Gas porosity could sometimes be a problem, and seems especially prevalent in middle Western Zhou vessels, for instance, the pair of large *hu* from the former Morse Collection (now in The Metropolitan Museum of Art, Cat. no. 20). These have very large and visible gas porosity. Another well-known example is the *mao gong ding* in the collection of the National Palace Museum, Taipei.

One must also consider that bronze vessel production in China was a high art. In the West, casting is an industrial process, rendered as inexpensive as possible. Creating the dies, generally in hardened tool steel, is very expensive, but thousands of castings can be pulled from them. In ancient China, labor was very cheap and the molds were intended to be used only once. Careful comparison of vessels that have survived in pairs or groups, such as the two *jian* basins at the Freer Gallery of Art and the Minneapolis Institute of Art[28] and the group of four *Zuo ce fang ding*, one of which is represented here (Cat. no. 13), show that while the bronzes may look identical, the molds were not. In the case of mirrors, a later production, identical molds do seem to occur, perhaps because wax positives were being used as an intermediate step. Identical molds were also used for producing iron ware,[29] and in coinage, often in stack mold assemblies for casting hundreds of coins (Cat. nos. 43 and 44).

HISTORICAL DEVELOPMENT

Beginnings of Bronze in China

The beginnings of bronze metallurgy in China probably date to just before 2000 B.C. Sporadic evidence of bronze use occurs in the Longshan levels at Dachangshan, Tangshan, Hebei Province, and in Qijia culture levels in Gansu Province. While some of these finds are early brasses, most are tin bronzes or leaded tin bronzes with some leaded coppers. The first bronze vessels were found at the Erlitou site in Yanshi County, Henan Province, and include a group of *jue* and two *jia* vessels, weapons, and decorative elements, one inlaid with turquoise. Overall, however, evidence for the precise origins of bronze casting in China is still somewhat controversial.[30]

Erlitou bronzes, the earliest cast bronze vessels yet found in China, deserve special attention.[31] These are mostly *jue* with proportions ranging from squat and awkward to tall and attenuated. The rims of the vessels are doubled, suggesting to some observers the imitation of a rolled-over metal rim on a hammered vessel, but the handles appear to be cast on. They are similar to, but somewhat earlier than, the *jue* in this exhibition (Cat. no. 1). Both this *jue* and one of the Erlitou *jue*, which have recast legs, seem to have been cast with a two-piece mold. The interleg core piece would have shaped the bottom of the vessel and the two interior surfaces of each leg. The handles seem to have been precast and set in the mold, after which the vessel was cast onto them.[32]

Decoration appears on the Erlitou vessels. The earliest decoration is a rectangular frame around five bosses on one of the Erlitou *jue*.[33] This decoration is clearly incised in the mold and marks the beginning of the cast decoration that dominates Chinese bronze production from this period on. A good example of simple incised decoration on a slightly later bronze is a *jia* from the Royal Ontario Museum (Cat. no. 2).

The next step in the evolution of Chinese bronze casting comes from other excavations at Erligang, Zhengzhou, in Henan Province. Here we have vessels of a much more developed type with more sophisticated decoration. Vessels with hollow legs show up (Cat. no. 3), as do vessels cast in a number of steps; for example, in the large *fang ding* from Zhengzhou,[34] the four central panels (the two central panels on the sides and the two on the ends with handles) were cast separately from the rest of the vessel. One assumes that the panels were cast first, set into the mold for the vessel, and the vessel was cast onto them. The legs were then added in four additional castings. This is an exceptionally thin vessel for its size, and its manufacture is a triumph of the caster's art.

The alloying practice also progresses with time. Before the highly developed foundry practice of the later Shang, alloys varied widely and may have contained much lead. It is interesting to contrast the *jia* (Cat. no. 2), which has an extremely high lead content (26%), with the *ding* in this exhibition (Cat. no. 3), which has no detectable lead. The analysis of vessels from Erlitou shows very low lead contents; the later vessels from Panlongcheng have variable, sometimes extremely high, lead contents.[35] Perhaps in the earliest periods the ancients used lead-bearing copper deposits but did not yet know how to separate the lead from the copper. In developed Shang casting at Anyang, lead values seem to have been controlled, with the founders consciously manipulating the alloy content.

Bronzes at Anyang

With the move of the Shang capital to Anyang, we enter into the developed phase of Shang bronze technology. From the Anyang foundries comes the *Si mu wu fang ding* mentioned earlier. This is the largest bronze casting known from antiquity. Also at Anyang, the recently excavated tomb of Fuhao yielded some 1600 kilograms of bronze artifacts.[36]

The evolution of decoration on the bronzes through the end of the Shang has been well set forth by Max Loehr.[37] Bronzes of the styles Loehr designates as I through V are all present in our exhibition. Style I bronzes, decorated in simple raised line, have a limited vocabulary of geometric and zoomorphic figures (Cat. no. 11B). In Style II, the lines are replaced by wide raised bands (Cat. no. 4). Bronzes in these two styles have been found in abundance at the city sites at Erligang near Zhengzhou in Henan Province and at Panlongcheng in Hubei Province. By the end of the Zhengzhou period, Style III presents the image as closely packed raised spirals (Cat no. 5). The separation of a foreground motif in Style IV through the use of a background of tight spirals, called *leiwen*, reflects an awareness of painterly rather than ceramic decoration (Cat no. 7). In this style, a black fill often appears to have been deliberately rubbed into the recessed lines to increase the contrast. In Style V, the foreground figure is raised in relief on a recessed ground of *leiwen* (Cat. no. 14). This simplified picture of the development of Shang bronze decoration from the Zhengzhou period to the Anyang, or Yinxu, period does not take into account the regional variations and the reemergence or survival of earlier styles in the late Shang and early Western Zhou bronzes. The evolution outlined here does not represent absolute dating criteria.

In terms of casting, however, the evolution of this decoration is very interesting. The earliest bronzes, and those of Loehr's Style I, appear to have decoration executed exclusively by incision into the mold surface, with very little finishing subsequent to casting. On late Style II and Style III there is a change, perhaps due to more intensive finishing after casting, so that the decoration lines are flattened at the top, eroded by abrasives. The approach to creating the mold and the aesthetic also change.[38] At this stage, some of the decoration must have been made in the model itself and then transferred to a mold. It becomes very difficult to say with certainty what was done in the model and what was done in the mold, but some of the decoration simply must have been done in the mold, for example, the small raised circles found on many early bronzes. However, much of the decoration was probably made on the model. In Style V, the interplay of fine lines against coarser lines and the juxtaposition of flat areas and large areas in lower or higher relief on the bronzes are beautiful and complex. Their high degree of finish makes it difficult to identify the vestiges of the mold tooling that would allow a definitive statement about casting methods.

The late Shang founder perfected his skill in casting with complex mold constructions. Large cast-on pieces, such as the capped post of the *fang jia* from the Albright-Knox Art Gallery (Cat. no. 6), and the swing handles of *you* vessels (Cat. nos. 14 and 15) were prevalent from the late Shang period into the early Zhou. The *gu* vessel type, with its complicated foot-core construction, also flourished in the late Shang dynasty.

A notable technical innovation in the late Shang, legs made with copper cores, is prevalent on *ding* vessels with cylindrical legs. Some legs seem to have been cast solid, others with a conventional ceramic core, and some with a core of solid copper. The solid copper is precast and may be held in the mold with extensions on the copper that are cut and finished off later. These copper cores probably prevent the excessive shrinkage in the legs that occurs when a large mass of solid metal (i.e., the legs) is cast against a much larger area of thin metal (i.e., the vessel body). Differences in the solidification rate between the body and legs also tend to create hot tearing, and these precast copper cores were probably included to prevent such tearing.

One further technical innovation seen in the late Shang and continuing into the Zhou dynasty is the markings on the bottoms of bronzes which are often referred to as "Karlbeck" lines in honor of Orvar Karlbeck, the Swedish archaeologist who devoted much study to the question. These markings are often in the form of diagonal crisscross lines that produce a diamond pattern (Fig. 7). Sometimes they can be in the form of pictorial designs in relief. Their exact function is still not precisely known, although they may have served at least two purposes: one, to allow venting of gases as the metal was poured; and, two, to allow better alignment of the foot cores and possibly to define the surface of the actual vessel

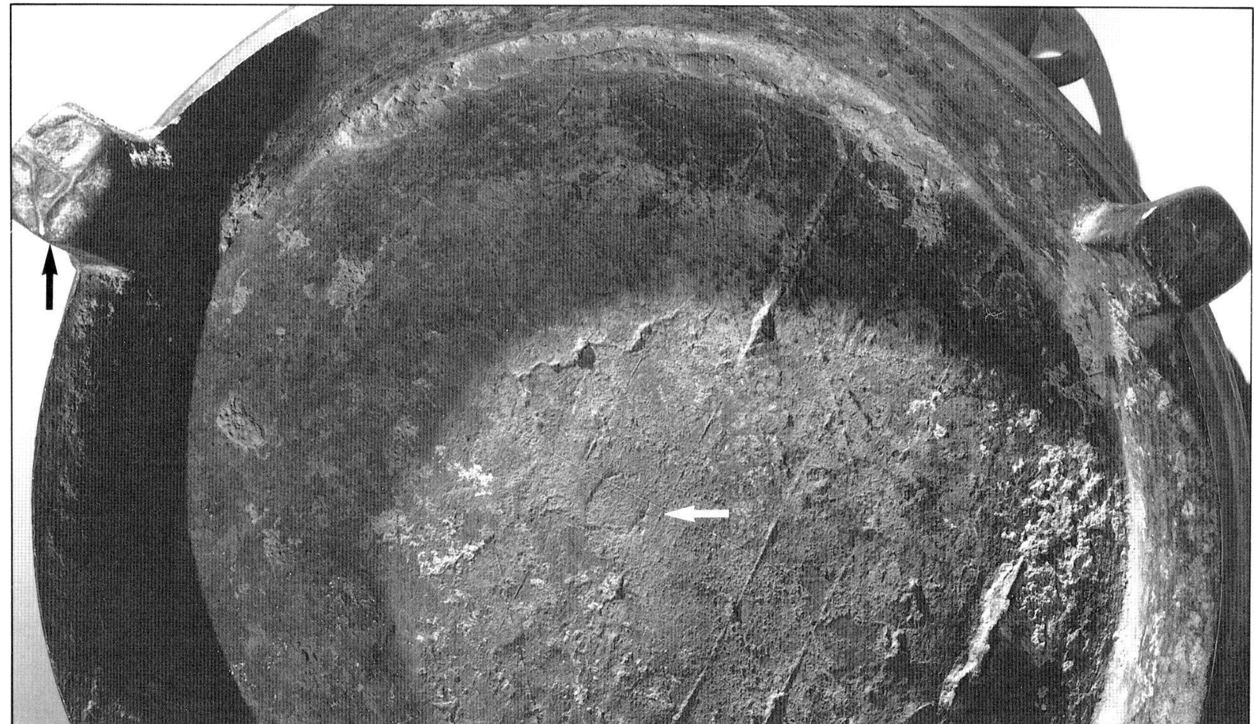

Fig. 7. Crisscross lines popularly known as "Karlbeck lines" on the base of a *gui* (Cat. no. 19). Remains of the core and a chaplet (indicated by arrow) can also be seen. Ground down sprue marks (indicated by arrow) are seen on the bottom of one of the feet.

core before it was cut down to establish the casting space. On a late Zhou *bian hu* belonging to Robert H. Ellsworth (Cat. no. 28), three vertical lines can be seen on the inside of the foot. On X-radiographs, these extend upward inside the vessel. This must have been a location device. The "Karlbeck" lines may have served a similar function.

Regional Styles

In Shang cities outside the Anyang capital area, different regional styles of bronze casting developed. Areas in the South developed an animistic style that often incorporated cast-on animal heads.[39] Another regional style, not yet securely dated, are the large masks and statues from the Guanghan finds in Sichuan Province.[40] These are remarkably large bronzes, mostly figural, which were found in the same sacrificial pit with bronze *zun* of the Shang southern regional style. Casting methods seem to be generally the same as in the central area of China, although technical examination of these bronzes still remains to be done.

The Zhou Conquest and Its Effect on Bronze Styles and Production

Probably the most interesting area of study is the question of Zhou regional styles prior to the Zhou conquest of Shang.[41] Technical developments after the conquest include larger and more flamboyant bronzes. A particularly good example is a *you* in the Freer Gallery of Art (30.26), which, with its matching *gui* (31.10), has many cast-on parts including large vessel flanges. These vessels present a very spiky and protruding appearance. Many of the earliest Western Zhou bronzes seem to have been an outgrowth of Shang bronze production, but affected by a different aesthetic.

Shortly after the conquest, bronze production seems to have diminished somewhat in quality. While inscriptions became much longer, the technical quality of the bronzes, particularly in terms of porosity, became much worse.

Deliberate manipulation of the color of the bronze surface seems to have occurred in the Western Zhou period. A number of bronzes are a beautiful shiny black, which does not seem to be a product of later repatination. A good example is the *gong* in the Art Museum of Princeton University (65-3) and its mate in the Avery Brundage Collection in the Asian Art Museum, San Francisco (B1004).[42] A set of vessels from Fufengxian in Shaanxi Province also appears to have very divergent patinas on the three pieces. It may be that intentional coloration was used here too.[43]

Inscriptions on Western Zhou bronzes become much longer. A great deal has been written on these inscriptions and their production,[44] but exactly how they were made remains a mystery. If it is true that the firing temperatures for the cores of these vessels were not as high as for the outer molds, then the cores were very friable and did not survive; and it may be that inscriptions, which are generally present on the interior of a vessel, are simply created by those parts of the mold assembly that no longer survive. The idea of Matsumaru Michio, that inscriptions were originally incised into leather from which a mold impression was taken, seems to be a good one. On the other hand, these inscriptions might have been simply incised into clay and the clay pieces then set into the mold. It is common in modern Japanese casting practice to include medallions or pieces with inscriptions in them as part of the mold assembly.[45]

Eastern Zhou

As we move into the Eastern Zhou dynasty in the eighth-century B.C., we find continuity with the Western Zhou, with large vessels, especially *hu*, becoming popular. Some of these seem to have a connection with southern regional styles.[46] The *hu*, often highly decorated, appears to have had religious and magical connotations for the later Zhou people; it becomes a very common type as one can see from the inclusion of a number of *hu* in our exhibition.

The early use of lost wax can also be traced to regional developments in the early Eastern Zhou period.[47] Lost-wax parts can be seen on a set of large *ding* made for a sixth-century royal prince of the Chu kingdom, excavated from a tomb in Xiasi, Xichuan County, Henan Province.[48] Here, a number of openwork parts were made in lost wax; the vessel body, made in the standard piece-mold construction technique, was then cast onto the parts. Multiple parts made of lost wax are much more evident on bronzes from the tomb of the Marquis of Yi at Suixian in Hubei Province.[49] The various parts of these vessels made by lost wax (or at least by some kind of investment casting) are cast together and joined with various soldering methods to create a remarkable tour de force of bronze casting.[50] With its first appearance in southern Henan Province, lost-wax casting seems to have rapidly become a prerogative of the South, especially in the Chu culture area. The exhibition includes a small openwork ornament (Cat. no. 33), an openwork sphere (Cat. no. 35), and two openwork belt hooks (Cat. no. 34), all made by lost wax and probably from the same area. The prevalent period of lost-wax casting in central China takes us into the late Eastern Zhou dynasty.

The Eastern Zhou period was a time of great technological innovation in China. Among the causes was the lack of a strong central bureaucracy, which permitted local technical innovations to flourish. The rise of iron casting and the increase in agricultural production produced by iron tools added to the prosperity of the middle class and created a large demand for sumptuary objects. Technical innovation in bronze production also increased, not only in the area of casting but also in decoration, inlay, and plating. The lack of religious proscriptions also allowed the use of bronzes for other purposes. Changes in warfare styles to accommodate mounted cavalry required new hardware, especially belt hooks and other sorts of buckles. These innovations make the Eastern Zhou a particularly exciting period to study in terms of bronze casting and bronze fabrication techniques.[51]

In terms of bronze production itself, the most exciting development early in the period was the extensive use of pattern blocks to produce decoration. Their use is particularly evident in bronzes of the so-called Liyu style, many of which were probably produced at the Houma foundry. Pattern blocks of various sizes and types have been discovered at the Houma foundry site in Shanxi Province.[52] Our exhibition includes a block for a Houma-style vessel with an animal mask on it (Cat. no. 42) as well as a number of vessels that were produced with block-impressed decoration (Cat. nos. 22-28). These pattern blocks formed the basis of the aesthetic for this period.

Interest in surface coloration also arises during the late part of Houma foundry production. A *hu* vessel from the collection of the Arthur M. Sackler Gallery in Washington, D.C. (Cat. no. 30), shows the combined use of Liyu-type molds to make parts of the decoration, including the feet and handles, and copper and silver inlay to decorate the rest of the vessel. It also has a light gray, shiny patina which seems to have been produced from the removal of copper from the surface and the retention of tin. Deliberate patination was applied to the bronze surface. Many of the bronzes of this period that have a light grayish-green coloration may have been treated to surface pickling. The handles, which seem to have been produced from a different alloy, have a black patina. Other forms of surface coloration was applied to many bronzes during this period. Gilding with mercury amalgam is common; silvering or two-color gilding was introduced late in the period and is more prevalent during the Han dynasty. Knowledge of surface coloration was particularly useful in producing pattern-etched weapons (Cat. no. 36),[53] and a type of sword made out of higher and lower tin alloys.[54]

Inlay methods cover a wide range. The inlay was done either by hammering metal wire into grooves (Cat. nos. 30 and 31) or by incorporating precast members in the form of sheets into the mold (Cat. no. 28). These sheets were held in place by chaplets and the vessel cast around them (Fig. 8). Often the sheet inlay is in the tradition of Eastern Zhou pictorial decoration (Cat. no. 29).[55] Pieces of metal were also incorporated in the mold to achieve a two-color effect. A particularly good example is the *bian hu* with intersecting bands of copper on the body and copper triangles encircling the neck (Cat. no. 28). Semi-precious stones, such as turquoise or malachite, were also used in the elaborate inlaid designs of late Eastern Zhou bronzes (Cat. no. 32). Other methods of inlay are only now being discovered, for instance, silver and gold amalgam.[56] Also, some vessels have particularly fine lines with copper inlay, which has the appearance of sheet metal. It is possible that this is an amalgam inlay as well, although none of these vessels has been tested.

Another type of inlay, the use of colored pastes, has only recently emerged. These pastes seem to have been made from mineral constituents, including azurite. It would be difficult to give credence to vessels with this inlay if several of them had not been discovered in a controlled excavation, such as the Taiyuan site.[57] The paste inlay, which would easily be washed out by water in damp tombs, may explain why some vessels have totally lost their inlay.

Qin and Han Metalwork

The technical innovations of the Eastern Zhou carry on into the Qin and Han dynasties. In the area of coloration, these innovations are clearly seen on the weapons retrieved from the pits surrounding the tomb of Qin Shihuangdi. While some of these are simply bronze-colored with green corrosion, others have a black patination, and some, notably the long sword, have a silvery color. A similar range of patination is seen on the objects from the late-second-century B.C. tombs of Liu Sheng and Dou Wan in Man Cheng, Hebei Province. Among the mirrors in this find one is green, one is partly green and partly black, and one is very black.[58]

Use of lost-wax casting also shows up in the Man Cheng tombs with the famous *boshanlu* censer, which is also finished black and inlaid with gold.[59] The sumptuous nature of Han metalwork is also evident in the small hill-shaped lid in this exhibition (Cat. no. 38). It was produced by lost-wax casting and gilding. The Han tradition of mercury gilding and silvering can still be seen in the pair of Tang dynasty roundels from The Metropolitan Museum of Art (Cat. no. 39).

Mirrors, which appear in abundance in the Han dynasty, are of particular interest because of the specialized technology required to produce them. The mirror in our exhibition (Cat. no. 37) is a superb example of a two-colored mirror. A soapstone mold also in this exhibition (Cat. no. 45) may possibly have been used to make wax models rather than the actual bronze mirrors. This is suggested by the location of the decorative band of triangles on the very edge of this mold. Normally there is an additional band of metal on a mirror beyond this band of decoration.

During the later Zhou and Han dynasties, the importance of ritual and ceremonial vessels declined, but the importance of cast metal, both bronze and iron, increased. Industrial casting was carried out on a massive scale. The use of stack molds (Cat. nos. 43 and 44), in which the individual plates within the stack were produced from bronze masters, made the production of vast numbers of coins and other small objects (such as buckles) possible.[60] Iron masters were produced to make ceramic molds for casting iron, particularly for such tools as plowshares.[61]

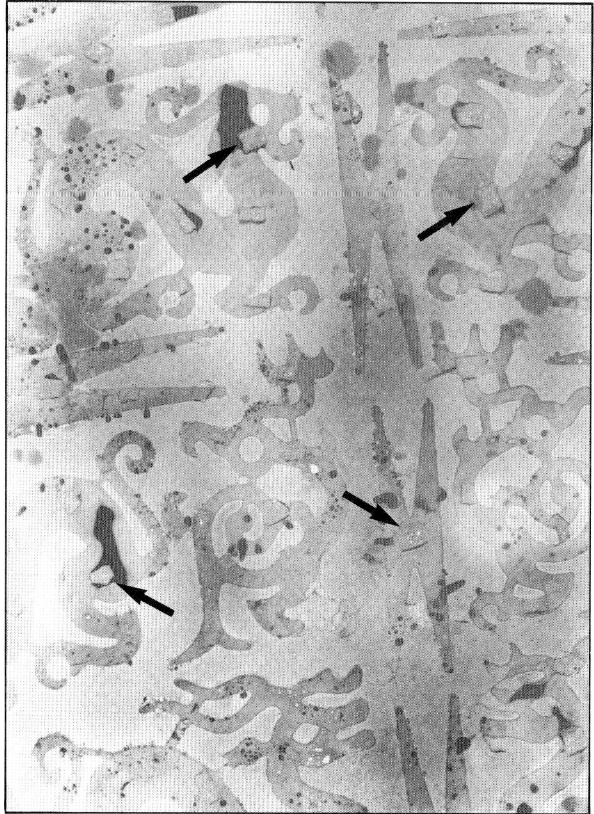

Fig. 8. Radiograph of inlaid copper *hu* from The Metropolitan Museum of Art, New York; Bequest of Mrs. H.O. Havemeyer, The H.O. Havemeyer Collection (29.100.545). Chaplets (indicated by arrow) hold the inlaid copper ornament in the mold prior to casting. Radiograph courtesy of Department of Objects Conservation, The Metropolitan Museum of Art.

Toward the end of the Han dynasty, Chinese metallurgy changed. Thereafter, most castings were done by the lost-wax process. The history of later metallurgy in China and in Asia continues to be an important subject for research.[62]

ANTIQUARIAN INTEREST, THE VOGUE FOR REPRODUCTIONS, AND REPAIRS

Ancient vessels have been collected since at least the Qin dynasty in the third century B.C. The story of Qin Shihuangdi's attempt to recover one of the *ding* from the Nine Tripod Set is depicted in the second-century stone carvings of the Wu family shrine in Jiaxiang, Shandong Province. This antiquarian interest can also be seen as early as the Song dynasty in the writing of Shen Kua and continues up to the present day. The exhibition includes two examples of repaired bronzes, the famous *pou* from the Princeton University Art Museum (Cat. no. 51), which has been extensively repaired, and a *gu* from the Freer Gallery of Art (Cat. no. 50), of which only five pieces of the foot are original. Two of these contain parts of an inscription. The history of repair methods, of patination methods for making new bronzes appear old, and of techniques for making complete bronzes out of fragments is still to be written. It is clear that the esteem in which Chinese bronzes are held, not only in China but also in the international art market, has stimulated a surprising range of technological innovations in the past and today as well.

FUTURE DIRECTIONS

The current state of studies in ancient Chinese bronze technology is one of great activity and flux. Recent discoveries in China, such as the Guanghan and Taiyuan bronzes, present us with technical innovations that have never been seen before. Studies now going on in various centers in Asia (Beijing, Hefei, Xian, Taipei, and Tokyo) and the West are all adding to our knowledge of the materials and techniques used to produce ancient Chinese bronzes. Because the field is so active, some of the concepts explored in this exhibition are rather different from what they would have been a year ago, and undoubtedly some will change again later.

Some issues now being studied include the effect of the relationship between mold and model on the fabrication of decoration, particularly in the early development of bronze casting through the Shang dynasty; inlay techniques, such as amalgam or paste; patination techniques and the corrosion-resistant patination on Chinese mirrors;[63] the possible use of lost wax in late Zhou and Han casting, especially for mirrors; metal sources and lead isotope analysis;[64] casting materials and casting conditions; and finally, a subject not touched on in the above essay, corrosion and preservation of bronzes. Many Chinese bronzes, especially those from southern sites, have bronze disease caused by chlorides, which can lead to recurring corrosion and eventual disintegration of the bronze. Current methods for treatment are either not economic or change the appearance of the bronzes. New methods for treatment of this problem are essential, but they require that we understand both the fundamental mechanisms of bronze production and the manner in which the metal solidifies in order to assess the strength and understand the structure of the metal when it was new. This basic knowledge must be related to corrosion studies so that we can understand what has happened during the two thousand years that these objects have lain in the ground and attempt to treat them so they will survive for many more years.[65]

Shen Kua, the eleventh-century Song dynasty archaeologist and collector, writing in his *Dream Pool Essays* (Meng Qi Bi Tan), sums up well the aim of study and conservation of these objects from the past. This summation also makes a fitting close to this essay:

> The ancients made mirrors according to the following methods. If the mirror was large, the surface was made flat (or concave); if the mirror was small, the surface was made convex. If the mirror is concave it reflects a person's face larger; if the mirror is convex it reflects the person's face smaller. The whole of a person's face could not be seen in a small mirror, so that is why they made the surface convex. They increased or reduced the degree of convexity or concavity according to the size of the mirror, and could thus always make the mirror correspond to the face. The ingenious workmanship of the ancients has not been equalled by subsequent generations. Nowadays, when people get hold of ancient mirrors, they actually have the surfaces ground flat. So perishes not only the ancient skill, but even the appreciation of ancient skill.[66]

By studying and conserving ancient Chinese bronzes, we try to preserve these tangible reminders of ancient skill. By reading this catalogue and seeing the exhibition, we hope that you may increase your appreciation of the amazing and wonderful mastery of technical processes of the ancient Chinese foundryman. If so, we have been successful.

ENDNOTES

All references in this endnote section are in short citation form. Full titles and other details of publication are provided in the Bibliography at the end of the catalogue section.

1. Tan Derui, ***The Splendid Craft of Lost Wax Casting in Ancient China***, pp. 80-91.

2. Rose Kerr, ***Later Chinese Bronzes***.

3. Noel Barnard and Tamotsu Sato, ***Metallurgical Remains of Ancient China***, p. 45.

4. On the societal requirements for bronze casting see Ursula Franklin's essays "The Beginnings of Metallurgy in China: A Comparative Approach" and "On Bronze and Other Metals in Early China"; and Noel Barnard, "From Ore to Ingot — Mining, Ore-processing, and Smelting in Ancient China."

5. Doris Dohrenwend, "The Early Chinese Mirror," p. 86; W. Thomas Chase and Ursula Franklin, "Early Chinese Black Mirrors and Pattern-etched Weapons," p. 234.

6. W. Thomas Chase, "Chinese Belthooks in the Freer Gallery of Art," pp. 151-158.

7. See Archaeometallurgy Group, p. 302, on early leaded bronzes from Gansu.

8. W. Thomas Chase and Thomas O. Ziebold, "Ternary Representations of Ancient Chinese Bronze Compositions," fig. 1.

9. Wu Kunyi and Li Xiuhui, "The Effect of Lead on the Properties of Bronze Drums," p. 6.

10. W. Thomas Chase, "Bronze Casting in China: A Short Technical History," p. 103.

11. Martha Goodway and Harold C. Conklin, "Quenched High-tin Bronzes from the Philippines," p. 4.

12. See Edward Biot, trans., ***Le Tcheou-li ou Rites des Tcheou***, vol. 2, p. 491; and Chase, "Bronze Casting in China: A Short Technical History," pp. 108 ff.

13. Barnard and Sato, ***Metallurgical Remains of Ancient China***, pp. 19 and 21.

14. An Zhimin, "Some Problems Concerning China's Early Copper and Bronze Artifacts," p. 278; Archaeometallury Group, p. 290.

15. Paul T. Craddock, ***2000 Years of Zinc and Brass***, p. 56.

16. Chase, "Bronze Casting in China: A Short Technical History," p. 116.

17. For a good general discussion of chaplets see Rutherford J. Gettens, ***The Freer Chinese Bronzes***, vol. 2, pp. 98-107.

18. Ibid., p. 74.

19. Ibid.

20. Ibid., p. 93-97.

21. Illustrated in Li Xueqin, ***The Wonder of Chinese Bronzes***, no. 23, and in Robert W. Bagley, ***Shang Ritual Bronzes in the Arthur M. Sackler Collections***, fig. 223.

22. Bagley, ***Shang Ritual Bronzes in the Arthur M. Sackler Collections***, p. 18; Nigel Wood, "Ceramic Puzzles from China's Bronze Age"; Pieter Meyers and Lore Holmes, "Technical Studies of Ancient Chinese Bronzes: Some Observations"; Chase, "Bronze Casting in China: A Short Technical History."

23. Marshall Becker, "Sardinian Stone Moulds: An Interesting Means of Evaluating Bronze Age Metallurgical Technology."

24. Barnard & Sato, ***Metallurgical Remains of Ancient China***, p. 73.

25. Bagley, ***Shang Ritual Bronzes in the Arthur M. Sackler Collections***, pp. 17-18.

26. Hubei Provincial Museum, ***Suixian Zeng Hou Yi Mu***.

27. A good demonstration with pictures of the various steps in modern lost-wax casting of Buddhist images can be seen in W. T. Chase, ***Bronze Disease and Its Treatment***, ch. 3.

28. Barbara W. Keyser, "Decor Replication in Two Late Chou Bronze *Chien*."

29. Li Jinghua, "The Casting Process of the Han Dynasty Iron Ploughshares," and Hubei Provincial Museum, ***Han dai die shu***.

30. For good surveys see Bagley, ***Shang Ritual Bronzes in the Arthur M. Sackler Collections***; Li Xueqin, ***The Wonder of Chinese Bronzes***; Han Rubin, "Metalcasting in Ancient China" and "Archaeometallurgy in China"; Noel Barnard, "From Ore to Ingot Mining, Ore processing, and Smelting in Ancient China"; and An Zhimin, "Some Problems Concerning China's Early Copper and Bronze Artifacts."

31. See Bagley, ***Shang Ritual Bronzes in the Arthur M. Sackler Collections***, p. 16; Wen Fong, ***The Great Bronze Age of China***, pp. 69 ff.; and Noel Barnard, "Thoughts on the Emergence of Metallurgy in Pre-Shang and Early Shang China," pp. 22-35.

32. Barnard, "Thoughts on the Emergence of Metallurgy in Pre-Shang and Early Shang China," p. 27.

33. See Fong, ***The Great Bronze Age of China***, figs. 17 &

34. Fong, ***The Great Bronze Age of China***, pls. 10 & 11.18; and Bagley, ***Shang Ritual Bronzes in the Arthur M. Sackler Collections***.

35. Chase, "Bronze Casting in China: A Short Technical History," p. 108.

36. Bagley, ***Shang Ritual Bronzes in the Arthur M. Sackler Collections***, p. 17.

37. Max Loehr, "The Bronze Styles of the Anyang Period (1300-1028 B.C.)"; see also Alexander Soper, "Early, Middle, and Late Shang: A Note."

38. Bagley, ***Shang Ritual Bronzes in the Arthur M. Sackler Collections***, pp. 38ff.

39. Robert W. Bagley, "P'an-lung-ch'eng: A Shang City in Hupei" and ***Shang Ritual Bronzes in the Arthur M. Sackler Collections***; Virginia Kane, "The Independent Bronze Industries in the South of China Contemporary with the Shang and Western Zhou Dynasties."

40. Robert W. Bagley, "A Shang City in Sichuan Province"; Jessica Rawson, ***Western Zhou Bronzes from the Arthur M. Sackler Collections***, pls. 1 and 2.

41. Virginia Kane, "The Chronological Significance of the Inscribed Ancestor Dedication in the Production of Shang Dynasty Bronze Vessels," pp. 340-342. The exact chronology and stylistic evolution of Western Zhou bronzes are discussed by Rawson in ***Western Zhou Bronzes from the Arthur M. Sackler Collections***.

42. See Rawson, ***Western Zhou Bronzes***, no. 117.

43. Fong, ***The Great Bronze Age of China***, nos. 45-47.

44. Gettens, ***The Freer Chinese Bronzes***, vol. 2, pp. 141-157; Rawson, ***Western Zhou Bronzes***.

45. Private communication from Jim Stewart.

46. Jenny F. So, "*Hu* Vessels from Xinzheng: Toward a Definition of Chu Style."

47. Tan Derui, ***The Splendid Craft of Lost Wax Casting in Ancient China***.

48. Robert L. Thorp, ***The Son of Heaven: Imperial Arts of China***, pp. 56 and 57; Bagley, ***Shang Ritual Vessels in the Arthur M. Sackler Collections***, fig. 222.

49. Hubei Provincial Museum, ***Suixian Zeng Hou Yi Mu***.

50. Li Xueqin, ***The Wonder of Chinese Bronzes***, pls. 23 and 24; Bagley, ***Shang Ritual Vessels in the Arthur M. Sackler Collections***, fig. 223.

51. Chase and Franklin, "Early Chinese Black Mirrors and Pattern-etched Weapons"; Cho-yun Hsü, ***Ancient China in Transition***; Li Xueqin, ***Eastern Zhou and Qin Civilizations***.

52. Barnard and Sato, ***Metallurgical Remains of Ancient China***, pl. 3.

53. Chase and Franklin, "Early Chinese Black Mirrors and Pattern-etched Weapons."

54. R. F. Tylecote, "Ancient Metallurgy in China"; Chen Peifen, "Composition and Casting Technology of Ancient Bronze Weapons and Mirrors."

55. For more information on inlaid pictorial decoration during the Eastern Chou period, see Charles Weber, ***Chinese Pictorial Bronze Vessels of the Late Chou Period***.

56. Emma Bunker, ***Ancient Chinese Inlaid Bronzes***, p. 12.

57. Zhu Qixin, "Bronze Vessels from a Spring and Autumn Period Tomb."

58. W. Thomas Chase, "What is the Smooth Lustrous Black Surface on Ancient Bronze Mirrors?"

59. Chinese Academy of Social Sciences, ***Man Cheng Hanmu fajue baogao***, color pl. IX.

60. Henan Provincial Museum, ***Han dai die zhu***.

61. Li Jinghua, "The Casting Process of the Han Dynasty Iron Ploughshares."

62. Craddock, ed., ***2000 Years of Zinc and Brass***, p. 40.

63. This has been discussed in the meeting on surface coloration at the British Museum ("Surface Colouring and Plating of Metals," June 14-16, 1990) and is also the subject of ongoing work at the University of Science and Technology of China in Hefei: Chen Yuyun et al., "An Experimental Imitation of the 'Hei-qi-gu' Bronze Mirror."

64. Lead isotopes have proven their usefulness particularly in the case of the bronze drums of Guangxi and Yunnan. Work is currently going forward in this field as a collaborative research project between the Smithsonian Institution, the Tokyo National Research Institute for Cultural Property, and The Institute for the Study of the History of World Religion in Beijing.

65. Wang Zhangsui et al., "Research on Powdery Corrosion of the Ancient Bell from Cai Hou Tomb," p. 639.

66. As quoted in Joseph Needham, ***Science and Civilization in China***, vol. 4, p. 93.

CATALOGUE OF THE EXHIBITION

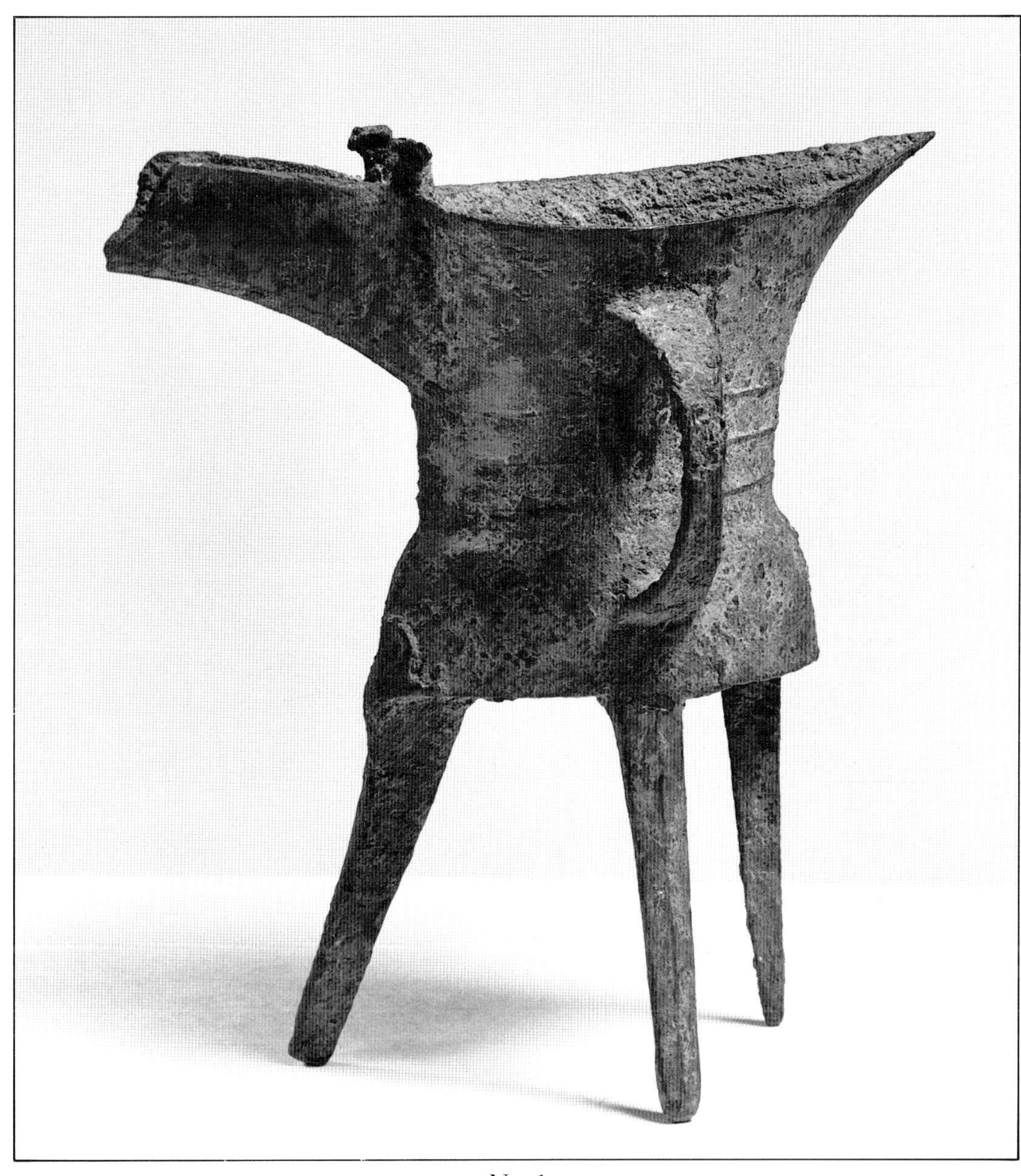

No. 1

1
JUE
Bronze
Shang dynasty, Erlitou period
19th-16th century B.C.
Height: 5-3/4 in. (14.7 cm)
Lent by Dr. Paul Singer

This primitive version of the *jue* shows all the characteristics expected of an early *jue* from Erlitou. It has thin walls and three flimsy-looking legs of triangular section. The piece was cast in a four-part mold, and the stumpy posts on the rim may indicate the sprues or ingates. A mold mark is clearly visible on the leg under the handle. The rim is doubled, with an extra thickness cast inside. It is not clear if the handle was made first, set in the mold, and the vessel then cast onto it, but this construction has been seen on Erlitou vessels. The simple decoration (three bowstrings) was carved into the mold. The front leg under the spout is an ancient repair, cast onto the vessel. These early vessels may have variable and high lead contents (see Cat. no. 2), but we do not as yet have an analysis of this piece.

Two other *jue* of primitive form have been discovered at Erlitou (Fong, *The Great Bronze Age of China*, p. 71, fig. 15, pp. 74-75, color pl. 1). They are similarly thin-walled, and their rims doubled, suggesting the imitation of hammered sheet-metal prototypes (Bagley, *Shang Ritual Bronzes*, pp. 15-16). The stumps on the rim also appear on a primitive *jia* from the Royal Ontario Museum (Cat. no. 2) and are precursors to the decorative capped posts on later *jue* (Cat. nos. 5, 47, and 48) and *jia* (Cat. nos. 4 and 6).

Published: Paul Singer, "Pre-Dynastic and Dynastic Shang Material," *Oriental Art*, 6 (1960), p. 42, fig. 1; Loehr, *Relics of Ancient China*, no. 6; Jean J. Young, *Art Styles of Ancient Shang from Private and Museum Collections* (New York: China Institute in America, 1967), no. 7; Jan Fontein and Tung Wu, *Unearthing China's Past* (Boston: Museum of Fine Arts, Boston, 1973), no. 5; *Selections of Chinese Art from Private Collections*, no. 20.

2
JIA
Leaded bronze (copper 67%, tin 7%, lead 26%)
Shang dynasty, Zhengzhou (Erligang) period
16th-14th century B.C.
Height: 9-3/4 in. (24.8 cm)
Royal Ontario Museum, Dr. J. M. Menzies Collection (960.234.12)

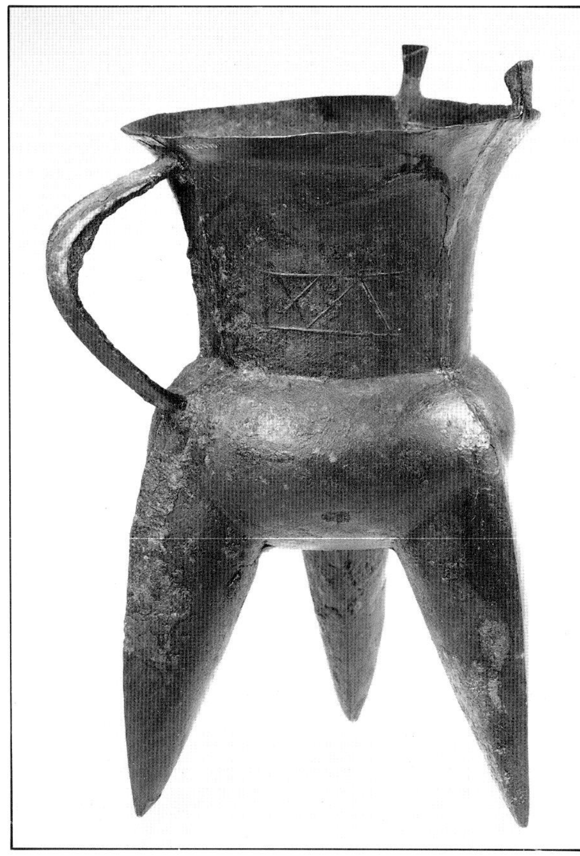

No. 2

This early form of the *jia* vessel has three hollow legs opening into a squat, bulbous body. The tall, flaring neck is decorated with a simple raised-thread diamond pattern between two horizontal lines. A simple strap handle is attached above the rear leg and just below the rim. Two short posts of triangular section rise from the rim above the front legs. The rim is doubled, as on the previous vessel.

Mold marks are very clearly visible, in line with each leg, indicating the use of a three-piece mold. Another mold mark runs up the inside of the handle. Two raised lines run down the neck parallel to the outer edges of the handle. The rudimentary posts may have been used as ingates. The raised line decoration was incised into the mold.

The composition of this *jia* is of great interest. The reported analyses (by Ursula Franklin) are as follows (Barbara Stephen, "Early Chinese Bronzes in the Royal Ontario Museum," *Oriental Art*, n.s. 8 [1962], p. 67):

TABLE I

	Tin	Lead	Zinc
Body	7-8%	26-28%	-
Repair	5%	5%	-

Copper (by difference) is 67 percent and 90 percent, respectively. The same sort of variation in composition is seen in the other early bronzes. Several old repairs are present in the upper part of the vessel. The dark and shiny patina may be due to extensive repair and restoration of the vessel by Dr. Menzies, who acquired the piece in China. It is reported to have been unearthed ten or twelve *li* north of the Anyang railway station during 1913 or 1914.

The posts on this vessel, like those on Dr. Singer's *jue* (Cat. no. 1) are precursors of the more elaborate post and caps of later *jia* (Cat. no. 4) and *jue* (Cat. no. 5). A *jia* of similar shape, but with posts of more developed form on the rim, was excavated from tomb no. 3 at Baijiazhuang, a village northeast of Zhengzhou (Fontein and Wu, p. 30, fig. 2).

Published: Barbara Stephen, "Early Chinese Bronzes in the Royal Ontario Museum," *Oriental Art*, 8 (1962), pp. 62-67; Jan Fontein and Tung Wu, *Unearthing China's Past* (Boston: Museum of Fine Arts, 1973), pp. 30-31, no. 2; Robert Bagley, "P'an-lung-ch'eng: A Shang City in Hupei," *Artibus Asiae*, 39 (1977), p. 203, fig. 23.

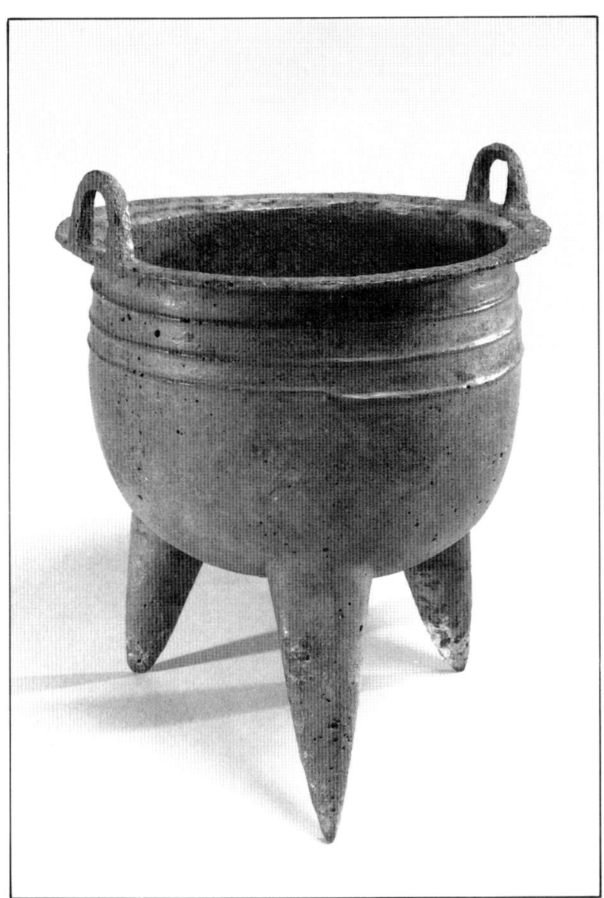

No. 3

3
DING
Bronze (copper approx. 90%,
tin approx. 10%, no lead)
Shang dynasty, Zhengzhou (Erligang) period
16th-14th century B.C.
Height to handles: 7-5/8 in. (19.4 cm)
Height to rim: 6-3/4 in. (17.2 cm)
Diameter: 6-5/16 in. (16.0 cm)
Lent by Richard J. Salisbury

The deep U-shaped bowl of the *ding* is decorated with three horizontal ribs, or "bowstrings," below a flat rim with two simple loop handles. Its three tapering legs are hollow and open onto the interior of the bowl. One leg is considerably shorter than the others, causing the vessel to sit unevenly. The rim has the doubled appearance typical of early bronzes. A pale turquoise-green patina covers the exterior.

This vessel was cast using a three-part mold with the seams running down the center of the legs. Vestiges of the seam marks that have been tooled off can still be seen under the rim. An ancient metal fill can be seen in what appears to be a casting flaw on the interior.

This *ding* was examined in the Freer Gallery of Art Technical Laboratory in 1981. Examination of a metallographic sample taken from the rim near the handle above a leg revealed this to be a tin bronze, with about 10 percent tin and no lead. This is not unlike the analysis of early *jue* from Erlitou (Fong, *The Great Bronze Age of China*, p. 71, fig. 15, pp. 74-75, color pl. 1).

Although thin, the patina does penetrate inward along grain boundaries. It consists mainly of malachite, with some eriochalcite ($CuCl_2 \bullet 2H_2O$), which could arise from previous treatment with hydrochloric acid; not much cuprite can be seen. Some repainting is seen in ultraviolet light on the outside. This *ding* has probably been cleaned and repatinated to improve its appearance.

Of interest is the heavy porosity in the bottom of the body and the legs, suggesting that this vessel was cast upside down.

The shape of this *ding* is related to that of a much larger vessel (height, 21-1/4 in.) excavated in 1974 from Panlongcheng in Hubei Province (Fong, p. 104, no. 4). In both vessels, the legs were probably cast hollow to conserve metal and minimize flaws caused by shrinkage as the metal solidifies. The cylindrical legs of later *ding* vessels (Cat. no. 7) are cast with separate cores that are encased by the metal. Another indication of the early date of these two *ding* are the thin, everted rims with a doubled edge. The same type of rim appears on Cat. nos. 1, 2, and 4.

4
JIA
Bronze
Shang dynasty, Zhengzhou (Erligang) period
16th-14th century B.C.
Height: 9-1/2 in. (24.1 cm)
Lent by Dr. Paul Singer

This vessel has a swelling belly, slightly convex bottom, and tall, flaring neck. It is supported on three hollow legs of triangular section. A simple strap handle is situated on the side of the vessel above one of the legs. Two posts with conical caps are situated on the mouth rim over the remaining two legs. A simple whorl circle in sunken line decorates the top of each cap. The decorative frieze around the waist of the vessel consists of a *taotie* mask on the central axis between the two posts and two halves of a mask separated by the bare area under the handle.

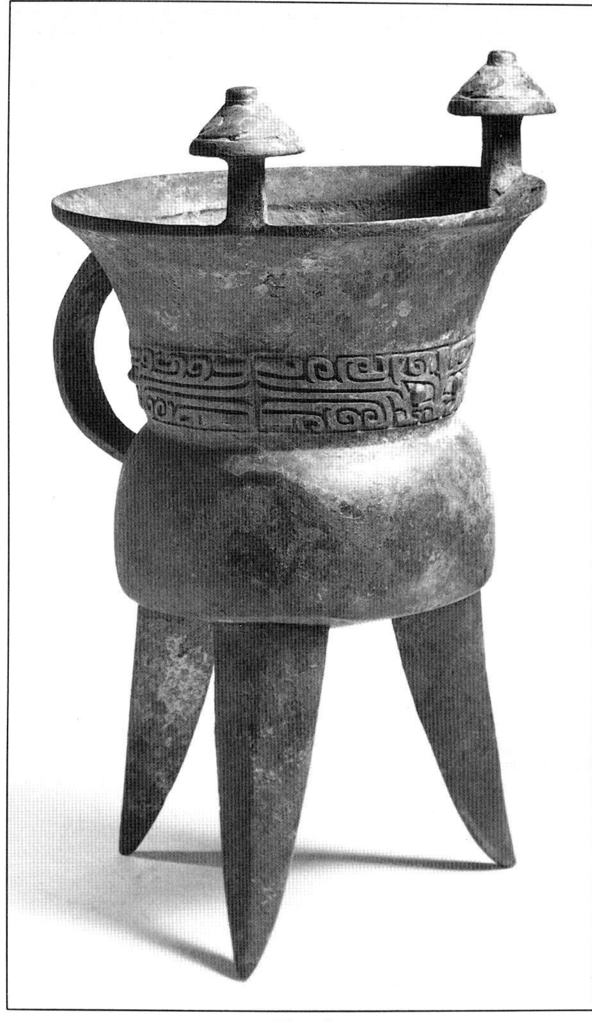

No. 4

The raised ribbonlike bands of the *taotie* mask are characteristic of the second phase of bronze ornament (Loehr's Style II) in the early Shang period. They were probably carved into the mold, just like the bowstrings and diamond patterns of the preceding bronzes. This decoration, however, was carefully finished with abrasives (probably stones) after casting. The even, planar character of the surface of the decoration is determined by the abrasive finishing employed. Where the cast grooves have been cut through by the plane of the abrasive, very sharp corners remain at the edges of the bands. The contrast of very sharp edges and a smooth, planar surface is what gives the decoration its emphatic character.

Characteristic of this early period, are the doubled rim and the high lead content of the alloy, which we infer from the grayish color of the patina.

Published: Loehr, *Relics of Ancient China*, no. 8; Minao Hayashi, *Conspectus of Yin and Zhou Bronzes* (Tokyo, 1984), no. 22.

5
JUE
Bronze
Shang dynasty, early Anyang period
13th century B.C.
Height: 8 in. (20.3 cm)
Inscribed
Hermitage Foundation Museum, Norfolk, Virginia (44.G.25)

This round-bottomed, tripod vessel is the mature form of the Erlitou period *jue* in this exhibition (Cat. no. 1). Its characteristic long, open spout and the pointed rim project in opposite directions. On the rim, at the base of the spout, are two posts topped by domical caps, each decorated with a whorl design in recessed line. The tapered legs of triangular section are asymmetrically arranged so that one leg projects out further than the other two and is placed below the single projecting loop handle on one side. Two *taotie* masks, rendered in Loehr's Style III, are formed by a dense design of raised, spiraling lines around pairs of projecting eyes. They fill a wide frieze encircling the sides of the vessel. Triangular blades decorated with recessed spirals rise from the frieze toward the rim. The decoration is very close to that produced by the mold fragment in the collection of the Seattle Art Museum (Cat. no. 41). Three notched flanges and the heavy handle subdivide the frieze into quadrants reflecting the four-part outer mold assembly. An inscription, probably a clan sign, is

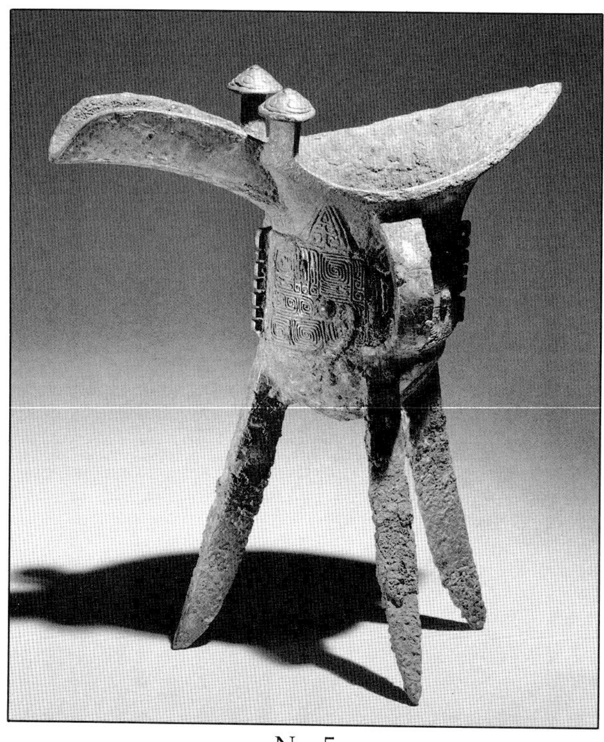

No. 5

located on the side of the vessel beneath the arch of the handle. The surface, particularly on the legs, is covered with a blistery corrosion product that is, in fact, exfoliating.

Lead *jue* vessels, such as Cat. nos. 46, 47, and 48, were left in a relatively unfinished state after casting and show the original appearance of bronze decoration before finishing. Mold seams on the lead vessels also reveal the original placement of the mold pieces.

Former collection: Yamanaka & Co.

6 (Color pl. I)
FANG JIA
Bronze
Shang dynasty, Anyang period
13th-11th century B.C.
Height: 12-1/8 in. (30.8 cm)
Albright-Knox Art Gallery, Buffalo, New York, Bequest of Arthur B. Michael, 1953 (53:2)

This four-sided version of the *jia* vessel has four tapering and splayed legs of triangular section. Its strongly curving sides have an S-shaped profile. Two large, rectangular pillars rising from the rim at the narrow sides are each surmounted by roof-shaped caps. Scored flanges line the corners and ridges of the caps as well as the corners of the vessel. A sturdy handle modeled with an animal mask has been placed on one of the broad sides along the central axis. The vessel is fitted with a flat lid with a central handle in the shape of two birds in the round, sitting back to back and connected at their crests.

The surface is richly covered with flat geometric and animal motifs on a *leiwen* spiral ground inlaid with a black paste. There are simple spirals on the caps and confronting dragons on the legs. The broad sides are decorated from top to bottom with profile dragons, whorl circles, and a bodied *taotie* mask arranged in three registers. The narrow sides are each decorated with an owl. Its large eyes and beak are modeled in low relief, while its horns and split body as well as a pair of dragon heads are rendered flat to either side of a central flange. The lid is decorated with a border frieze of confronting birds separated by a short ridge.

The large, architectonic capped posts illustrate one of the methods used by the ancient artisan to attach various pieces. Each cap was cast separately. The end of the post, cast with the vessel, and the cap were incorporated into a small mold in their

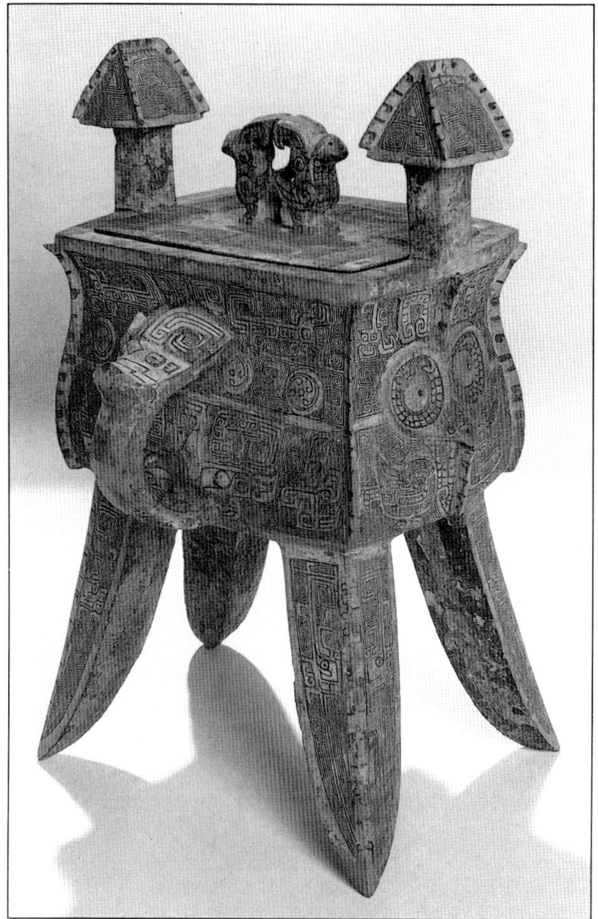

No. 6

correct relative positions. Bronze was then poured into the mold, filling the gap and joining the two pieces. This method was used in attaching the majestic caps on the large *fang jia* in the collection of the Freer Gallery of Art (35.12; Gettens, *The Freer Chinese Bronzes*, vol. 2, p. 94, figs. 97-100).

According to laboratory analysis of the lid carried out in 1977 by Steven Weintraub at The Metropolitan Museum of Art, there is evidence that the edges had been cut down. Although the authenticity of the lid has not been questioned, this has led to some speculation that the lid may not originally have been a part of this vessel (Nash, *Painting and Sculpture from Antiquity to 1942*, p. 78).

Provenance: Reportedly found at Anyang shortly before 1944

Former collections: Dr. Otto Burchard; Mathias Komor

Published: Eleanor von Erdberg Consten, *Das alte China* (Stuttgart: Gustav Kilpper Verlag, 1958), p. 28; P. J. Kelleher, in *The Buffalo Fine Arts Academy Gallery Notes*, 18 (Jan. 1954), no. 2; Loehr, *Ritual*

Vessels of Bronze Age China, no. 31; *Far Eastern Art in Upstate New York* (Ithaca: Herbert F. Johnson Museum of Art, 1976), no. 4; Christian Deydier, *Chinese Bronzes* (New York: Rizzoli, 1980), no. 24; Steven Nash et al., *Painting and Sculpture from Antiquity to 1942* (New York: Rizzoli, 1979), p. 78, illus. p. 17.

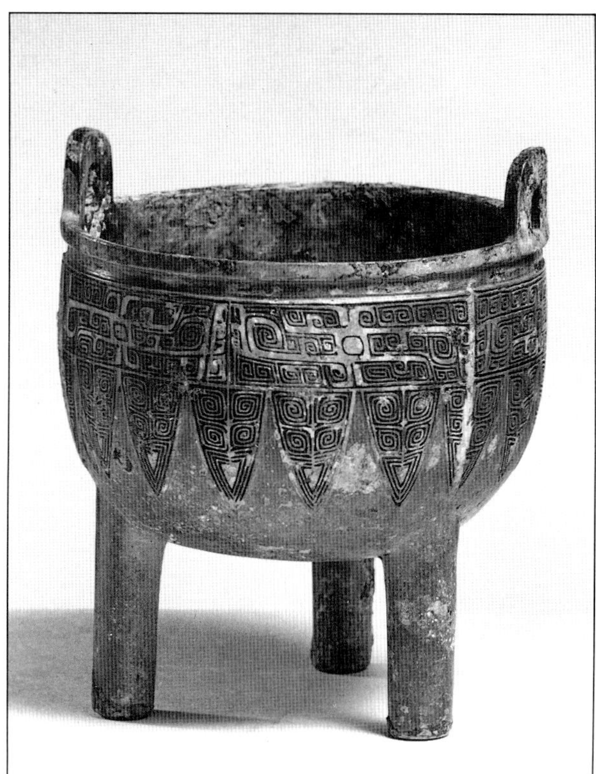

No. 7

7 (Color pl. II)
DING
Bronze
Shang dynasty, Anyang period
13th-11th century B.C.
Height: 4-3/8 in. (11.2 cm)
Three-character inscription in bottom of bowl
Lent by Dr. Paul Singer

The small tripod vessel has cylindrical legs and a pair of small loop handles on the rim. It is decorated with a flat design of monoculi, single eyes at the center of hooked bands, in a horizontal frieze below the rim. Below this, pendant blades circle the belly of the vessel. The *leiwen* spiral background of the monoculi frieze and the spirals in the blades are inlaid with a black fill. The mold seams clearly coincide with divisions of the decoration.

In this phase of Shang bronze decoration (Loehr's Style IV), there is a strong desire to distinguish the figure from the background. The black fill in the *leiwen* seems to be a deliberate attempt to heighten the contrast. Investigation of this filling on the Freer bronzes by Gettens has determined that the material contains carbonaceous material and scattered particles of quartz, and is possibly the residue of black lacquer (Gettens, *The Freer Chinese Bronzes*, vol. 2, pp. 197-204).

Published: Loehr, *Relics of Ancient China*, no. 10.

8
DING
Bronze
Shang dynasty, Anyang period
13th-11th century B.C.
Height: 6-1/2 in. (16.5 cm)
Width: 5-3/4 in. (14.7 cm)
Three-character inscription on interior has been rendered as *zi yu ji*
Yale University Art Gallery, Gift of Mrs. William H. Moore for the Hobart and Edward Small Moore Memorial Collection (1955.4.145)

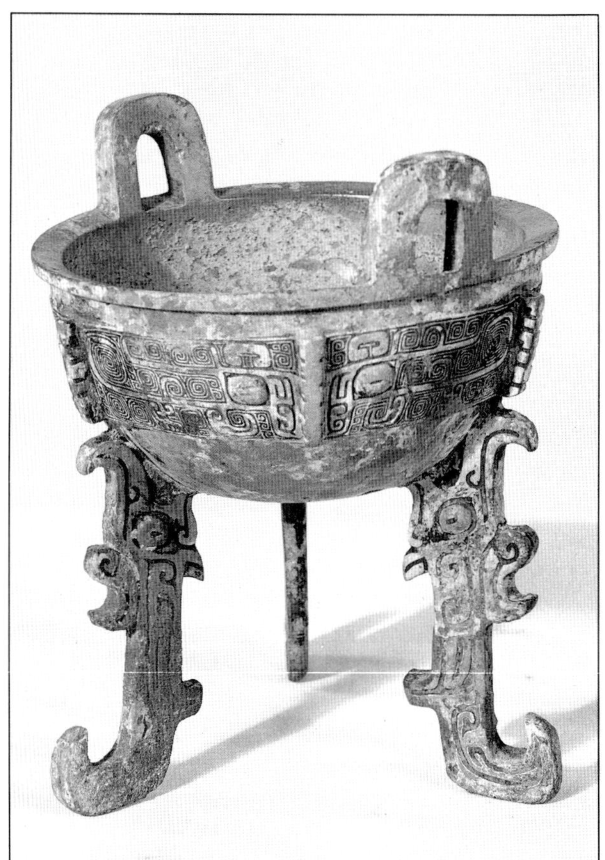

No. 8

This tripod vessel, known as a *ding*, has a bowl-shaped body with a pair of heavy loop handles on its everted rim. Its flat legs are in the shape of one-legged *kui* dragons with upturned heads, gaping mouths, and protruding eyes. The frieze around the belly of the vessel is decorated with three *taotie* masks with bulging eyes and flat horns, jaws, and a thin scrolling body spreading out flush against a *leiwen* spiral background. Each mask is centered between the legs. Heavy vertical flanges are located at the center of each mask and over each leg.

Mold seams are visible above and through the legs. The vessel appears to have been cast in a three-piece outer mold with the legs cast as one with the body.

Published: Bernard Karlgren, "New Studies on Chinese Bronzes," *BMFEA* 9 (1937), pl. 29; Phyllis Ackerman, *Ritual Bronzes of Ancient China* (New York: The Dryden Press, 1945), pl. 58; Eleanor von Erdberg Consten, "A Terminology of Chinese Bronze Decoration," *Monumenta Serica*, 16 (1957), pp. 287-314, fig. 5; Chen Mengjia, *Yin Zhou*, no. A81, vol. 1, p. 19 and no. 116, p. 200, vol. 2, pp. 361-62; Neill, *The Communion of Scholars*, p. 23, no. 2; Lee, *Selected Far Eastern Art in the Yale University Art Gallery*, p. 3 no. 2.

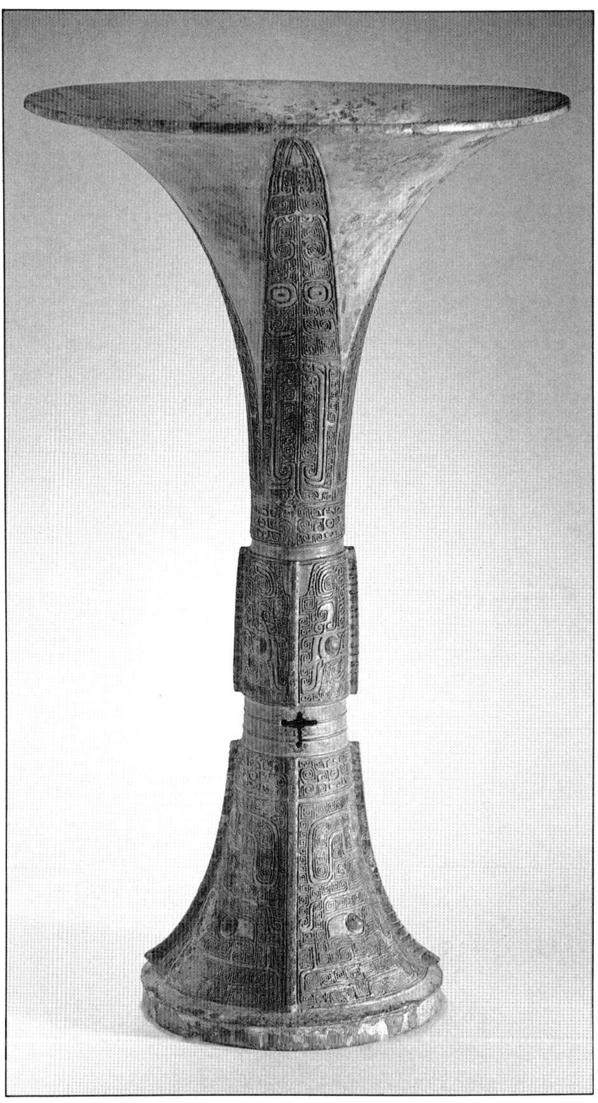

No. 9

9
GU
Bronze
Shang dynasty, Anyang period
13th-11th century B.C.
Height: 11 in. (27.9 cm)
Inscribed in the foot
Hermitage Foundation Museum, Norfolk, Virginia (43.G.35)

The trumpet-shaped neck of the *gu* is decorated in Loehr's Style IV with four slender cicada blades rising to the mouth rim from a narrow collar of "eyed" scrolls. Within each blade a pair of eyes and scrolls are cast against an intricate, squared spiral (*leiwen*) background, all in uniform low relief. The central bulb is decorated in a similar manner with four descending *kui* dragons with protruding eyes. A plain band separating the bulb from the flaring foot is decorated with two raised rings. At the top of the foot is a narrow band of eyed scrolls above four large profile dragons dissolved into the background *leiwen* pattern. The dragons on both the foot and the bulb are symmetrically paired so that they can also be read as *taotie* masks with protruding eyes. Narrow vertical flanges divide both the bulb and the foot into quadrants.

A single cross-shaped opening on the plain band of this vessel is clearly visible, but the expected opening on the other side cannot be seen on the exterior. These openings are formed by cruciform extensions from the core to the outer mold which maintain the casting space. One extension was not in contact with the mold when the molten bronze ran in, and so, did not create a cross mark on the outside. The marks left from these extensions are often visible only on the inside of the foot.

Former collection: Yamanaka & Co.

10
GU
Bronze
Shang dynasty, Anyang period
13th-11th century B.C.
Height: 10-5/8 in. (27 cm)
Inscribed in the foot
Lent by Richard J. Salisbury

The decoration of this *gu* is similar to that on Cat. no. 9. Instead of "eyed" scrolls, the narrow bands at the base of the neck and the top of the foot are filled with simple interlocking spirals. A pictograph on the underside of the foot depicts a kneeling figure.

The two cross-shaped openings usually seen on *gu* vessels are closed here. These openings are the result of extensions from the ceramic core which would have been in contact with the outer mold and which held the foot core in place when the molten metal ran into the mold. If the core shifts slightly, metal can run into the gap and the perforation will not be visible from the outside. In the *gu* from the Hermitage Foundation Museum (Cat. no. 9), only one perforation is visible, suggesting a shift of the core in that direction. The tapering shape of the extensions from the core outwards towards the mold can be seen inside the foot (Fig. 4).

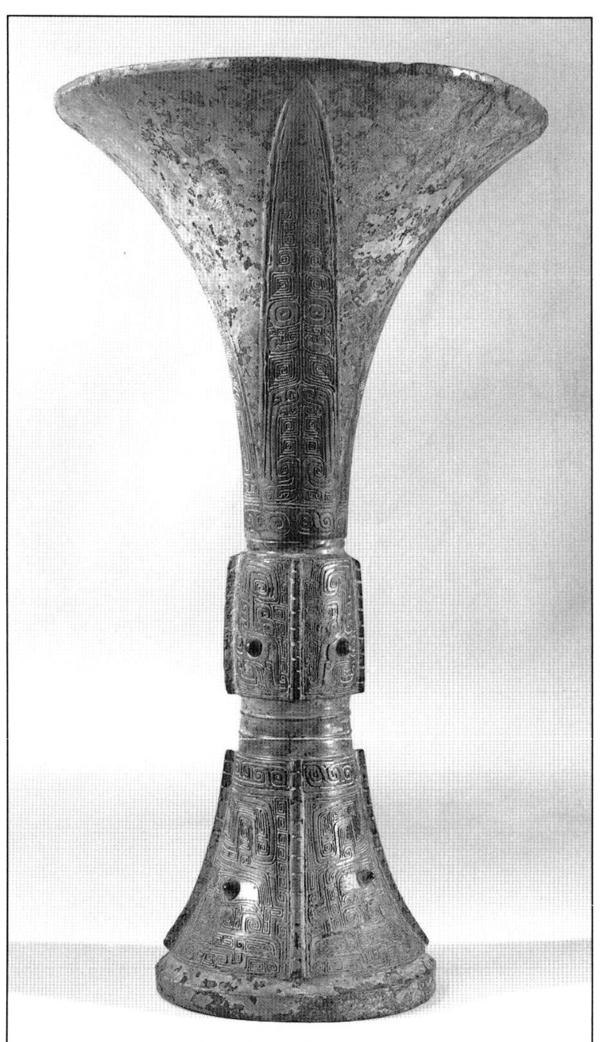

No. 10

Also visible on the underside are buttresses and a chaplet. See Fig. 3 (a) and (b) for a cross section of a *gu* in the Freer Gallery of Art Study Collection clearly showing the different metal used for the chaplet. There is blistery corrosion on the trumpet-shaped mouth of this *gu* and a large restored crack in the mouth.

11A
FANG DING
Bronze
Shang dynasty, Anyang period
13th-11th century B.C.
Height: 13 in. (33.0 cm)
Inscribed
The Metropolitan Museum of Art, Rogers Fund, 1943 (43.25.2a)

11B
LID OR ALTAR TABLE
Bronze
Shang dynasty, Anyang period
13th-11th century B.C.
Height: 4-1/2 in. (11.5 cm)
Inscribed
The Metropolitan Museum of Art, Rogers Fund, 1943 (43.25.2b)

This four-legged, rectangular vessel has bulging sides with an S-shaped profile and two stout loop handles that are attached under the thick everted rim and project upward at an angle. The *fang ding* is decorated on each side with a *taotie* mask in low relief on a *leiwen* background. Above the mask, in a narrow frieze under the rim, is a pair of confronting dragonlike figures with a single, central eye and a scrolling body. Heavy flanges project from the center axis of each side and the corners of the vessel. The cylindrical legs are decorated in sunken line with a simple design of pendant blades below a band of scrolls.

An unusual offering table has been inverted and fitted into the mouth rim of this *fang ding* to function as a lid. Its four legs are decorated with an eye amid scrolls in a revival of the raised-line decoration of Loehr's Style I. The top of the table

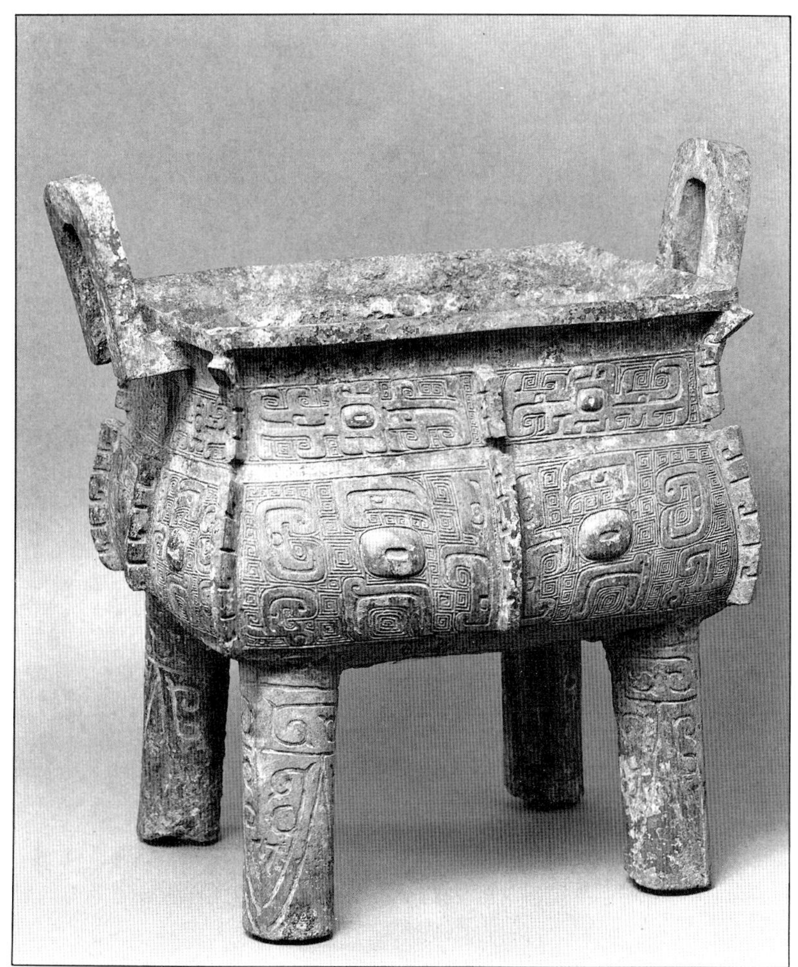

No. 11A

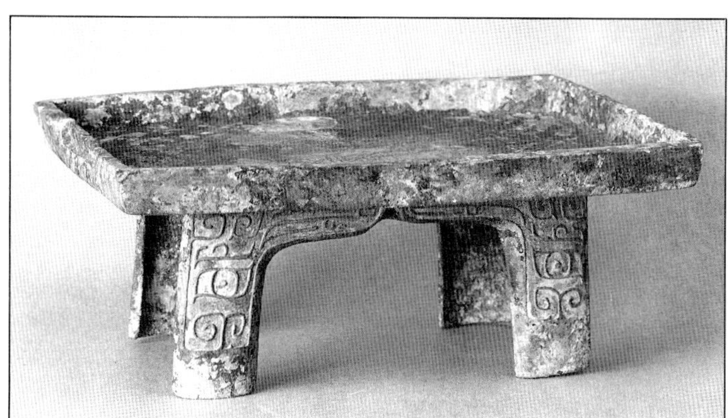

No. 11B

appears to have traces of black of the type found on the bottom of bronze vessels believed to have been used for cooking.

A single character or clan sign is inscribed on the center of the table and on the inside wall of the vessel body. Both inscriptions have been chiseled rather than cast. There is some conjecture that these two bronzes were not originally made for each other.

Former collection: C. T. Loo

Published: C. T. Loo & Co., *Exhibition of Chinese Arts* (1942), no. 46; Alan Priest, "Chinese Bronzes," *The Metropolitan Museum of Art Bulletin*, 4 (1945), p. 109; Phyllis Ackerman, *Ritual Bronzes of Ancient China* (New York: The Dryden Press, 1945), pl. 11.

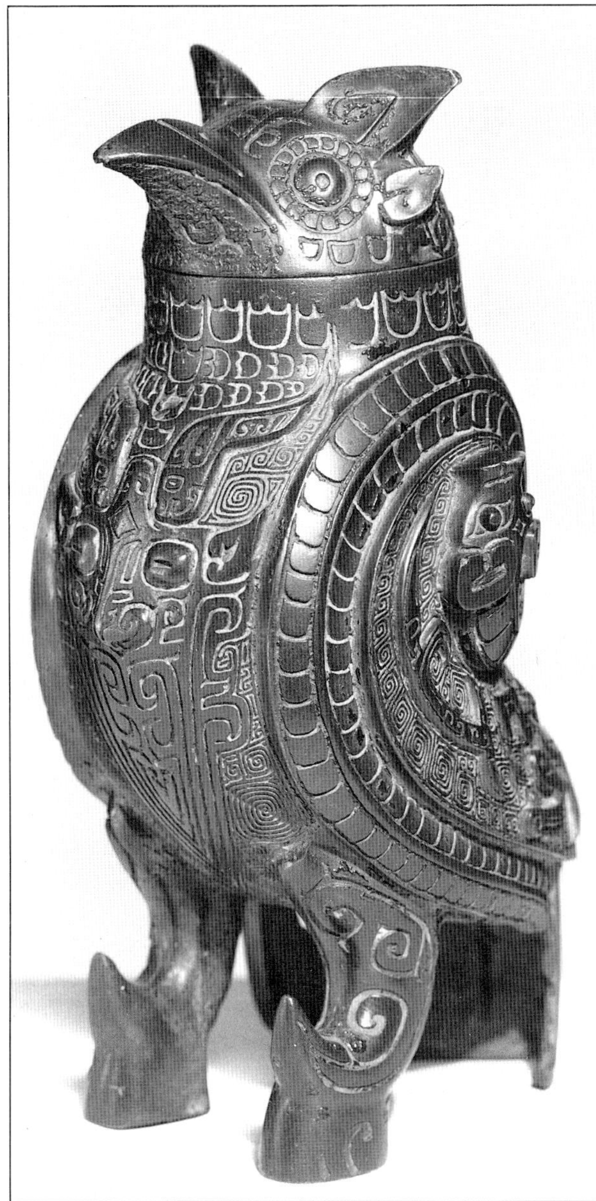
No. 12

12
OWL-SHAPED *ZUN*
Bronze (copper 79%, tin 13%, lead 3%)
Shang dynasty, Anyang period
13th-12th century B.C.
Height: 8-1/4 in. (21 cm)
Yale University Art Gallery, Gift of Mrs. William H. Moore for the Hobart and Edward Small Moore Memorial Collection (1954.48.7)

This wine vessel is cast in the shape of an owl in an upright position resting on its two legs and V-shaped tail. Its head serves as the removable lid.

The body of the owl is decorated with zoomorphic forms in relief against a fine *leiwen* spiral ground. A scaly serpent, dramatically outlining the wing on each side, terminates in a tiger head in high relief on each shoulder. Within the wing are a sweeping hooked band and a plumed bird in profile. On the chest of the owl is a large composite motif consisting of a cicada blade below an animal mask with a pair of goat's horns formed by profile dragons. Feathers and markings on the head, neck, spine, feet, and tail of the owl are indicated by scales and spirals in recessed line.

At one time this owl *zun* was believed to be an archaistic vessel of the Song dynasty (Lee, *Selected Far Eastern Art*, pp. 11-12). Scientific examination undertaken by Lynda A. Zycherman in 1982 at the Technical Laboratory of the Freer Gallery of Art determined the metal content of the alloy to be within the known range for Shang and early Zhou ceremonial bronzes. Thermoluminescent testing of a ceramic core sample from the owl reveals that it is authentic; the last firing of the core took place some time between 1271 B.C. and 221 B.C., roughly from the late Shang to the end of the Warring States period. Stylistic comparison and the popularity of the owl theme in Shang art narrows the range even further to the late Shang period. This is supported by excavated material, such as the carved stone owls from tomb 1001 at Xibeigang, Anyang (Chang, *Shang Civilization*, p. 115, fig. 33), and an owl-shaped *zun* excavated from the tomb of Lady Hao at Anyang (Fong, *The Great Bronze Age of China*, no. 29, p. 162).

X-radiographic analysis reveals that the legs and the body were formed in one casting in a four-piece mold assembly. Separate mold pieces consisted of two side sections, the chest section and an interleg core piece for the belly and inside edges of the feet. Mold seams are visible on the interior edges of the feet and along the "spine" of the bird. The head, which was cast separately in a two-piece mold, shows a mold seam running from front to back along the central axis. A repair patch to the tiger head on the proper right shoulder was made in antiquity and can be detected from the inside and on radiographs. The bright green encrustations scattered over the surface are botryoidal malachite, a type of corrosion which takes a long time to form. Examination indicates recent cleaning or polishing of the surface corrosion.

Former Collections: Peytel Collection, Paris; C. T. Loo

Published: Chen Mengjia, *Yin Zhou*, no. A669, vol. 1, p. 127, vol. 2, pp. 964-965; Christian Deydier, *Chinese Bronzes* (New York: Rizzoli, 1980), no. 36, cat. 68; Neill, *The Communion of Scholars*, pp. 26-29, no. 4; Zycherman, "Technical examination of two owl-shaped *Tsun*," pp. 59-91; for a more complete bibliography see Lee, *Selected Far Eastern Art in the Yale University Art Gallery*, pp. 11-12, no. 15.

13
FANG DING
Bronze (copper 77.5%, tin 14.1%, lead 6.4%, iron 0.1%, zinc 0%)
Early Western Zhou dynasty
Late 11th-early 10th century B.C.
Height: 10-3/4 in. (27.4 cm)
Inscription of forty characters on interior wall
Hermitage Foundation Museum, Norfolk, Virginia (50.G.11)

This rectangular vessel has two loop handles rising from the everted rim on the narrow ends. The heavy flanges on the corners are decorated with an alternating straight line and T-pattern and have blunt projections. A horizontal frieze at the top of each side is decorated with an undulating split-bodied serpent and whorl circles in relief on a *leiwen* spiral. Below this frieze is a small plain panel framed on the sides and bottom by three rows of bosses. The four tall, cylindrical legs are decorated at the top with *taotie* masks and flanges in relief above two bowstrings.

This vessel is referred to as the *Zuo ce fang ding* or *Da zuo ce fang ding*, after "Recorder Da," who is named in the inscription as the maker of the vessel. There are four similarly decorated *fang ding* bearing the same forty-character inscription. Of the two in the National Palace Museum, Taipei, one is considered by Chen Mengjia to be spurious; though overcleaned in the past, this vessel is, in fact, authentic and shows no significant difference in construction, composition, or fabrication methods from the others. Another one is in the collection of the Freer Gallery of Art (50.7). The lengthy inscription documents a specific event and securely dates the vessel to the early Zhou period (Pope et al., *The Freer Chinese Bronzes*, vol. 1, p. 194).

Investigations of these four almost identical *fang ding* show that the vessels were cast with a four-piece outer mold with an interleg core assembly, as shown in Figures 1 and 2. The underside of the vessel has double, parallel ridges crisscrossing between the legs; these are duplicated on one of the Taipei *fang ding*; on the other two *fang ding* of the set, these ridges take on different configurations. Three of the vessels have three chaplets on the underside; one of the Taipei vessels

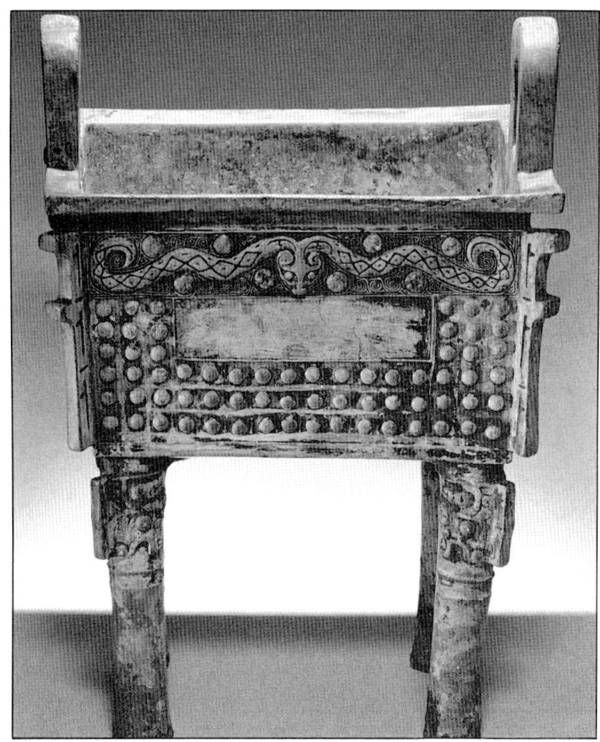

No. 13

has four. The Freer vessel and one of the Taipei vessels have chaplets located in the undecorated panel on each side; the other Taipei vessel and this vessel do not show chaplets in the side walls, even by X-radiography (Gettens, *The Freer Chinese Bronzes*, vol. 2, p. 73, fig. 52; p. 103, fig. 123; p. 205, fig. 276). Analysis of the black filling in the recesses of the decoration of the Freer vessel reveals a mixture of carbonaceous material and quartz. Other carbon deposits on the surface may support the view that these vessels were actually used in cooking during the Shang and Zhou rituals (Pope et al., *The Freer Chinese Bronzes*, vol. 1, pp. 193-194).

From careful examination of these four vessels one builds a picture of Early Western Zhou casting that is close to what one might see in a modern foundry. While all four vessels were made to look the same on the exterior, the individual chaplet placement, lines on the underside, and finishing display some variation. One can almost see the artisans making these pieces, taking great care with the steps that show, and "tossing off" the steps that don't.

Former collection: T. L. Yuan

Published: A. G. Wenley, "The Appearance of a Fourth *Ta tso tsu ting* as Proven by the Inscriptions," in *Akten des XXIV. internationalen Orientalistenkongresses* (Munich, 1957), pp. 632-633.

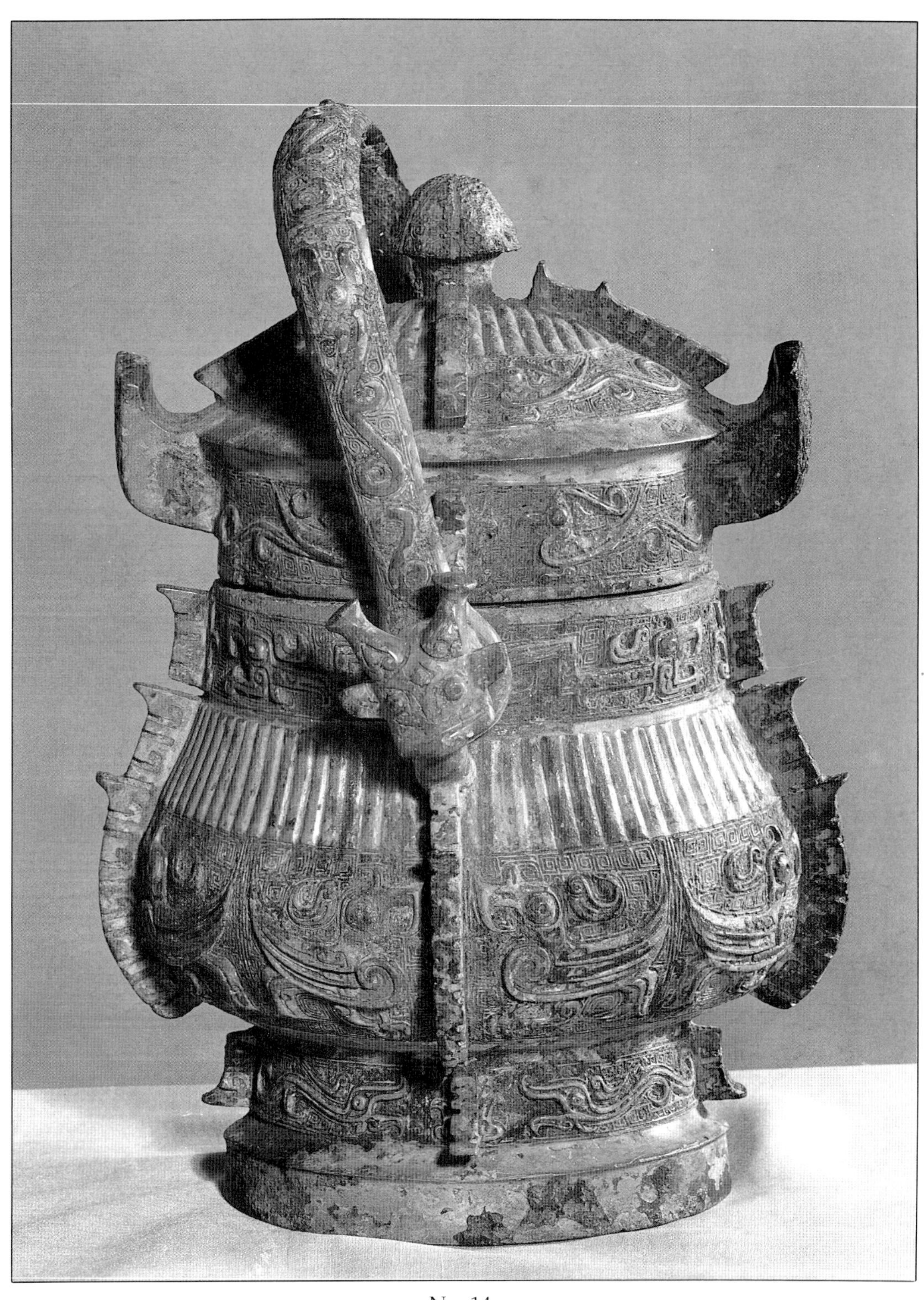

No. 14

14
YOU
Bronze
Shang dynasty, Anyang period
11th century B.C.
Height: 9-7/8 in. (25.1 cm)
Worcester Art Museum, Worcester, Massachusetts (1940.18)

The oval container with bulging sides rests on a stepped foot. It has a swing handle and a domical lid with a conical knob and wide collar. Heavy barbed flanges dividing the vessel into quadrants, and the hornlike projections on the lid give the silhouette an aggressive appearance. A band of vertical ribbing circles both the knob on the lid and the container on its shoulder. The rest of the vessel surface is covered with decorative friezes consisting of stylized birds or dragons cast in relief on a *leiwen* spiral background. The outer edge of the handle is decorated with a band of undulating profile dragons. Animal heads with blunt-tipped horns in high relief cover the ends of the handles; the handles are attached to the vessel at the center of the neck on the broad side.

A very similar *you* from the Pillsbury Collection in The Minneapolis Institute of Arts is dated by Loehr to the late Shang period. Both vessels are typologically related to the *you* in The Metropolitan Museum of Art altar set that was reportedly unearthed near Baojixian in ancient Zhou territory. (The various arguments for either a Shang or a Western Zhou date for this set are presented in Loehr, *Ritual Vessels of Bronze Age China*, pp. 96-100.)
The movable swing handle is one of the technical accomplishments of the Shang bronze caster (see Cat. no. 15).

Published: Phyllis Ackerman, *Ritual Bronzes of Ancient China* (New York: The Dryden Press, 1945), pl. 28; P. B. Cott, *Art Through Fifty Centuries* (Worcester, Mass.: Worcester Art Museum, 1948), fig. 25.

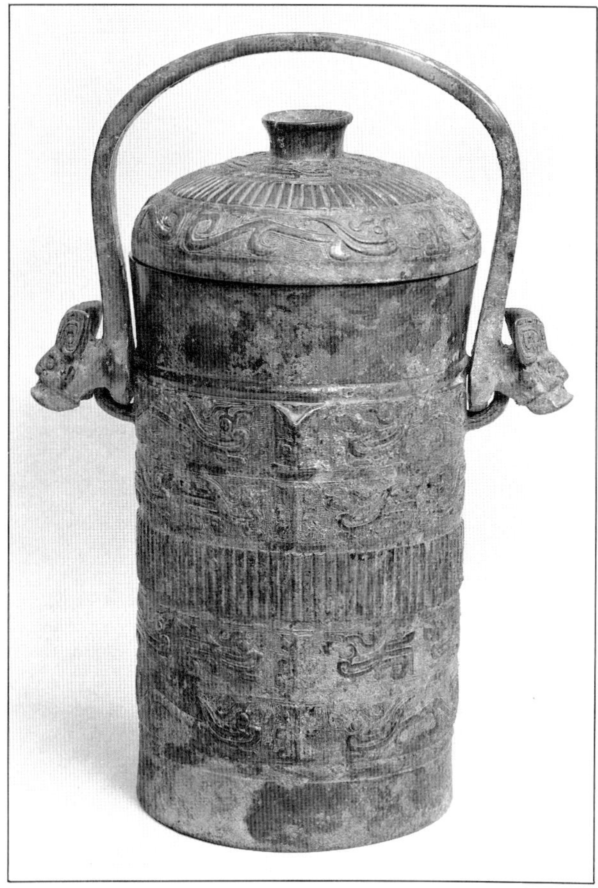

No. 15

15 (Color pl. III)
YOU
Bronze
Shang dynasty, Anyang period
11th century B.C.
Height: 10-7/8 in. (27.7 cm)
Three-character inscription in lid and on base
The Metropolitan Museum of Art, Bequest of Addie W. Kahn, 1949 (49.135.5a, b)

This cylindrical variation of the preceding *you* vessel (Cat. no. 14) is covered with a similar program of decoration. There are four horizontal friezes of confronting, long-tailed birds on a *leiwen* ground and a central frieze of vertical ribs. The lowest band and the slightly flaring neck are left bare. A simple raised mask on the top register marks the central axis of each side. The domical lid has a small knob in the shape of a flaring ring surrounded by two concentric zones of confronting birds separated by a band of vertical ribs. A horned animal head decorates each end of the swing handle. The surface of the vessel is covered with a light green patina with several large bald patches revealing the original yellowish color of the metal.

The swing handles on this vessel and the *you* from The Worcester Art Museum (Cat. no. 14) were made by the same method. A protruding ring on each side of the neck was cast as one piece with the vessel. The handle was cast separately, with a U-shaped opening at each end. The vessel and the handle were assembled in a mold with an open space corresponding to the gap in the handle end. Molten metal was then poured into this gap to complete the handle ring. When the mold was removed, the handle swung freely.

Provenance: This vessel was brought from China by Jörg Trübner who was told that it was found in Henan Province.

Published: Jörg Trübner, *Yu and Kuang: Zur Typologie der chinesischen Bronzen* (Leipzig, 1929), pls. LIX, LX; Otto Kümmel, *Jörg Trübner zum Gedächtnis* (Berlin, n.d.), pl. 14, 15; Umehara, *Seika*, pl. 85; Umehara, *Kodōki keitai*, pl. XVII, no. 6; Rong Geng, *Shang Zhou*, p. 329, no. 17, fig. 630; Phyllis Ackerman, *Ritual Bronzes of Ancient China* (New York: The Dryden Press, 1945), pl. 47; Aschwinn Lippe, "A Gift of Chinese Bronzes," *The Metropolitan Museum of Art Bulletin*, 9 (1950), p. 105, illus. p. 103.

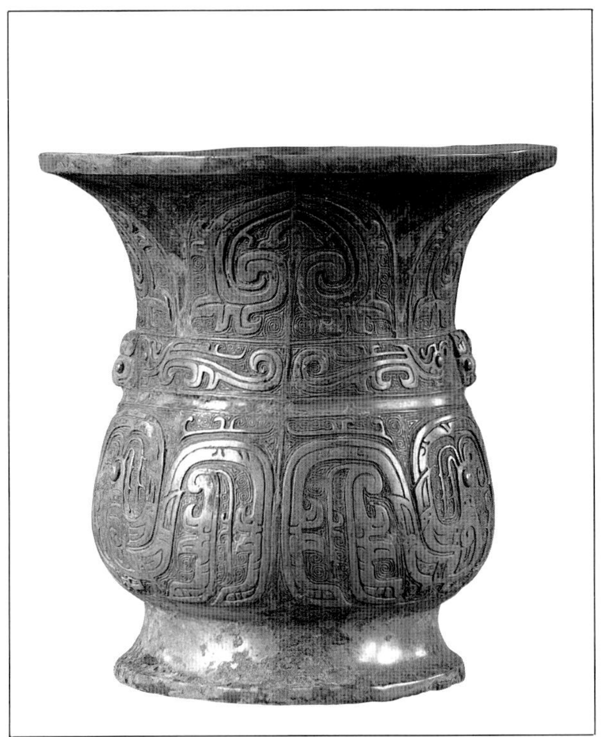

No. 16

16 (Color pl. IV)
ZUN
Bronze
Early Western Zhou dynasty
11th-10th century B.C.
Height: 6-7/16 in. (16.4 cm)
Diameter at mouth: 6-11/16 in. (17 cm)
The Art Museum, Princeton University, Museum Purchase, Carl Otto von Kienbusch, Jr., Memorial Collection (y1952-58)

This *zun*-type wine vessel has curved sides, a flaring mouth, and a splayed foot. The decoration, arranged in three zones, is done in flat relief on a *leiwen* spiral background. Two pairs of confronting birds with bulging eyes and spiraling bands of plumage occupy the main frieze at the belly. A narrow band of confronting birds circles the neck. Above this, a frieze of blade-shaped panels rises up from the neck band to the flaring mouth. These panels are filled with broad bands conforming to the shape of the blade and ending in scrolls at the base. The abstract bands, embellished with a median groove and flamelike barbs, are derived from the confronting birds or dragons that usually fill such panels in the late Shang and early Western Zhou dynasties (compare Cat. no. 17). The surface is covered with a beautiful green patina.

Chaplets are clearly visible in the bare areas between the rising blades. The symmetrical disposition of these plugs of metal distinguish them from ancient repairs. They are used to keep the outer mold and the core separated and to maintain an even casting space. Their location in this type of vessel was noted by Gettens in his study of a *zun* in the collection of the Freer Gallery of Art (54.122; Gettens, *The Freer Chinese Bronzes*, vol. 2, p. 99, fig. 112).

Published: *The Carl Otto von Kienbusch, Jr., Memorial Collection*, The Art Museum, Princeton University, 1956, no. 135; Loehr, *Ritual Vessels of Bronze Age China*, no. 52; Ruth Spelman, *The Arts of China: A Retrospective*, (Greenvale, Long Island: C.W. Post Art Gallery, 1977), no. 23; Christian Deydier, *Chinese Bronzes* (New York: Rizzoli, 1980), no. 26; *Selections from The Art Museum, Princeton University* (Princeton, NJ, 1986), illus. p. 193.

17
ZUN
Bronze
Early Western Zhou dynasty
11th-10th century B.C.
Height: 9-1/2 in. (24.1 cm)
Diameter at mouth: 8-1/4 in. (21 cm)
Loaned by The University Museum, University of Pennsylvania, Philadelphia (C352)

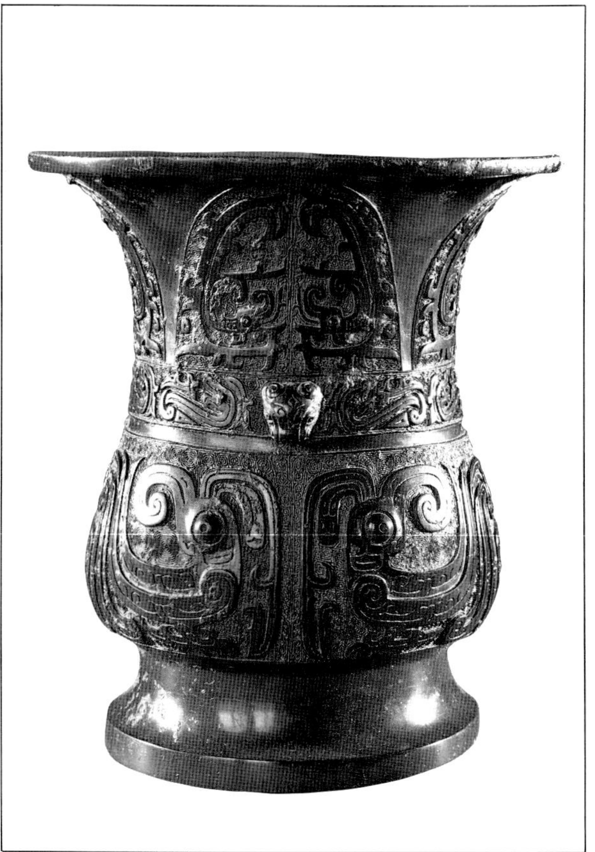

No. 17

A wide, flaring rim and the curving sides of the *zun* create an elegant S-curve profile. Its shape and decoration are reminiscent of the preceding vessel. Two pairs of large, addorsed birds with protruding eyes occupy the frieze on the swelling belly. Their beaks and plumage are arranged in sweeping spirals and curves. Circling the shoulder of the vessel is a narrow band of S-curved dragons with everted heads that is interrupted by two projecting feline heads at opposite sides. Wide petal-shaped panels rise from this band to the rim. Each panel is filled with a pair of confronting profile dragons with upswept bodies or plumage of grooved barbed bands. A four-character inscription reads *zuo bao zun yi*, "made [this] precious sacrificial vessel."

Although very similar in form and decoration to the *zun* in The Art Museum, Princeton University, the surface appearance is very different. The smooth, blackish patina is presumably caused by a high tin content, in this case about 14 percent tin.

Published: Umehara, *Seika*, vol. 1, no. 27; Umehara, *Kodōki keitai*, pl. 8:10; Rong Geng, *Shang Zhou*, fig. 545; Loehr, *Ritual Vessels of Bronze Age China*, no. 51.

18
GUI
Bronze
Early Western Zhou dynasty
11th century B.C.
Height: 6 in. (15.3 cm)
Width: 10-1/8 in. (25.7 cm)
Lent by Dr. Paul Singer

The wide bowl with a flaring mouth rim rests on a high ring foot with a stepped rim. The heavy handles at the sides are cast in the shape of an animal head and curving bird body, with the tail and leg cast in relief on the pendant lugs. The sides are decorated in relief with confronting spiral-bodied creatures on a *leiwen* ground. Their eyes and fangs are cast in particularly high relief. The creatures are separated along the central axis by a small mask in relief over a short flange on a hooked shield. The foot is decorated in very low relief with a pair of confronting, undulating dragons on a spiral ground.

A raised pattern of crisscrossing (Karlbeck) lines is visible on the underside of the bowl. Similar lines are found on the base of the *gui* in the collection of Mr. and Mrs. Myron S. Falk, Jr. (Cat. no. 19; Fig. 7).

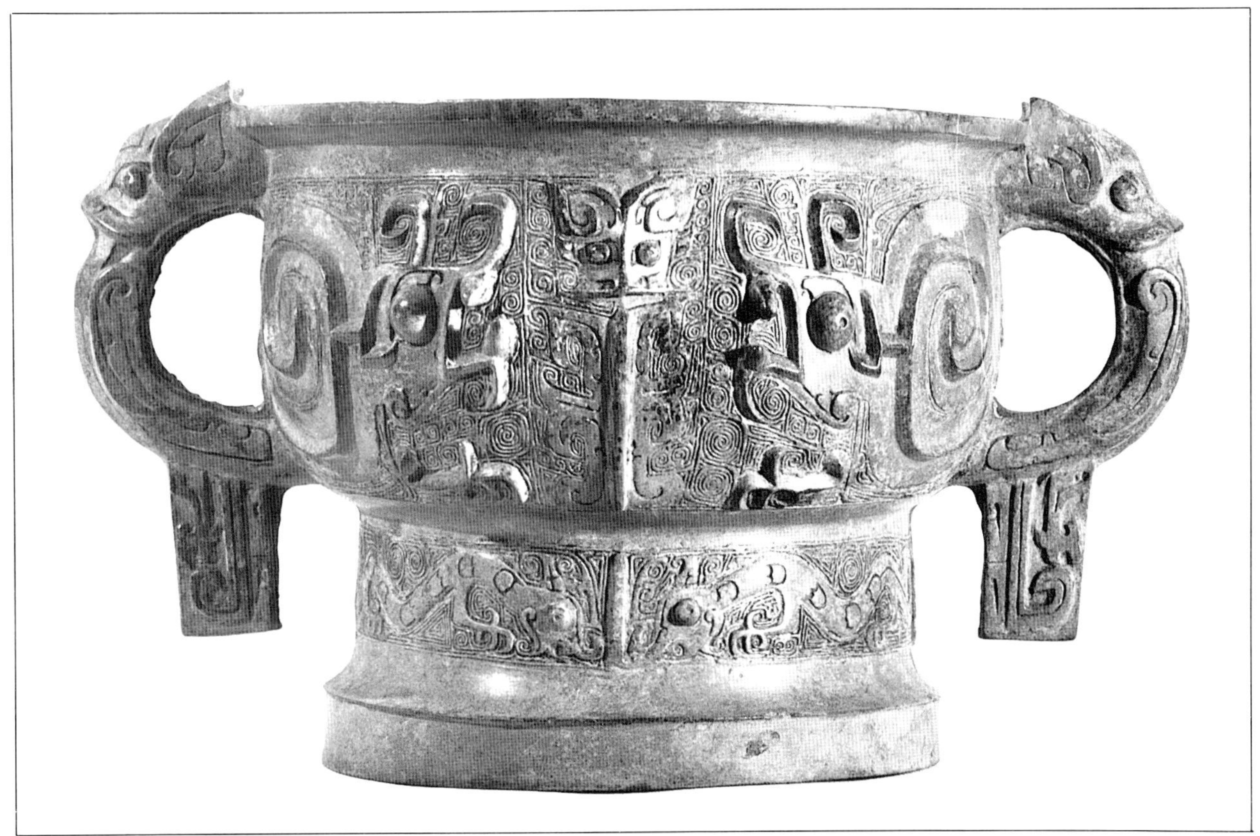

No. 18

Published: John D. La Plante, *Arts of the Chou Dynasty* (Palo Alto: Stanford University Museum, 1958), no. 13; Ruth Spelman, *The Arts of China: A Retrospective* (Greenvale, Long Island: C. W. Post Gallery, 1977), no. 22; Loehr, *Ritual Vessels of Bronze Age China*, no. 40.

19
GUI
Bronze
Late Western Zhou dynasty
9th century B.C.
Height: 9 in. (22.9 cm)
Diameter without handles: 9-1/4 in. (23.5 cm)
Lent by Mr. and Mrs. Myron S. Falk, Jr.

The round, covered container has a flaring ring foot raised on three short legs descending from animal heads overlaid on the foot. Its domed lid is surmounted by a flaring ring that serves both as a knob and as a foot when the lid is inverted. Above the horizontally fluted belly, the slanting neck is decorated with a wide frieze of grooved scrolls and eyes in flat relief suggesting a dissolved zoomorphic design. Another frieze of the same design is repeated on the lid. The foot is decorated with a band of grooved diagonals and hooks in flat relief. Two loop handles in the shape of animal heads with spiral horns, cast onto the vessel at the neck, hold loose rings.

It is conjectured that the two perforations at the base of the knob were used to tie the lid to the rest of the vessel; or more likely they may be the result of the supports used to align the core of the knob during casting. The underside of the vessel is marked with a grid of raised crisscrossing lines known as Karlbeck lines (Fig. 7). There are various conjectures for the presence of these lines. One possible explanation is that they were used in aligning the core in the assembly. Also visible in the photograph are the sprue marks on the feet.

Published: John D. La Plante, *Arts of the Chou Dynasty* (Palo Alto: Stanford University Museum, 1958), no. 43.; Loehr, *Ritual Vessels of Bronze Age China*, no. 60; K. M. Linduff, *Tradition, Phase and Style of Shang and Chou Bronze Vessels* (New York & London: Garland, 1979), pl. 21.

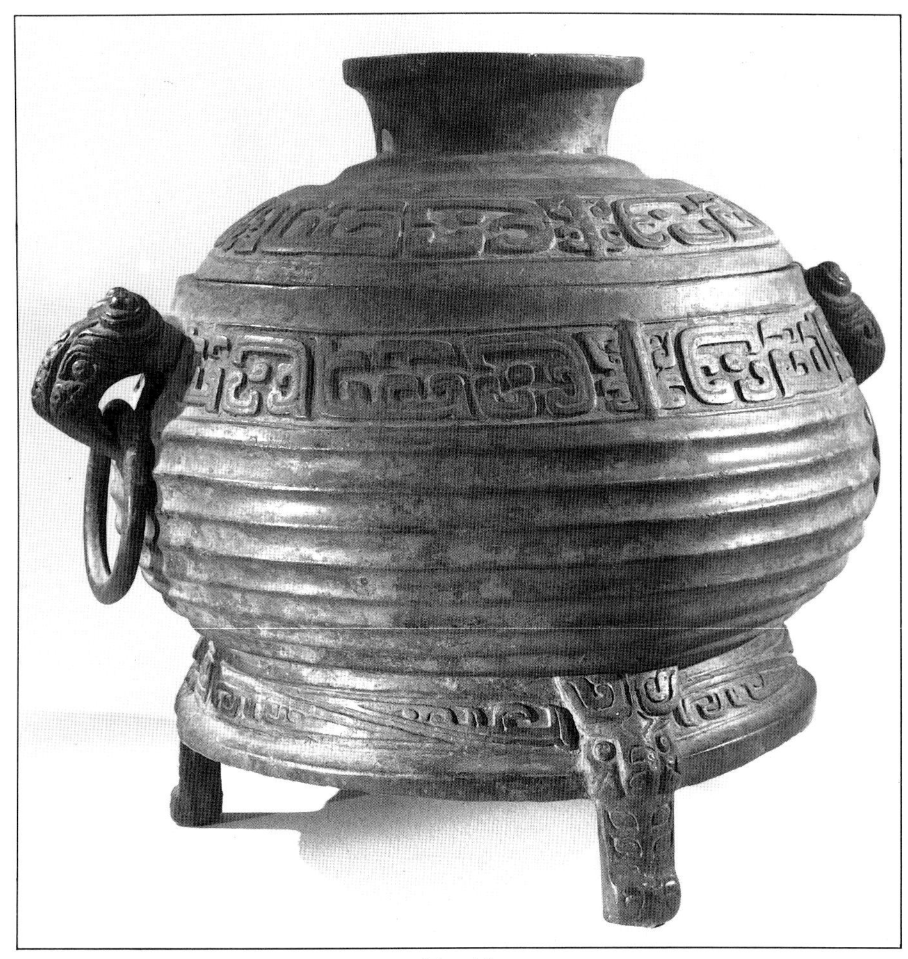

No. 19

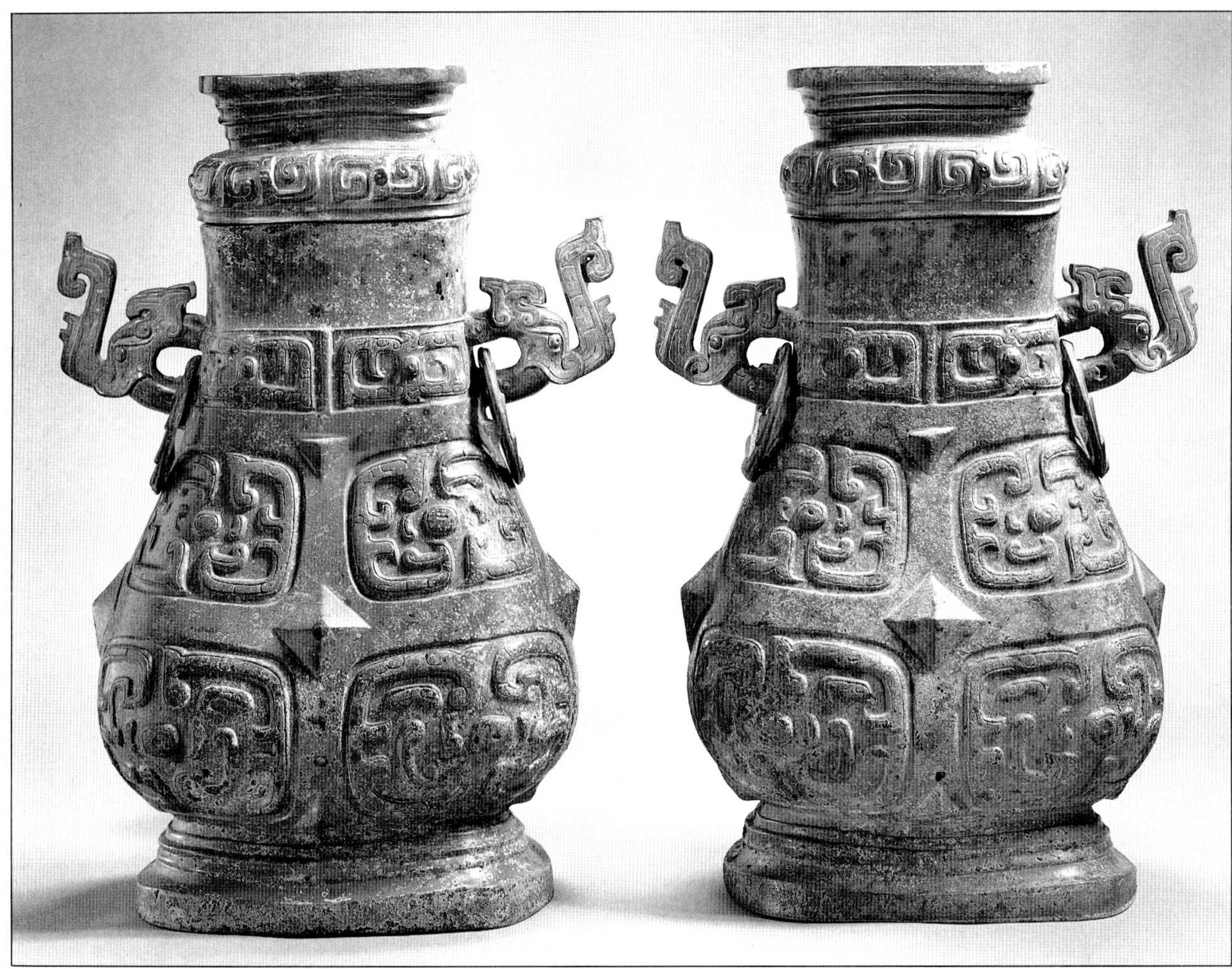

No. 20

20
PAIR OF *HU*
Bronze
Late Western Zhou dynasty
9th-8th century B.C.
Height: 21-5/8 in. (55 cm)
Inscription on the lid: *wei*
The Metropolitan Museum of Art, Charlotte C. and John C. Weber Collection, Gift of Charlotte C. and John C. Weber through the Live Oak Foundation, 1988 (1988.20.4ab, 5ab)

Each of the massive *hu* vessels has a pear-shaped body with a tall, straight neck and a flattened oval cross section. The vessel rests on a molded ring foot. The lid is surmounted with a flaring ring resembling the foot in an inverted position. Wide intersecting bands divide the belly of the *hu* into four sunken panels on each side, with large diamond-shaped studs marking the crossing. Each panel is decorated in relief with a single eye and spirals resulting from a distortion of the old *taotie* image. A band of raised eyes and spirals at the neck and on the lid are conventionalized images of profile dragons. The lid is decorated on the top with a shield consisting of a central eye surrounded by swirls. Elaborate loop handles at the base of the neck carry loose rings and are surmounted by animal heads with large trunklike extensions.

The numerous large holes in the neck result from the entrapment of gas bubbles as the molten bronze cools. This porosity is seen in many Western Zhou bronze vessels. There are various possible reasons for its occurrence, including changes in casting practice after the Zhou conquest.

Former collection: Mr. and Mrs. Earl Morse

Published: Fong Chow, *Animals and Birds in Chinese Art* (New York: The China Institute in America, 1968), no. 9; Loehr, *Ritual Vessels of Bronze Age China*, no. 58; Thorp and Bower, *Spirit and Ritual*, p. 35, nos. 20, 21.

21
LEI
Bronze
Early Eastern Zhou dynasty
8th-7th century B.C.
Height: 10-7/8 in. (27.6 cm)
Diameter: 11-13/16 in. (30 cm)
Worcester Art Museum, Worcester, Massachusetts; Gift of Mrs. F. Harold Daniels (1957.1)

This wide-shouldered vessel, sometimes called a *pou*, rests on a flat bottom and has a narrow, straight neck with a broad, everted mouth rim. Two loop handles are cast onto the shoulders. Broad, interlocking bands of dragons are arranged in two wide friezes on the body. The scrolling bands, which terminate in profile dragon heads at each end, are raised in flat relief and embellished with grooves. Large, projecting bosses mark the eyes of some of the dragon heads.

The large-scale dragon design here heralds a change in taste and production technique. In the following centuries such designs began to condense into complex repeat patterns, ideal for the use of pattern blocks.

Published: Worcester Art Museum, *News Bulletin and Calendar*, 22, no. 5 (1957), p. 27, and *Annual Report* (1957), p. 13 (listed); Loehr, *Ritual Vessels of Bronze Age China*, no. 61.

22
DOU
Bronze
Eastern Zhou dynasty, late Spring and Autumn period
Late 6th century B.C.
Height: 10-1/2 in. (26.7 cm)
The Metropolitan Museum of Art, Rogers Fund, 1925 (25.20.2a, b)

This graceful *dou* is a bowl on a tall, pedestal foot. Its domical lid is surmounted by a flaring ring crown that becomes a pedestal foot when the lid is

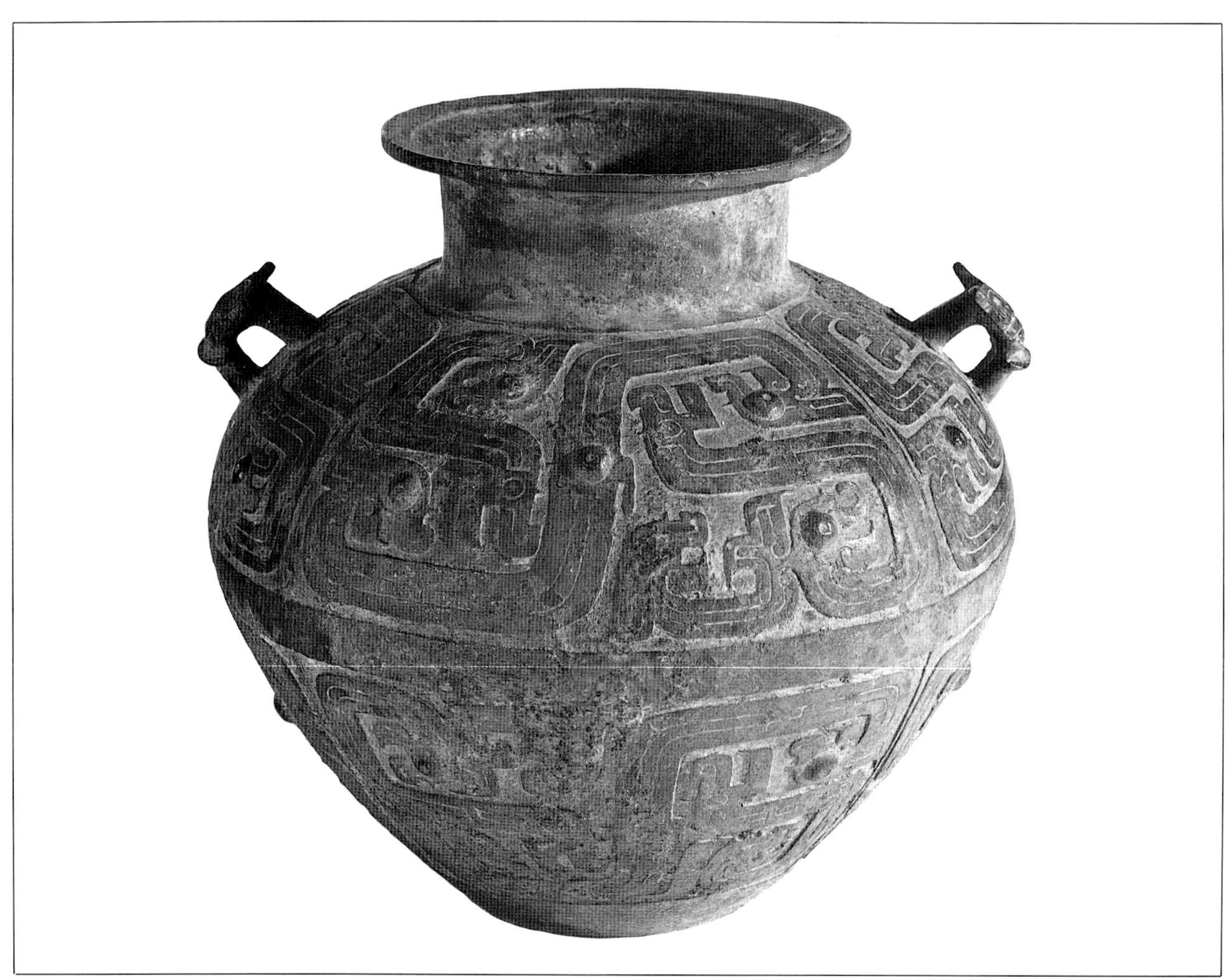

No. 21

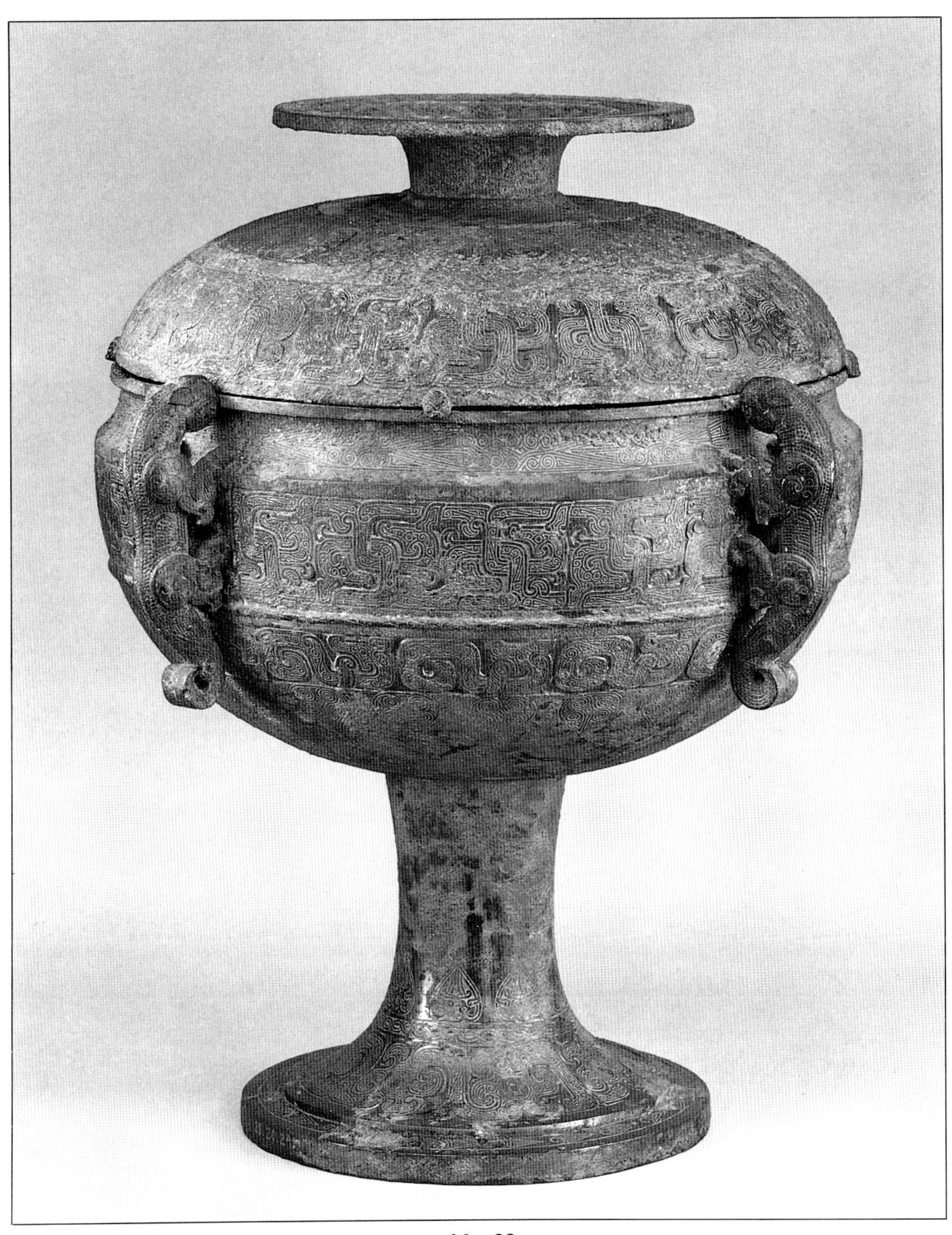

No. 22

inverted. The handles, in the shape of four large, sinuous felines, divide the vessel into four equal quadrants. They are covered with a fine pattern of granulae. Four tiny lugs in the shape of animal heads project from the rim of the lid.

The *dou* is decorated in the so-called Liyu style with repeat patterns of interlacing or meandering dragon bands in flat relief (see G. W. Weber, *The Ornaments of Late Chou Bronzes*, pp. 402-403). They are arranged in two concentric friezes on the lid and in two horizontal friezes separated by a half-round molding on the sides of the bowl. Delicate heart-shaped petals border the lower frieze. A fine pattern of spirals and triangular volutes in sunken line embellish the petals, the dragon bands, and the concave band around the neck of the bowl. Another dragon band frieze decorates the spreading stem foot below a rope-twist band and a border of heart-shaped petals. The rim of the foot is decorated with a simple border of spirals and triangular volutes. Two bands of cusped meanders encircle the interior of the flaring crown.

This is a fine example of late Zhou piece-mold casting and the use of pattern blocks. Chaplets can be clearly seen, symmetrically placed in the clear band on the top of the lid. The handles were cast first, and the vessel was cast onto them; a similar construction is seen in the large *hu* in the Freer Gallery of Art (57.22; Pope et al., *The Freer Chinese Bronzes*, vol. 1, p. 501, no. 97). The vessel has a silvery color, very similar to a *dui* also in the Freer Gallery (32.13; Pope et al., p. 528 ff., no. 103). The Freer *dui* has a composition of 70 percent copper, 14 percent tin, 13 percent lead; one suspects that our *dou* has a similar composition. The large band of decoration on the *dou* running under the handles appears to be identical with that on the *dui*; perhaps both were produced from the same pattern block.

Provenance: Reportedly from Liyu, Hunyuanxian, Shanxi Province

Published: Osvald Siren, *A History of Early Chinese Art: The Prehistoric and Pre-Han Periods* (London, 1929), pl. 104; Umehara, *Sengoku*, pl. X; J. L. Davidson, "Toward a Grouping of Early Chinese Bronzes," *Parnassus* (April 1937), fig. 7; Umehara, *Kodoki keitai*, pl. VI:4; Mizuno Seiichi, *In Shu seidoki to gyoku* (Tokyo, 1950), p. 31, pl. 136; G. W. Weber, *The Ornaments of Late Chou Bronzes*, pp. 402-403; Maxwell Hearn and Wen Fong, "The Arts of Ancient China," *The Metropolitan Museum of Art Bulletin*, 32, 2 (1973-1974), no. 2, fig. 28; Christian Deydier, *Chinese Bronzes* (New York: Rizzoli, 1980), no. 39.

23
BELL (*ZHONG*)
Bronze
Eastern Zhou dynasty
Late 5th-4th century B.C.
Height: 11-3/8 in. (28.2 cm)
Lent by Dr. Paul Singer

This small bell has straight contours and a pointed oval cross section. A pair of S-shaped felines with winged bodies and taloned feet stand on the flat top of the bell. Their bodies are textured with fine striae, scales, and granulae. Rising from the heads of the felines is a U-shaped suspension loop decorated with a sunken pattern of spirals.

A large panel on the front and back of the bell is outlined and subdivided by thick ridges into five horizontal registers interrupted by a narrow trapezoidal panel in the center. Three of the registers are decorated with large bosses in high relief and textured with an overall pattern of raised curls. These alternate with two registers of hooks and curls in low relief similarly textured with fine granulae and spirals. A similar pattern borders the sides and top edge, as well as the very top of the bell. The lower panel on each side is decorated with a symmetrical, masklike arrangement of textured hooks and curls.

This bell is a masterful example of the method of casting with pattern blocks that was used in the bronze foundry site at Houma, Shanxi Province. Both sides of the handle are identical, having been created from the same pattern block. The long registers of decoration on the face of the bell were produced from another block. A third block was used for the bosses; this might have also carried the design around the bosses, as joints in the pattern are discernible on a line equidistant between the two bosses. Negative patterns for bosses (without surrounding design) have been discovered at Houma (Barnard and Sato, pl. III). The master pattern block for the

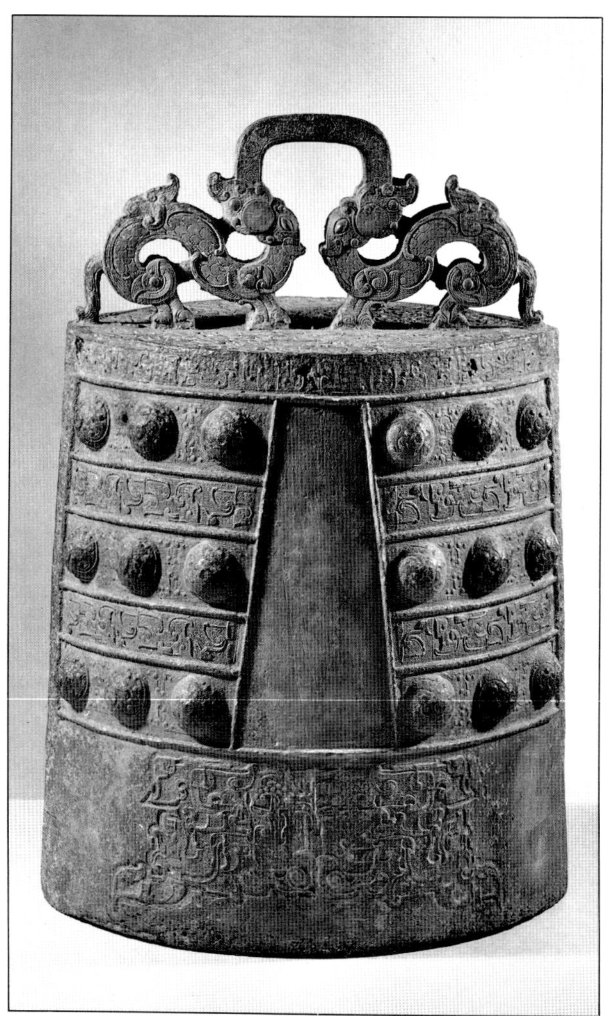

No. 23

bosses would have been positive (the boss would stand proud of the surface, as the bosses do on the bell). Thirty-six individual negative patterns for the bosses would have been pulled from the master pattern block and incorporated into the mold. A bell mold of this type, with the negative patterns included, was also discovered at Houma (Barnard and Sato, fig. 32). The raised lines on the bell, which would have been the last thing cut into the mold, serve to disguise the edges of the negative patterns. The decoration on the lowest section of the bell was produced from another pattern block.

Early Chinese bronze bells are cast with the same alloy used in the ritual vessels. Their tin content is normally not as high as in Western bells.

Published: Cheng Te-k'un, *Chou China: Archaeology in China* (Cambridge: W. Heffner & Sons, 1963), pl. 14; Loehr, *Relics of Ancient China*, no. 54; Kenneth S. Cooper, *Man and Change* (Morristown, N.J.: Silver Burdett Co., 1972), p. 194; *Selections of Chinese Art from Private Collections*, no. 24.

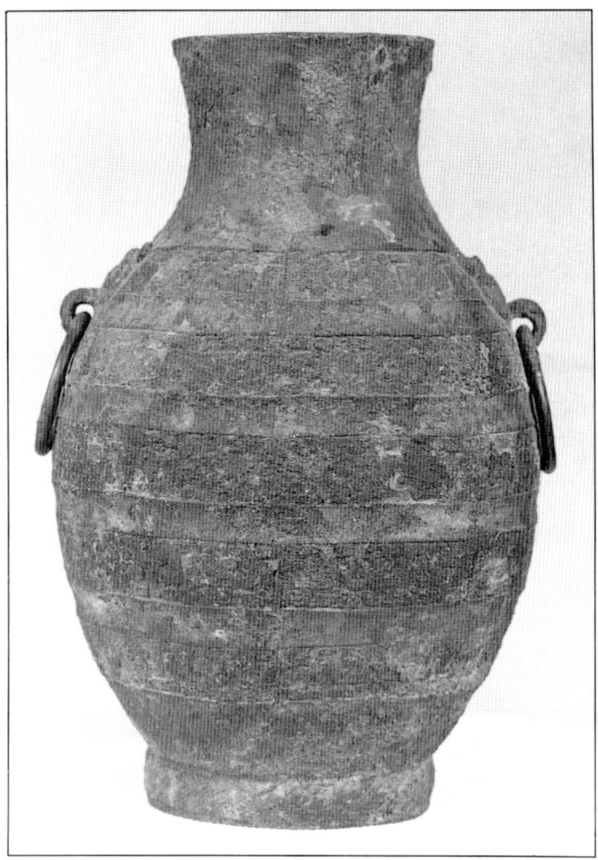

No. 24

24 (Color pl. V)
HU
Bronze
Late Spring and Autumn/early
Warring States period
6th-5th century B.C.
Height: 13-5/8 in. (34. cm)
Dr. and Mrs. David Morowitz, Bethesda, Maryland

Another example of the application of pattern blocks to piece molds can be seen here. This large, ovoid vessel with swelling sides and flaring neck is decorated with a repeating pattern of angular dragon meanders in five registers. The dragons, flat, interlacing bands textured with "raised-thread" spirals and striae, are raised in relief on a granulated ground. A large-scale twist pattern decorates the tall ring foot. Attached to the shoulders of the vessel is a pair of relief *taotie* masks holding loose ring handles, one of which appears to be a replacement.

It is likely that the pattern blocks here, as in the *zhong* (Cat. no. 23), were used to create impressions in pieces of clay that were then inserted into the larger mold for the vessel walls. The raised-line border probably hides the joint of the inset pieces.

This vessel has a particularly handsome and interesting dark green and red patination. One wonders if the red areas, which look like exposed cuprite (copper oxide), may have arisen from acidic stripping of heavy corrosion, thereby exposing the underlying patina.

The *hu* wine jar was one of the most popular bronze vessel forms of the Warring States period. The basically simple shape is often embellished with such additions as foliate crowns (Cat. no. 25), chain handles (Cat. no. 2), and tiger-shaped feet (Cat. no. 30). George W. Weber, who coined the term "raised-thread body band" for this decoration, identified it on two similar *hu*, one in the Royal Ontario Museum (Cat. no. 25) and the other formerly in the C. T. Loo Collection (G. W. Weber, *The Ornaments of Late Chou Bronzes*, pls. 69 and 70). He suggests a date in the first quarter of the fifth century B.C. for the group.

Former collections: Natanael Wessen; Earl and Irene Morse

Published: Bernhard Karlgren and Jan Wirgin, *Chinese Bronzes, The Natanael Wessen Collection* (Stockholm: Museum of Far Eastern Antiquities, 1969), no. 27, color pl. on p. 23, pl. 39; Christian Deydier, *Chinese Bronzes* (New York: Rizzoli, 1980), no. 72.

25
HU
Bronze
Late Eastern Zhou dynasty, early
Warring States period
5th century B.C.
Height: 18-3/4 in. (47.7 cm)
Inscribed around the neck
Royal Ontario Museum, Bishop W. C.
White Collection (933.12.76)

This *hu* vessel is similar in shape and decoration to the preceding vessel (Cat. no. 24). It has, in addition, a lengthy inscription around the neck and an elaborate lid with a crown of flaring petals. Each ogee-shaped petal, which is held in place with a flange, frames an openwork design of a modeled animal meander and animal head. The surface is decorated with circular and triangular volutes in sunken line. The petals have been repaired and pieces are missing. A band at the exterior base of the crown is decorated with the same dragon pattern that appears on the body.

The openwork lid here could have been produced either by the lost-wax casting process or by the prevalent piece-mold method. Certainly an interest in openwork designs made the lost-wax process more appealing.

Provenance: Reportedly from Luoyang

Published: W. C. White, *Tombs of Old Lo-yang* (Shanghai, 1934), p. 123, pl. CXIV; G. W. Weber, *The Ornaments of Late Chou Bronzes*, related object no. 59, pp. 326-331.

26
HU
Bronze
Late Eastern Zhou dynasty, early
Warring States period
5th century B.C.
Height: 12-1/2 in. (31.8 cm)
Lent by Richard J. Salisbury

The round body of this *hu*-type wine vessel has

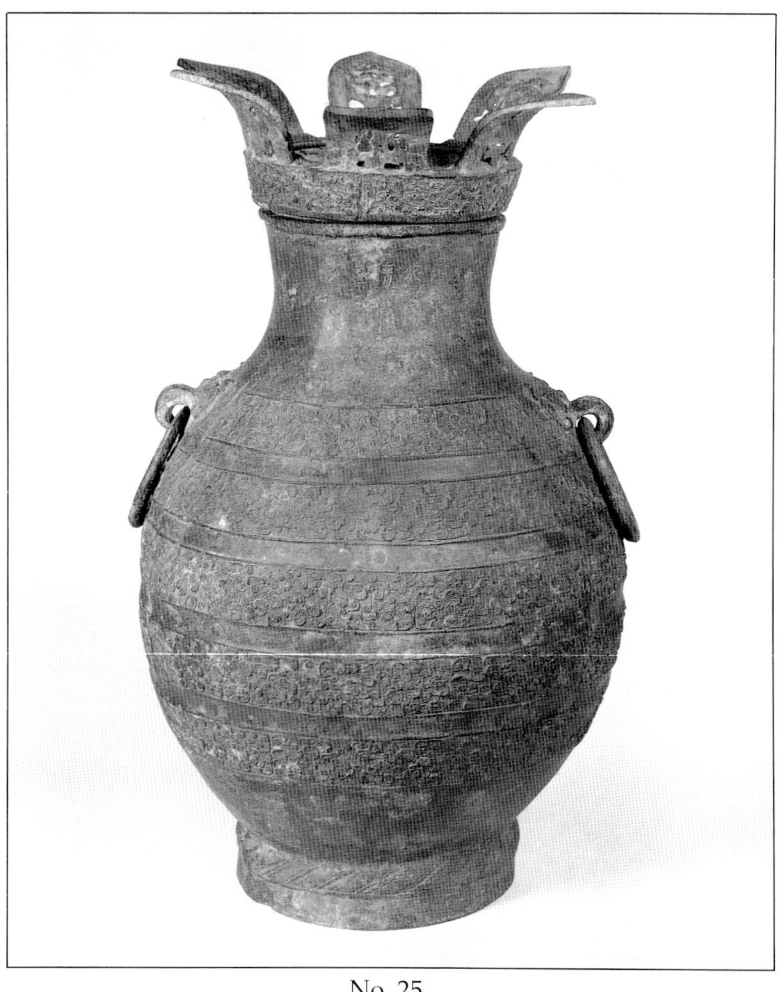

No. 25

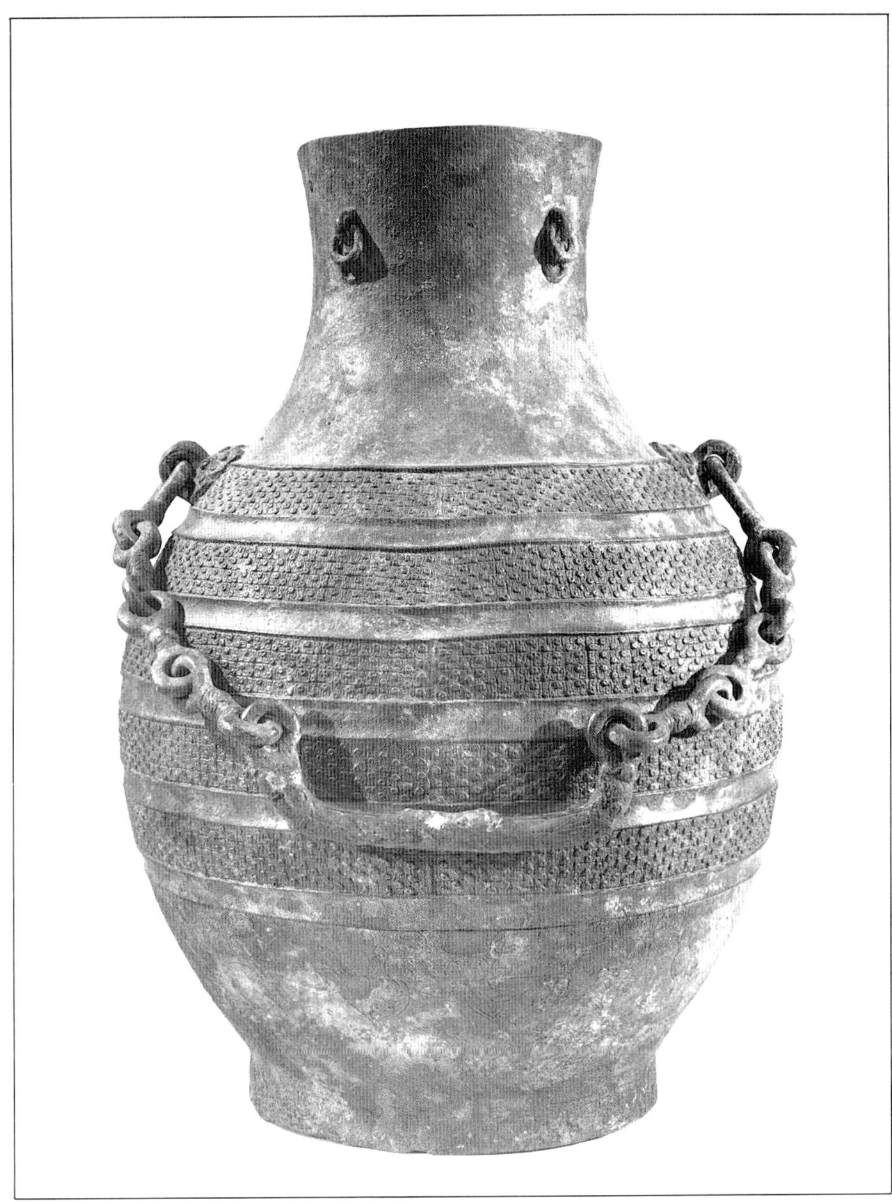

No. 26

five registers decorated in relief with densely packed meanders and raised circles. Below these relief bands are a subtle design of flat dragon heads repeated in a narrow frieze and a band of pendant petals. The large ring foot is decorated with a band of flat interlocking spirals. A chain-link handle consisting of a central grip and eight double-loop links is attached to animal-mask escutcheons with projecting rings at the shoulder. Four small rings are held by tiny masks on the neck. This vessel was probably originally crowned with an ornamented lid of some sort. The outer surface of the bronze seems to have been waxed.

Pattern blocks were also used in making this vessel. The design probably resulted from the simplification and condensing of animal interlace patterns as found on the preceding two *hu*. Because of the square shape of the basic meander unit, the term "waffle pattern" was coined for the decoration (G. W. Weber, *The Ornaments of Late Chou Bronzes*, pp. 174-175). The design was created using a pattern unit measuring 1-3/8 in. (3.4 cm) wide.

The body was cast with a four-part outer mold. Vertical mold seams are visible under the masks and at 90° intervals. The chain-link handle, popular in the Warring States period, is a tour de force of interlock casting (Fig. 6). Longitudinal mold joints are visible in the chain-links. Remains of the old core are found in the recessed base.

Published: Thorp and Bower, *Spirit and Ritual*, no. 25.

27
DOU
Bronze
Eastern Zhou dynasty
6th-5th century B.C.
Height: 7 in. (17.8 cm)
Hermitage Foundation Museum,
Norfolk, Virginia (47.P.11)

The bowl and cover of this *dou* fit together to form a spheroid on a spreading pedestal foot. The *dou* has a flaring crown on the lid that serves as a handle and, when the lid is inverted, as a foot. Two circular loop handles project like ears from opposite sides of the bowl just below the mouth rim.

A pattern block or a roller was used to produce the delicate repeating pattern of profile dragons arranged in three concentric zones on the lid and two zones on the body. The profile animal heads are defined by interconnecting, raised-thread scrolls and commalike hooks on a ground of granulae. A plaited rope pattern separates the zones.

The fine dragon design reappears on the spreading foot below a rope-twist band. The zone above the rope twist is decorated with the so-called waffle pattern, repeating square units of tightly interlocking bands with eyes. These units are probably highly stylized versions of the late Zhou interlacing dragon motif.

Published: G. W. Weber, *The Ornaments of Late Chou Bronzes*, pp. 276-279, pl. 58.

Former collection: C. T. Loo

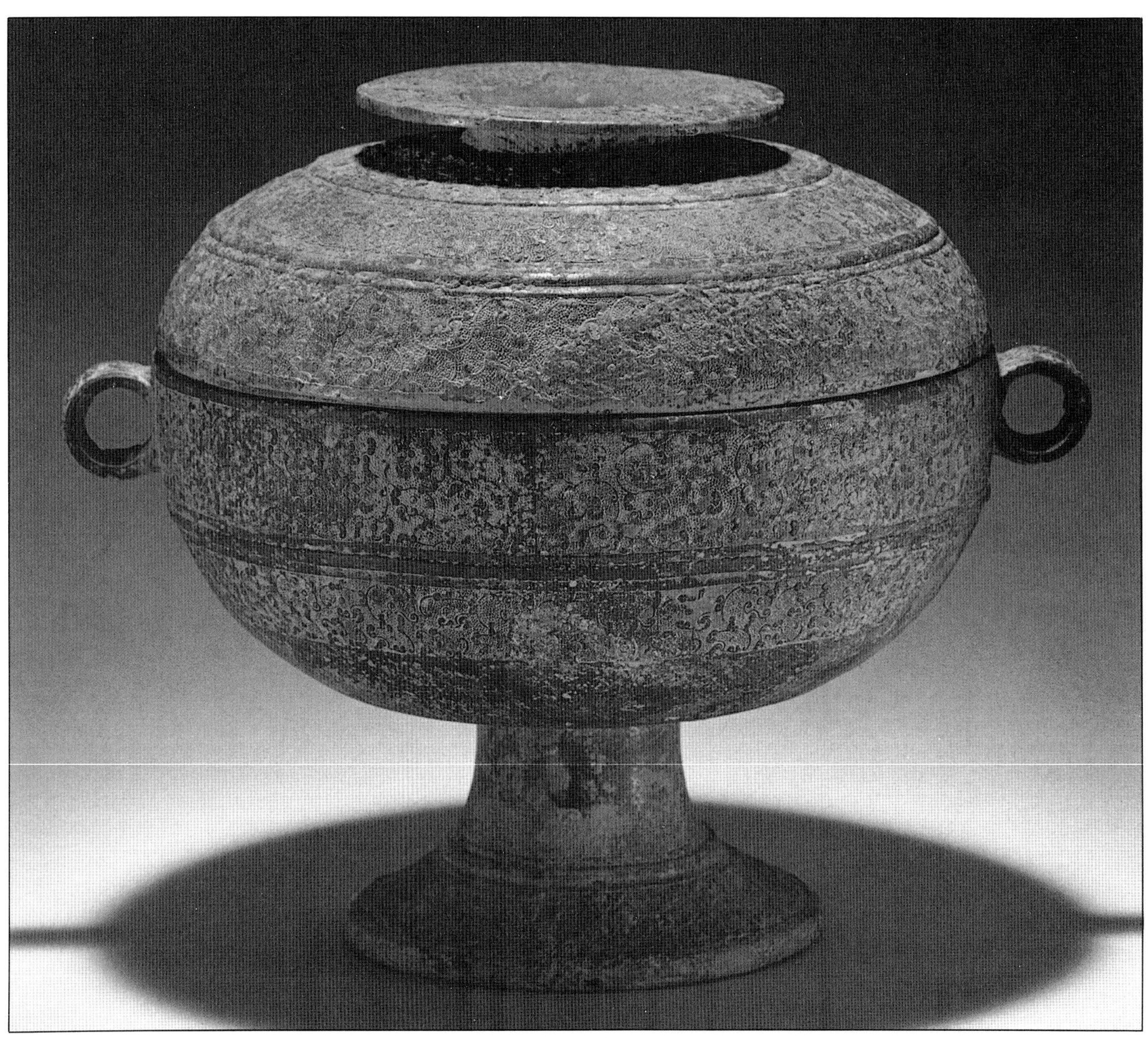

No. 27

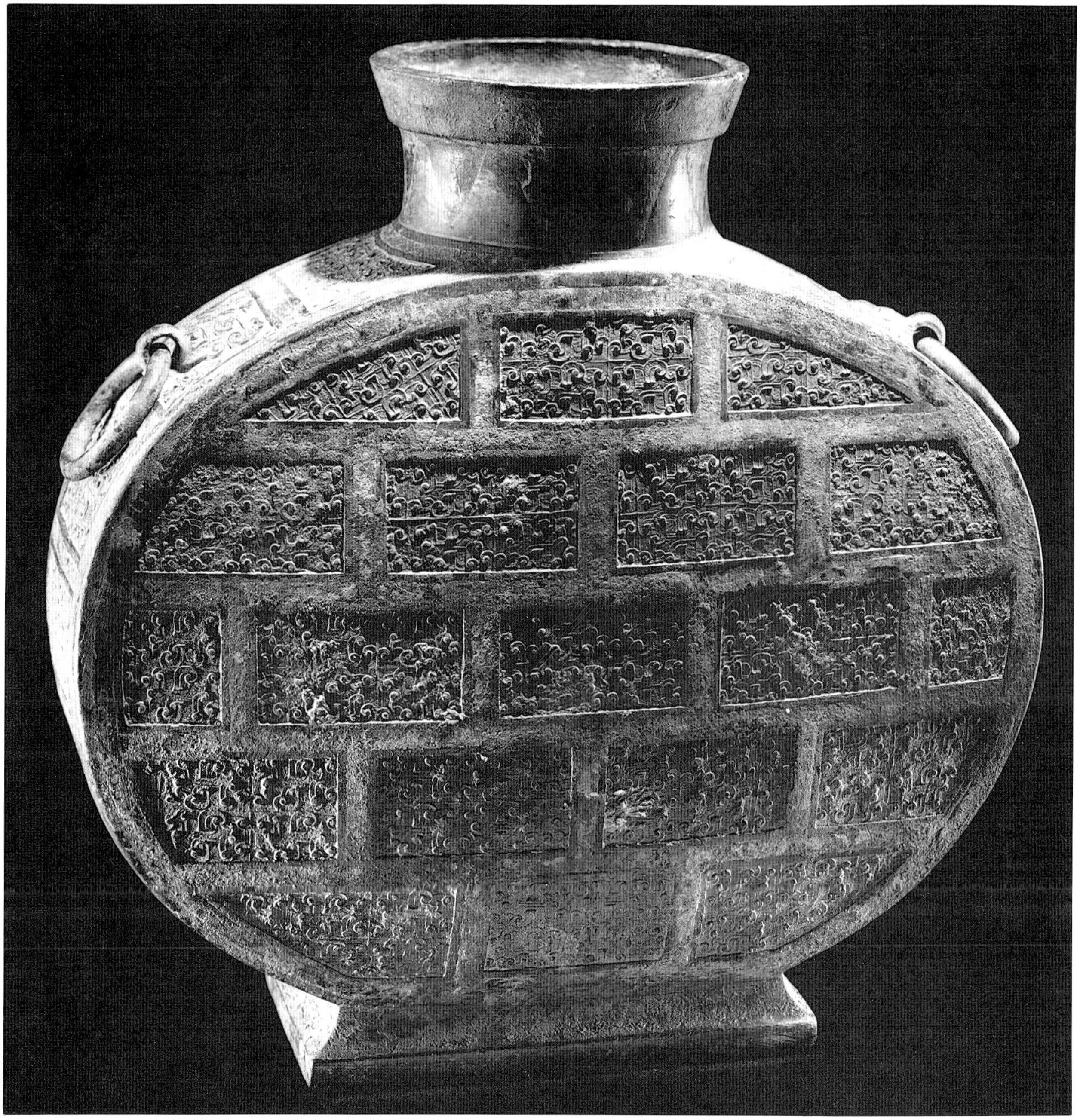

No. 28

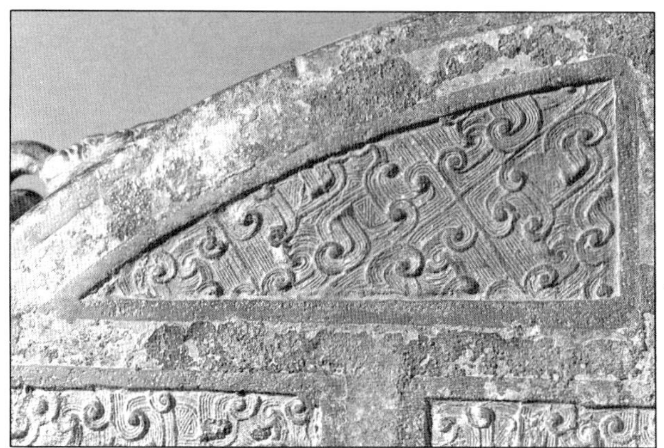

No. 28 (detail)

28
BIAN HU
Bronze (copper approx. 75%, tin approx. 8%, lead approx. 17%), with copper inlay
Late Eastern Zhou dynasty
5th century-4th century B.C.
Height: 12-3/8 in. (31.5 cm)
Width: 12-3/16 in. (31.0 cm)
Depth: 4-1/8 in. (10.5 cm)
Collection of Robert H. Ellsworth

This vessel in the shape of a pilgrim's flask is decorated around the slightly concave neck with downward-pointing copper triangles. The flat sides and narrow ends of the oval body have a design of recessed rectangular panels arranged like brick masonry and separated by a grid of copper bands. These panels are filled with an impressed pattern of feathery "commas." The mask handles on the shoulders were cast with the vessel, as were the projecting snouts. The precast loose rings must have been incorporated into the mold assembly with clay around them. After the casting was completed, the clay was removed and the rings remained loose within the circles formed by the snouts.

The casting method is typical of the late Zhou period, as seen at the Houma foundries. One interesting feature is the three parallel lines on one side of the inner foot core; these can be seen on a radiograph of the inside of the vessel as well, and suggest that the inner core was marked for alignment during final assembly before casting.

The inlay is of particular interest on this piece. The owner kindly consented to allow us to take two large samples for metallographic examination in cross section. One was taken from the edge of one of the rectangular panels just under the handle, near an old dent. The other was taken from the edge of one triangle on the side of the neck. Both reveal that the copper was cast first, fitted into the mold, held in place with chaplets, and the vessel metal then cast to it. The section from the neck also went through a main casting chaplet that held the core and mold in register.

This *bian hu* shares one mysterious characteristic with others of this type: the comma-shaped design in one of the upper panels is oriented diagonally rather than being squarely placed (see detail). One wonders if this is the same sort of intentional mistake that is made in Persian rugs?

29
HU
Bronze with copper inlay
Eastern Zhou dynasty
5th-4th century B.C.
Height: 17-5/8 in. (44.8 cm)
The Art Institute of Chicago, Lucy Maud Buckingham Collection (1928.143)

The large ovoid vessel has a tall, slightly flaring neck and a ring foot. Two animal-mask handles are attached to the shoulders. The exterior is profusely inlaid in copper with curvilinear figures of birds, felines, and antlered deer. These are arranged in confronting pairs separated by

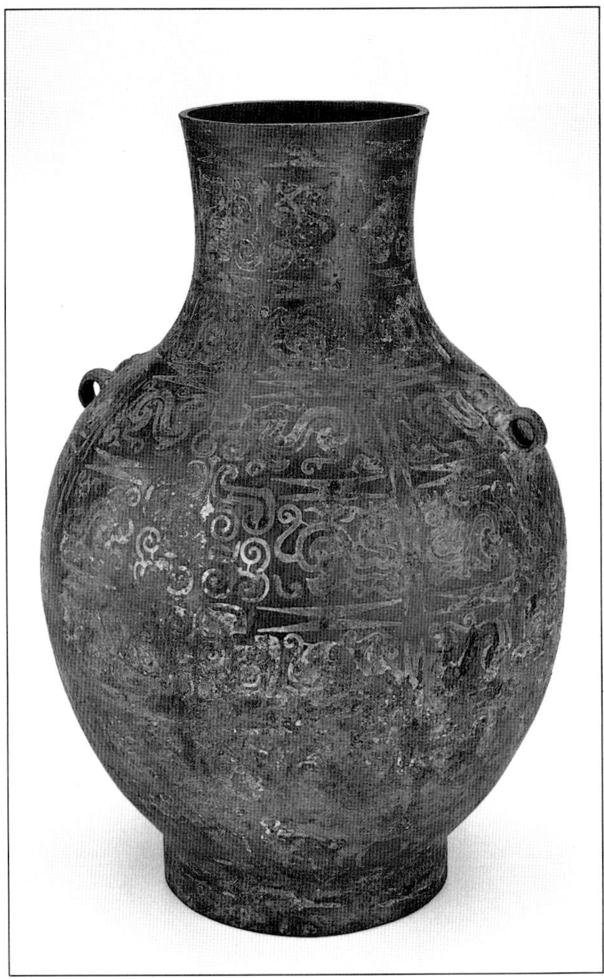

No. 29

horizontal and vertical rows of double triangles. Abstract, curvilinear figures derived from the *taotie* mask are inlaid along the four main axes of the sides. A row of double triangles circles the foot.

The figural inlay on this vessel was made by the same method as that on the *bian hu* above (Cat. no. 28). The inlay was cast to shape, after which chaplets were attached either with adhesives or soft solder; the inlay pieces were placed in the mold, and the vessel was then cast to them. Some spots where the inlay has floated out of place can be seen. The inlaid figure at these spots is incomplete, since it was partly submerged in the molten bronze. Extensive abrasive finishing has rendered the surface flat.

This type of construction has been clearly documented in X-radiography of the similarly decorated Havemeyer *hu* (Fig. 8) in The Metropolitan Museum of Art (29.100.545). (Pieter Meyers, "Applications of X-ray Radiography in the Study of Archaeological Objects," vol. 2, ch. 5 in *Archaeological Chemistry* [ed. Giles F. Carter,

American Chemical Society, Washington, D.C. 1978], p. 91, figs. 11 and 12.)

Published: C. D. Weber, *Chinese Pictorial Bronze Vessels*, p. 154, fig. 36b.

30 (Color pl. VI)
HU
Bronze (copper 71%, tin 15%, lead 13%)
inlaid with gold and copper
Eastern Zhou dynasty
Late 6th or early 5th century B.C.
Height: 17-3/16 in. (43.7 cm)
Arthur M. Sackler Gallery, Smithsonian Institution, Washington, D.C. (S1987.318)

This large pear-shaped vessel has a flaring neck and a spreading ring foot with a stepped rim. The foot is raised on three tigers cast in the round. Two monster masks attached to the shoulder of the vessel, which carry loose ring handles, are embellished with gold sheet onlay at the eyes. Five horizontal bands of raised rope-twists divide the body of the vessel into five friezes. The upper frieze is decorated with rising heart-shaped blades and the lower frieze with pendant heart-shaped blades in sunken line inlaid with copper. The remaining three friezes are decorated with an overall linear pattern of interlocking T's with curls inlaid with copper and accented with a gold center.

The vessel was cast in a two-piece mold assembly with joins running vertically through the handle areas. The guilloche, or rope-twist pattern, so common on the bronzes from Houma, was produced with the aid of pattern blocks. Impressions from these blocks were inset into the mold. The three tiger feet were cast onto the vessel; each has a sprue and riser visible on the other side of the foot ring (see detail). Three separate molds and castings were necessary to make the feet. All three molds, however, were constructed from the same model. The piece-mold joins in each foot are quite visible on the inside.

The extreme thinness of the vessel is especially observable in the lowest band, just above the foot, where some of the inlay has been lost. The vessel

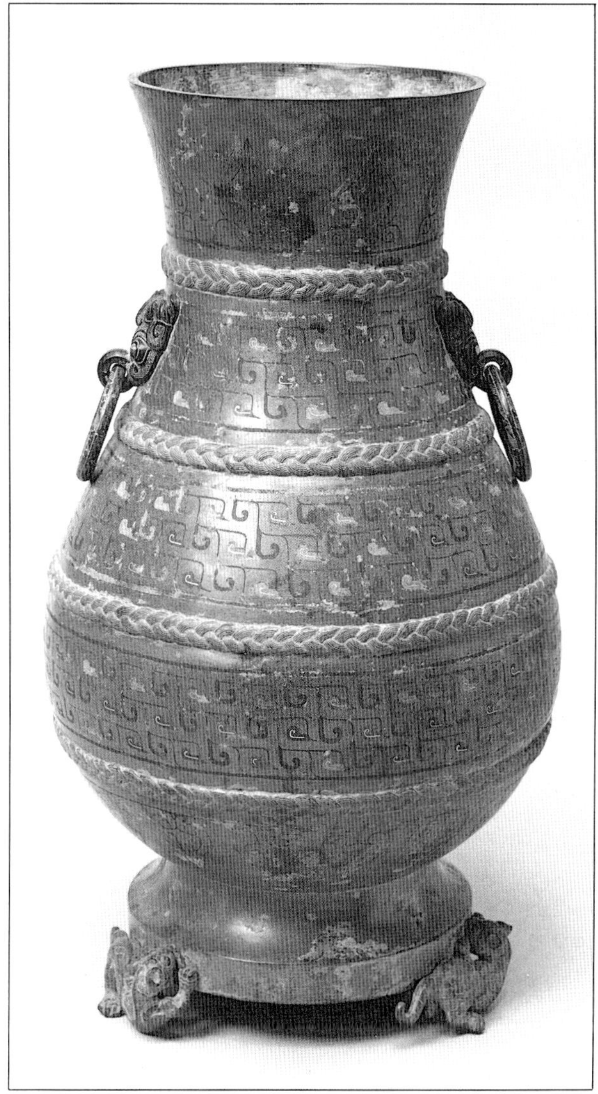

No. 30

is also quite brittle, and a break on the upper lip has been repaired with soft solder.

The light gray, shiny patina is similar to that seen on a large number of vessels from the Eastern Zhou period. The few samples available indicate that coloration seems to arise from the removal of copper from the surface and the retention of tin. This is the reverse of normal corrosion, and may well arise from "pickling" at the time the vessels were made. The black handles may be replacements. Fine finishing scratches remain after

TABLE II

	Weight %					Parts per million						
	Copper	Tin	Lead	Iron	Arsenic	Antimony	Zinc	Gold	Silver	Mercury	Cobalt	Nickel
Vessel:	71.3	15.3	13.1	-	0.4	900	-	29.7	1279	-	158.9	-
Foot:	69.8	9.1	17.4	-	1.1	1980	-	40.6	1469	-	188.8	-

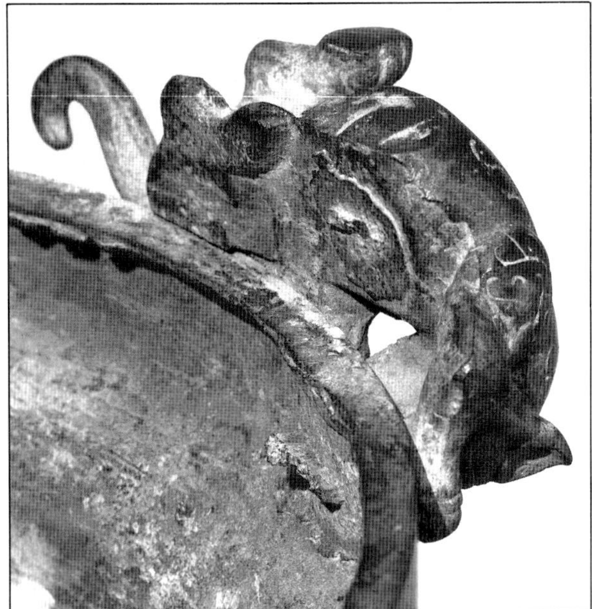
No. 30 (detail)

the outer surface of the vessel was ground down to leave the inlay flush with the bronze. Coarser finishing scratches can be seen inside the neck.

The inlay on this vessel is somewhat of a mystery. The copper is extremely fine; it is hard to believe that the same method used in the *bian hu* (Cat. no. 28) would have worked. It seems that here the copper was too fine to be held in the mold with chaplets while the vessel metal was running onto it. Nevertheless, the vessel metal does seem to come up and slightly over the edges of the copper inlay. More laboratory examination is needed.

The gold inlay is set into the centers of the copper curls. The corrosion, at some points, does run over the gold inlay, suggesting that the inlay is not a later addition. On the other hand, this is the only vessel that we know of where gold has been inlaid into the copper.

Both the foot and the vessel body were analyzed at Brookhaven by Edward Sayre, Pieter Meyers, and Lore Holmes for the Arthur M. Sackler Foundation. It is interesting that the foot is so much higher in lead (see Table II).

Lead isotope ratio analysis determined that the lead from both the vessel and the foot falls into the same group with many other vessels probably from the central (so-called metropolitan) area of Eastern Zhou bronze production. It is very possible that this vessel was made in the Houma foundries.

Published: Paul Singer, *Masterpieces from the Arthur M. Sackler Collections* (to be published); Jenny So, *Eastern Zhou Ritual Bronzes in the Arthur M. Sackler Collections* (to be published).

31
HU
Bronze (copper 74%, tin 12%, lead 7%)
inlaid with copper
Eastern Zhou dynasty
Late 5th century B.C.
Height: 13-9/16 in. (34.4 cm)
Arthur M. Sackler Gallery, Smithsonian Institution, Washington, D.C. (S1987.410)

This unusual ten-sided *hu* has a swelling belly and a pair of mask-and-ring handles attached at the shoulders. It is decorated with an elaborate inlaid pattern of curls and meanders arranged in horizontal friezes of triangular panels and zigzags. Each panel of the ten-sided foot ring is decorated with a simple X-shaped figure embellished with triangles and curls. The contrast of light yellow and dark red is created by bronze and copper, respectively. Coiled copper wire has been set into the cast recesses of the bronze, then beaten smooth and abraded. Much of the red and green patina of the vessel surface is restored. There are scattered plugs of metal on the sides that are probably early repairs. Most of the original ceramic core remains in the foot. The sprue was located in the bottom of the vessel.

This vessel was also analyzed at Brookhaven by Edward Sayre, Pieter Meyers, and Lore Holmes for the Arthur M. Sackler Foundation (see Table III).

Lead isotope ratio analysis revealed that the lead does not match that from the previous *hu* (Cat. no. 30); and that it is different than that of other vessels of Liyu type from the central (so-called metropolitan) area of Eastern Zhou bronze

TABLE III

	Weight %					Parts per million						
	Copper	Tin	Lead	Iron	Arsenic	Antimony	Zinc	Gold	Silver	Mercury	Cobalt	Nickel
Vessel:	74.0	11.7	7.4	0.13	0.24	1420	-	28.5	993	-	143	-

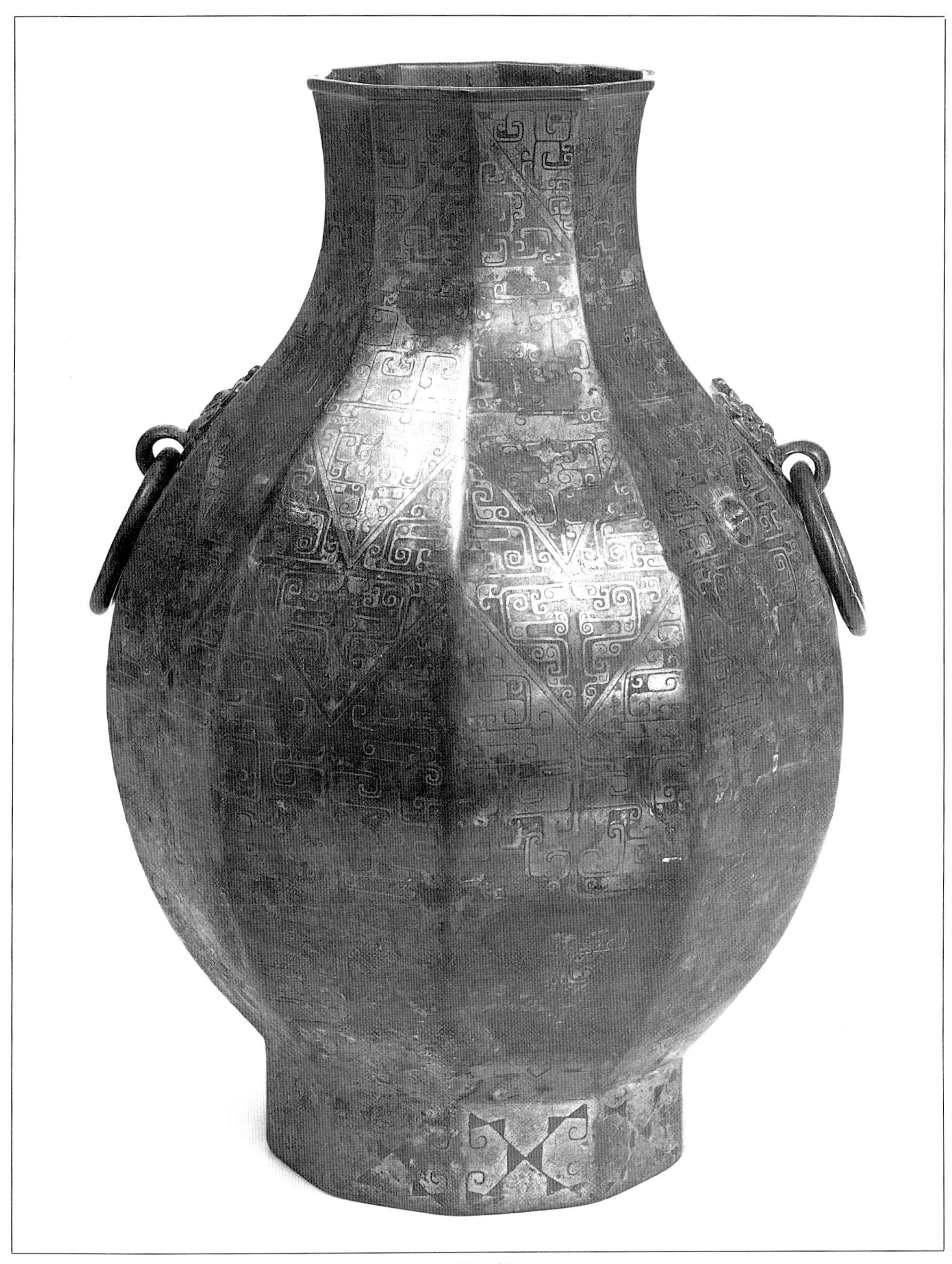

No. 31

production. At present, the lead isotope analyses do not help us in deciding where this vessel was made.

The inlaid pattern of this *hu* is found on a square *hu* excavated from tomb no. 1 at Liulige in Henan Province. (Compare this to a drawing in C. D. Weber, *Chinese Pictorial Bronze Vessels*, p. 152, fig. d; and a rubbing in Guo Baojun, *Shanbiaozhen yu Liulige*, pl. 89, no. 2.)

Published: Paul Singer, *Masterpieces from the Arthur M. Sackler Collections* (to be published); Jenny So, *Eastern Zhou Ritual Bronzes in the Arthur M. Sackler Collections* (to be published).

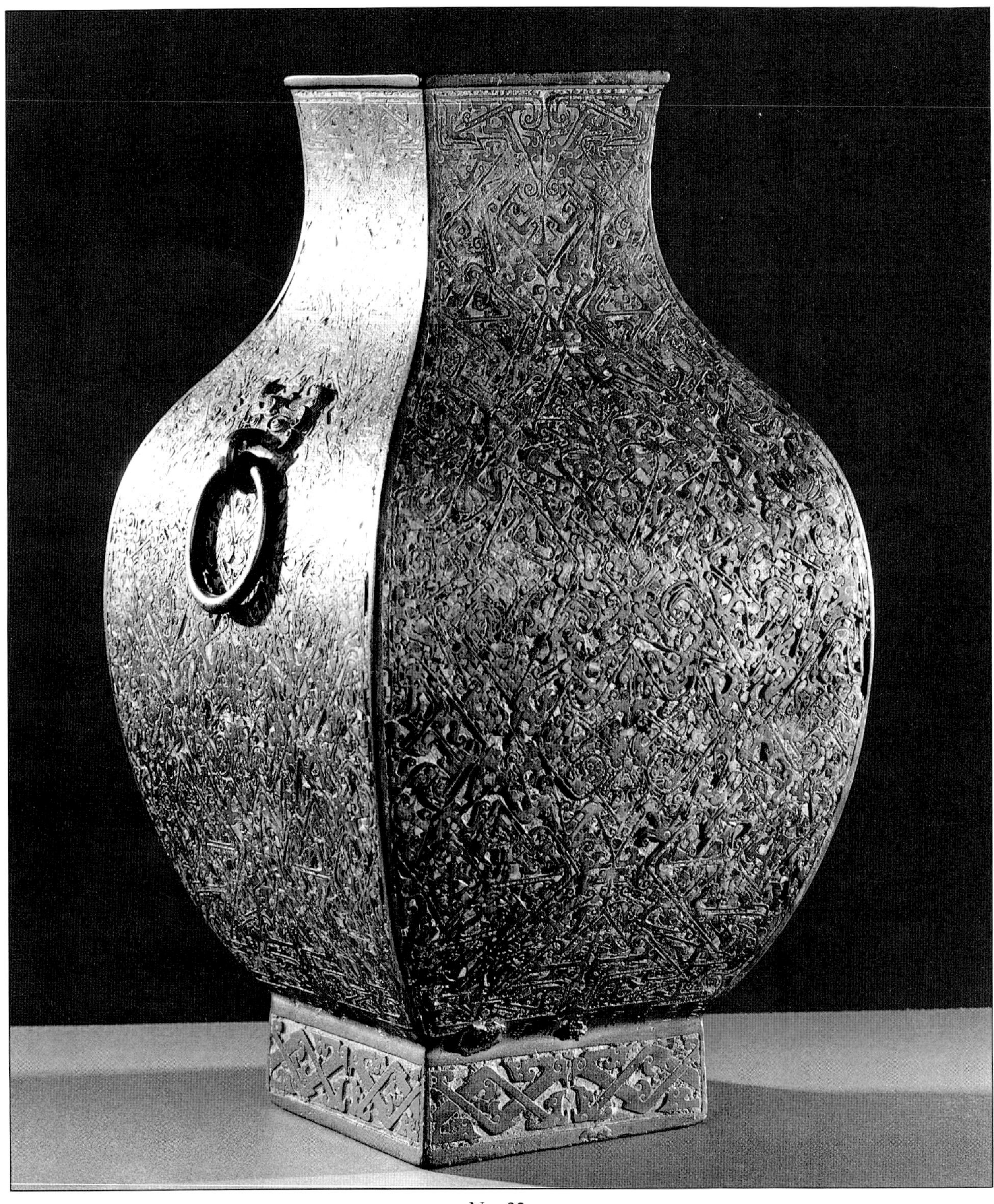

No. 32

32
FANG HU
Bronze inlaid with malachite
Late Eastern Zhou dynasty
4th century B.C.
29-character incised inscription
Height: 14-5/8 in. (37.2 cm)
Loaned by The University Museum, University of Pennsylvania, Philadelphia (C243)

This square *hu* has swelling sides and a slightly tapering foot. A pair of animal masks in relief, each holding large, loose ring handles, is attached at the shoulders on opposite sides. The vessel is decorated in raised, flat ridges with an extremely complex geometric design of flat zigzagging lines, small hooks, and curls. A relatively simpler zigzag design decorates the foot. The negative areas of the design are inlaid with chips of bright green malachite.

Many of the malachite chips, originally held in place with some kind of paste, have fallen out, leaving the design pitted with empty sunken areas. A related vessel in the Freer Gallery of Art (61.32) has a less complex geometric design embellished with the addition of gold and silver inlay (Pope et al., *The Freer Chinese Bronzes*, vol. 1, pp. 515-516). An almost identical vessel, reported from Jincun, is reproduced in W. C. White, *Tombs of Old Lo-yang*, pl. 109 (also Umehara, *Sengoku*, pl. 95:2; *idem, Rakuyo kinson*, pl. 16). A series of stylistically related vessels is listed by Loehr (*Ritual Vessels of Bronze Age China*, p. 154, note). Jenny So offers an update of this list in her discussion of a *fang hu* excavated in 1957 from Shanxian, Henan Province (in Fong, *The Great Bronze Age of China*, p. 312).

The inscription, which is incised above the foot, recounts a battle at Zhengdehong and is dated to "the King's fifth year." Two dates have been suggested for this vessel, 279 B.C. by Guo Moruo and 314 B.C. by Chen Mengjia (see Andersson, p. 27, for a summary of Guo Moruo's translation; Chen Mengjia, *Yin Zhou*, pp. 138-139). The fourth-century date is supported in a study of this inscription by Zhou Xiaolu (*Kaogu* [1988], no. 3, pp. 258-263).

Published: Umehara, *Seika*, p. 213, pl. 3; Andersson, "The Goldsmith in Ancient China," pls. 19, 20; Umehara, *Sengoku*, pl. 95:1; Rong Geng, *Shang Zhou*, fig. 774; Emma Bunker, *The Art of Eastern Chou* (New York: China House, 1962), no. 51, Loehr, *Ritual Vessels of Bronze Age China*, p. 154, no. 6; William Watson, *Art of Dynastic China* (New York: Abrams, 1983), pl. 30; I. Kominami, *Studies on Unearthed Objects* (Kyoto University, 1985).

33
OPENWORK ORNAMENT
Bronze
Eastern Zhou dynasty, Warring States period
5th-4th century B.C.
Length: 2-5/8 in. (6.7 cm)
Lent by Dr. Paul Singer

This object, possibly a finial or small lid, is rectangular in form, with the broad sides slightly concave. Its complex openwork design consists of small intertwining serpents with grooved bodies accented by small raised rings. Each of the four corners of the object is decorated with a large florette in the round.

The intricate shape of this object, particularly the raised floral petals that stand above the surface,

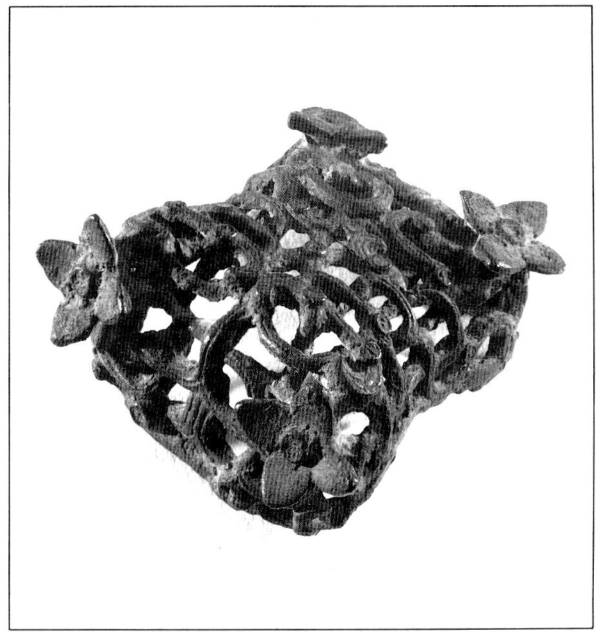

No. 33

must certainly have been made by an investment casting process, presumably lost wax. Similar use of openwork serpents as a major decorative element was found in bronze vessels from the late fifth-century B.C. tomb of the Marquis of Yi of the State of Zeng unearthed at Suixian, Hubei (Li Xueqin, *The Wonder of Chinese Bronzes*, nos. 22 and 23). A closer parallel is seen in the intricate openwork shell around the body of an inlaid bronze *hu* excavated in 1982 from Xuyixian in Jiangsu Province (*Kaogu* [1988], no. 3, pl. VI). This *hu* carries an inscription identical to the *fang hu* in The University Museum, University of Pennsylvania (Cat. no. 32).

Published: Paul Singer, "The 'Unique' Object in Chinese Art," *Oriental Art* 7 (1961), p. 32 ff.

34
PAIR OF BELT HOOKS
Bronze inlaid with turquoise
Eastern Zhou dynasty, Warring States period
5th-4th century B.C.
Length of each: 4-5/8 in. (11.7 cm)
Lent by Dr. Paul Singer

The nearly identical belthooks are each cast in a complex openwork design of two large, undulating felines biting and grasping serpents. A modeled *taotie* mask decorates the head of the projecting hook. The surface of the mask and the creatures are decorated with granulae, ribbing, and raised spirals. Pieces of teardrop and diamond-shaped turquoise are inlaid on the mask, on the heads and legs of the felines, and on the tails of the serpents.

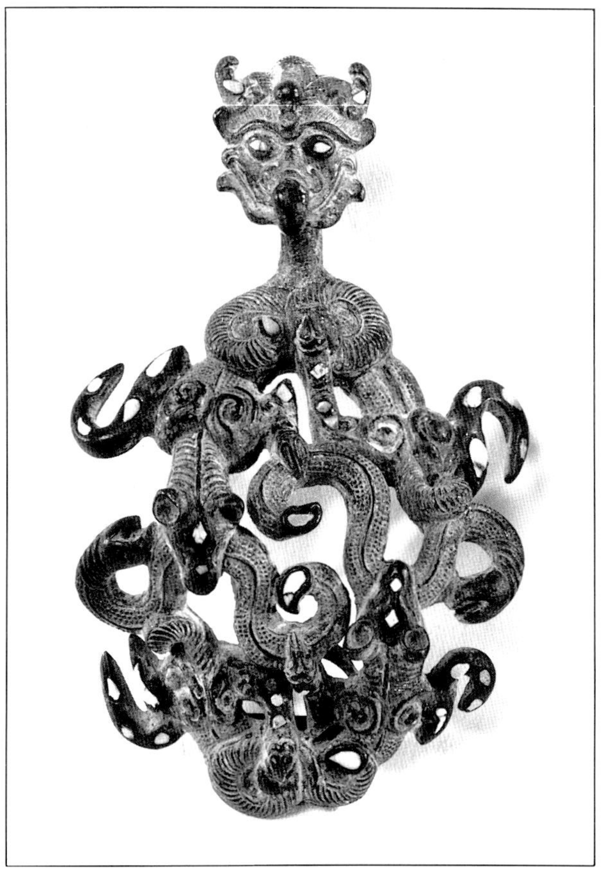

No. 34

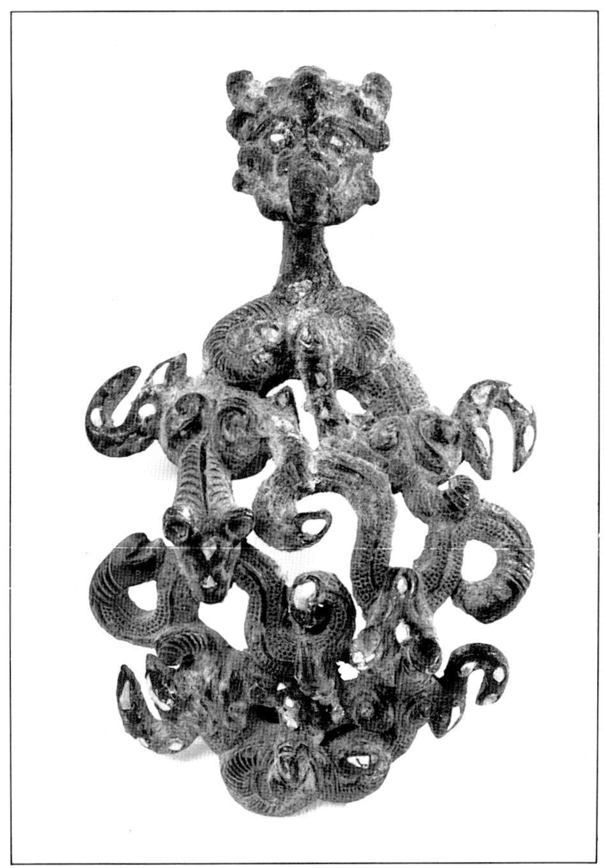

No. 34

These belt hooks are similar in style and manufacture to the other openwork objects in this exhibition (Cat. no. 33 and Cat. no. 35); they were undoubtedly produced with the lost-wax process. The stones were probably inlaid into cast recesses with some kind of adhesive.

35
SPHERICAL OBJECT
Bronze
Eastern Zhou dynasty, Warring States period
5th-3rd century B.C.
Height: 8-5/8 in. (21.9 cm)
The Metropolitan Museum of Art, Rogers Fund, 1947 (47.27ab)

The spherical object is raised on three feet in the shape of coiled serpents with upturned heads. Its sides are articulated with an openwork pattern of small intertwining serpents with raised circle accents. Four modeled animal heads holding loose rings are attached to a raised band embellished with simple scales running around the center of the object. A large bird with outspread wings sits on top of the sphere at the center of a circle of D-shaped lappets and a plain band. Four smaller birds sit on the shoulder with wings outspread and heads upturned. There is a circular opening on the back of the bird. A similar opening on the curved bottom of the object is surrounded by four radiating slots. The interior has a thin metal lining with corresponding circular openings. The function of the piece is still a mystery.

Evidence of the use of lost-wax casting is indicated by the break in the band of lappets surrounding the base of the large bird. This kind of damage occurs because of the fragility of the model and because the molds could not be inspected before casting. Except for the large bird, the various parts of the object were probably separately cast and assembled with soft solder.

The object was examined by Richard E. Stone of The Metropolitan Museum of Art, Department of Objects Conservation. He has determined that the solder holding all the protruding parts is modern. These parts may not belong together and the whole piece may be a pastiche made up of genuinely old parts.

Soldered composite vessels, however, are not unknown in the Warring States period. A stylistically related vessel from the tomb of the Marquis of Yi of the State of Zeng unearthed at

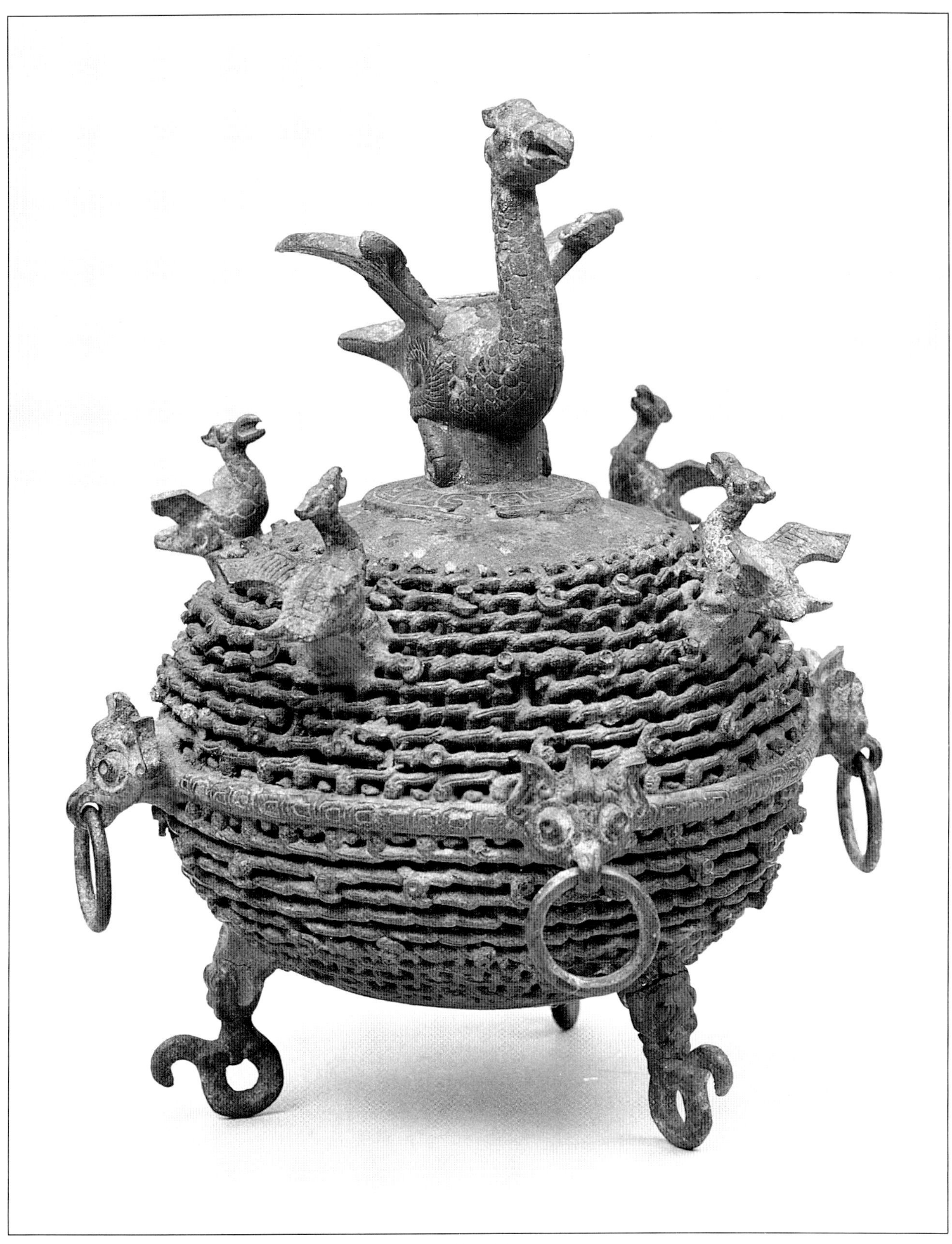

No. 35

Suixian is a composite *pan* and *zun* vessel, assembled with both hard and soft solder to create a single vessel (Li Xueqin, *The Wonder of Chinese Bronzes*, no. 23).

Published: Fong Chow, *Animals and Birds in Chinese Art* (New York: The China Institute in America, 1968), p. 20, no. 18; Christian Deydier, *Chinese Bronzes* (New York: Rizzoli, 1980), no. 86.

36
SPEAR BLADE (*MAO*)
Bronze with metallic inlay
Eastern Zhou dynasty
6th-4th century B.C.
Length: 10-3/4 in. (27.3 cm)
The Metropolitan Museum of Art, Gift of Ernest Erickson Foundation, Inc., 1985 (1985.214.27)

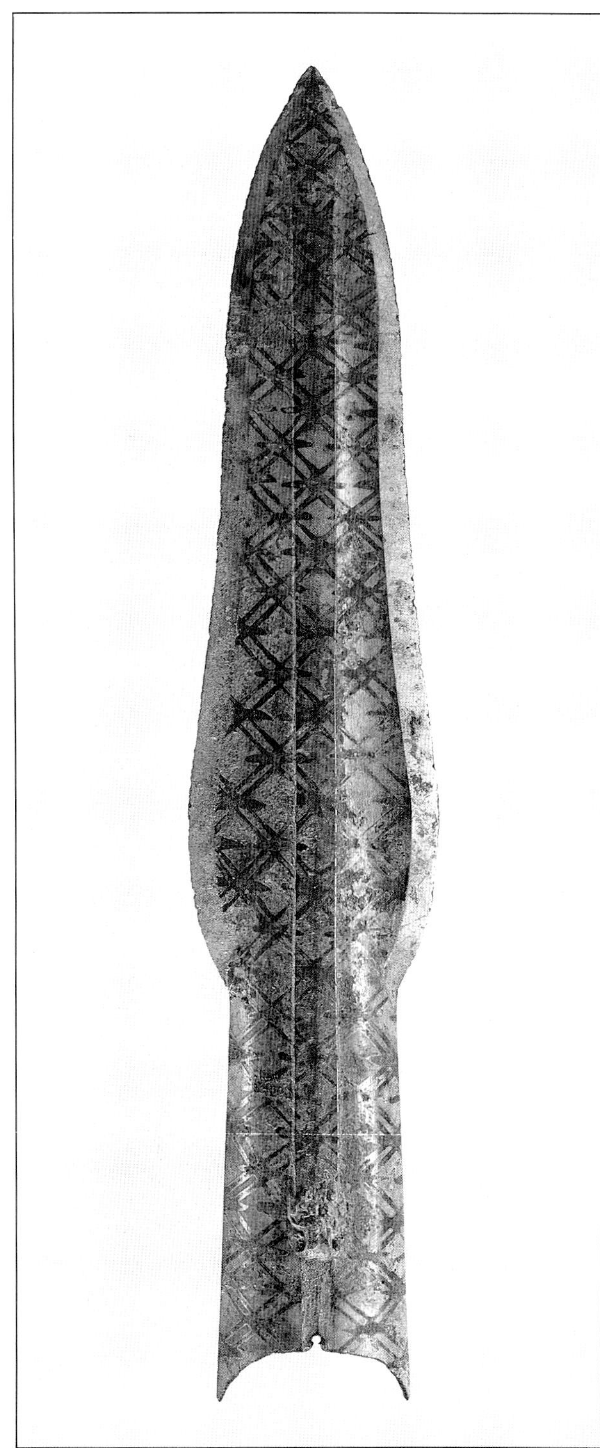

No. 36

This spearhead, when viewed along its thin edge, has a long wedge-shaped profile as it widens from its point to its socket. The wide profile has a tapering straight-sided socket with an arching cutout base and an elegant blade with subtly curving sides. The flat, central ridge on each side runs from the tip to the socket where it terminates in a tiny animal mask with a projecting loop. A grooved slot continues the line of this ridge to a small notch on the rim. The loop and groove probably aided in lashing the weapon to a wooden shaft, remnants of which still survive inside the socket.

The surface of the spearhead is covered with a pale, yellowish-green patina. With the exception of the cutting edge, the spearhead is decorated with an attractive grid of intersecting double-lines and diamond-shaped lozenges in a darker-colored metal. This variegated pattern is thought to have been created by either resist etching (possibly with ferric sulfate or ferric chloride) or surface deposition of tin. The exact method is not thoroughly understood and needs further study.

Both the spearhead shape and its decoration are associated with the southern kingdoms of Wu, Yue, and Chu during the Warring States period. An identical pattern decorates the surface of a sword excavated from a Chu tomb in Jiangling, Hubei Province. This sword is inscribed with eight characters stating that the sword belonged to Gou Jian, who reigned as king of Yue from 496 to 465 B.C. Its pattern is described as filled with an "alloy containing much tin and copper and a small amount of iron" (Ma Chengyuan, *Ancient Chinese Bronzes*, p. 83, illus. pl. 15c).

Published: Maxwell K. Hearn, *Ancient Chinese Art: The Ernest Erickson Collection* (New York: The Metropolitan Museum of Art, 1987), p. 44, no. 41, illus. p. 40.

37 (Color pl. VII)
TWO-COLORED MIRROR
Bronze
Eastern Han dynasty
2nd-early 3rd century
Diameter: 6-1/2 in. (16.5 cm)
Lent by D. H. Graham, Jr.

The back of this round mirror is decorated with a *shou dai* or "animal belt" design in contrasting silvery and black-colored metal. The main frieze, bordered on the top and bottom by a band of slanting lines, consists of seven figures cast in raised line separated by scallop-edged discs with nipples. The seven figures include the dark warrior (tortoise and serpent), a tiger, a dragon, a bird, a dancing immortal, a horned creature, and a deer. At the center, the round knob is encircled by a band of nine nipples alternating with nine trefoils in raised line followed by a plain band. The wide rim of the mirror is decorated in flat relief with a scrolling design incorporating a *xian* immortal and the animals of the four directions between an inner sawtooth band and an outer plain band. The four directional animals consist of the red bird of the south, the white tiger of the west, the green dragon of the east, and the dark warrior of the north.

The two-color decoration of this mirror is currently under investigation, for the method of production is still a mystery. One conjecture is that the design was masked off and the mirror dipped into a molten mix of tin and lead, which was followed by refiring and water quenching. Such a high tin content of the coating would result in a shiny, corrosion-resistant surface. Another possibility is the application of a tin-mercury amalgam to form the silvery areas.

Published: Rawson and Bunker, *Ancient Chinese and Ordos Bronzes*, p. 252, no. 172, illus. p. 253; *Bronze Mirrors of Ancient China: An Exhibition* (Honolulu: Honolulu Academy of Arts, 1990), no. 31.

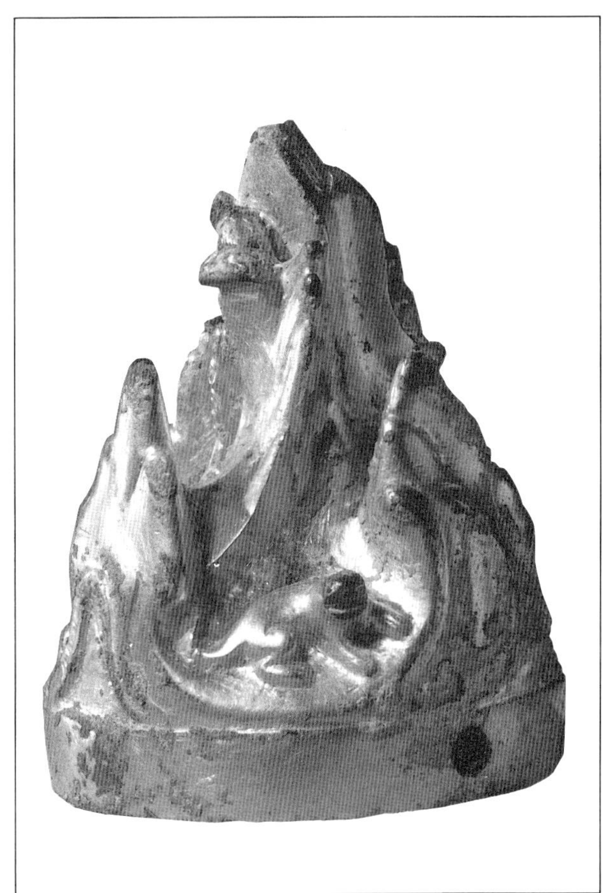

No. 38

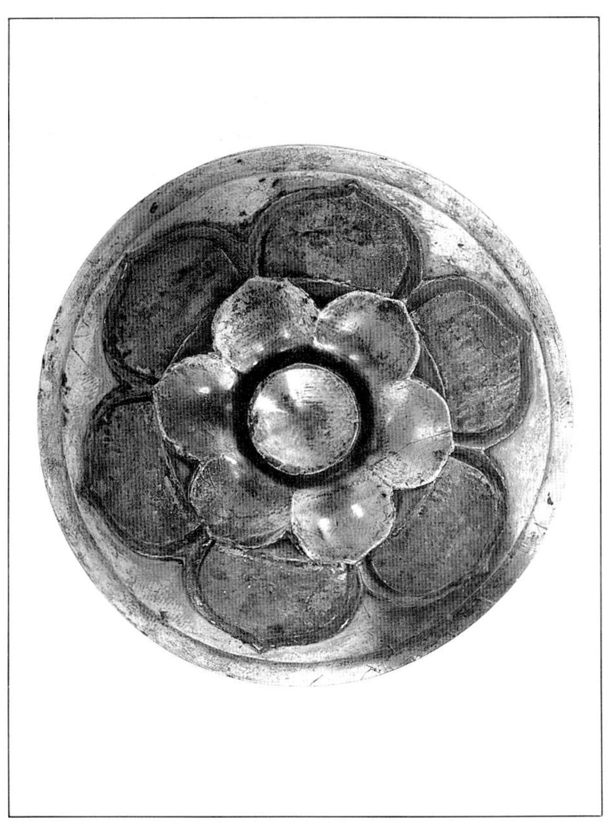

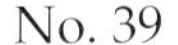

No. 39

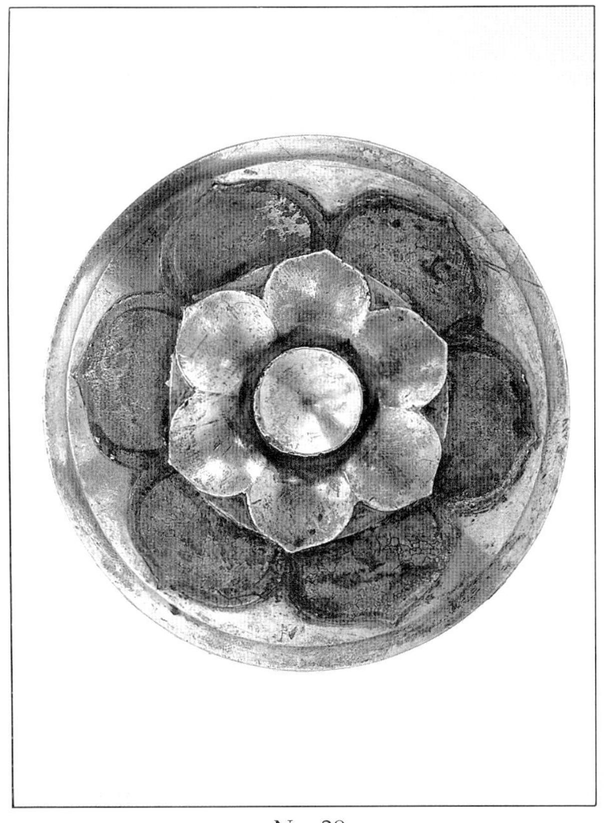

No. 39

38
CENSER LID
Gilt bronze
Eastern Han dynasty
2nd-3rd century or later
Height: 2-3/4 in. (7 cm)
The Metropolitan Museum of Art, Rogers Fund, 1915 (15.161.1)

This conical lid is strongly modeled in the shape of a mountain with sweeping peaks occupied by the figures of two immortals and a tiger. Tiny holes pierce the lid in the recesses of the peaks, presumably to allow the vapors of burning incense to escape. Two larger holes pierce the side walls of the base.

The complex shape of the hill with its undercut forms indicates the use of lost-wax casting, which by this time had supplanted the piece-mold method. Mercury or fire gilding was the likely method of decorating the surface of this piece. Gold and mercury were combined in a pasty amalgam and applied to the surface of the object. When the mercury was driven off with heat, the gold adhered to the surface.

Published: Maxwell Hearn and Wen Fong, "The Arts of Ancient China," *The Metropolitan Museum of Art Bulletin*, 32, 2 (1973-1974), fig. 54; Max Loehr, *Chinese Art: Symbols and Images* (Wellesley, Mass.: Wellesley College, 1967), pp. 20-21, no. 9; Laurance Roberts, *Treasures from The Metropolitan Museum of Art* (New York: China Institute in America, 1979), p. 21, no. 12.

39
PAIR OF ROUNDELS
Gilt and silvered bronze
Tang dynasty, 7th-8th century
7th-8th century
Diameter of each: 3-9/16 in. (9.1 cm)
The Metropolitan Museum of Art, Purchase, Arthur M. Sackler Gift, 1974 (1974.268.22)

Each of the domed roundels has a stepped base and is cast with six petals in flat relief surrounding a raised flower head. The exterior of the roundels has been gilt, except for the silvered band of six large petals, which is in corroded condition. The concave underside has been cast with radiating flanges inside the rim. A coupling device remains inside one of the roundels.

Silver was probably applied with mercury in a process paralleling fire-gilding. This combination of gilding and silvering on the same object was already in use during the late Eastern Zhou dynasty.

Former collection: Frederick M. Mayer

THE ANCIENT MOLDS

40
PIECE-MOLD FRAGMENTS
Pottery
Late Shang dynasty
14th-11th century B.C.
Length A: 1-7/8 in. (4.8 cm)
B: 1-3/4 in. (4.5 cm)
C: 2 in. (5.1 cm)
D: 2-1/2 in. (6.4 cm)
E: 3-1/16 in. (8 cm)
Lent by Dr. Paul Singer

The worn fragments contain the decoration of finished bronzes in reverse, and show what the surface of Shang molds would have looked like. Since a mold does not always pull away cleanly from the cast bronze, the decoration left in the

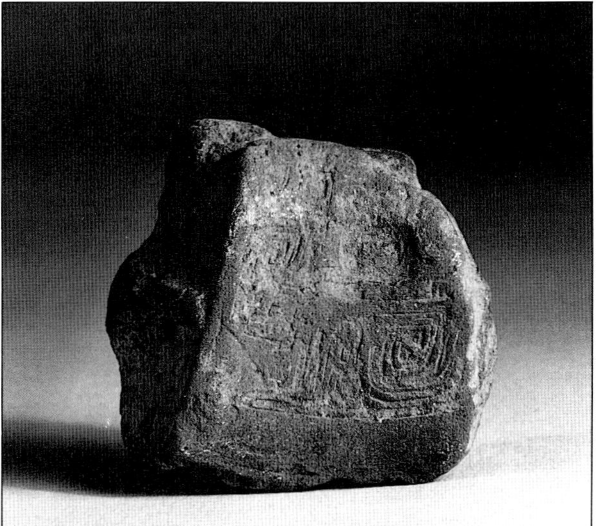

No. 40A

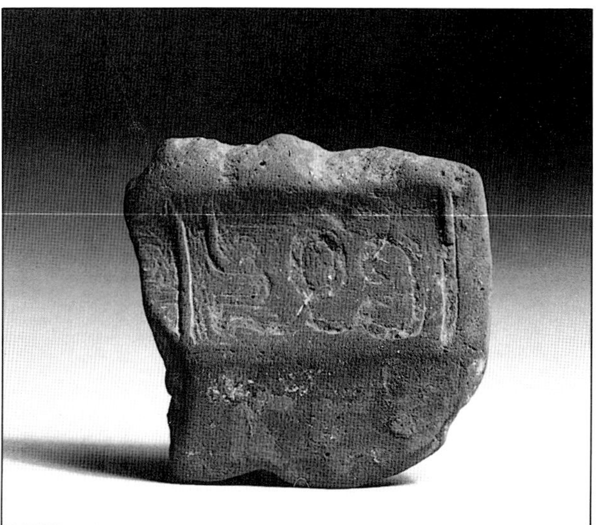

No. 40B

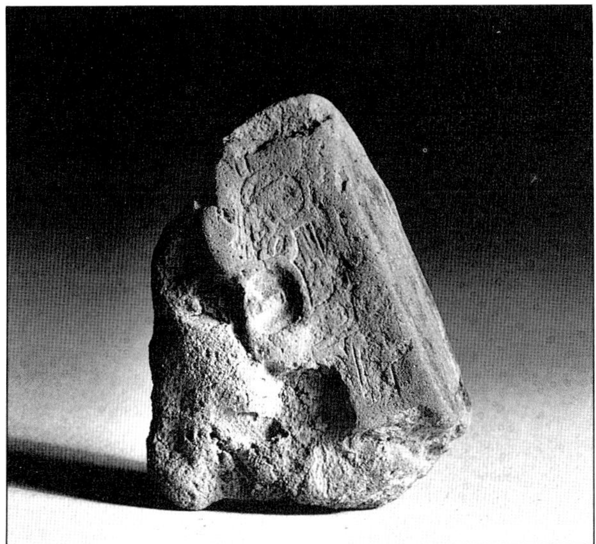

No. 40C

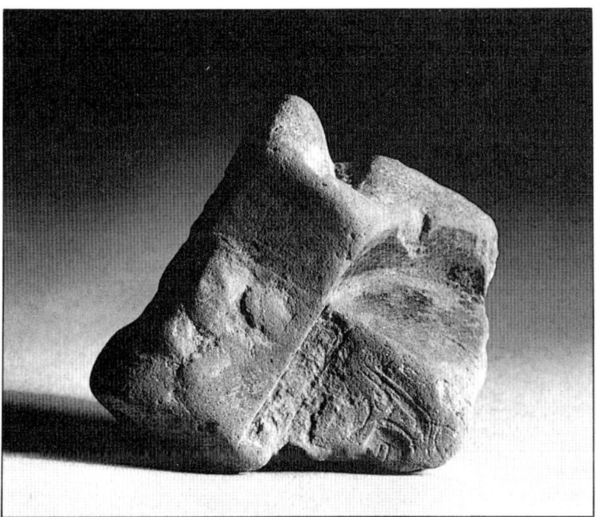

No. 40D

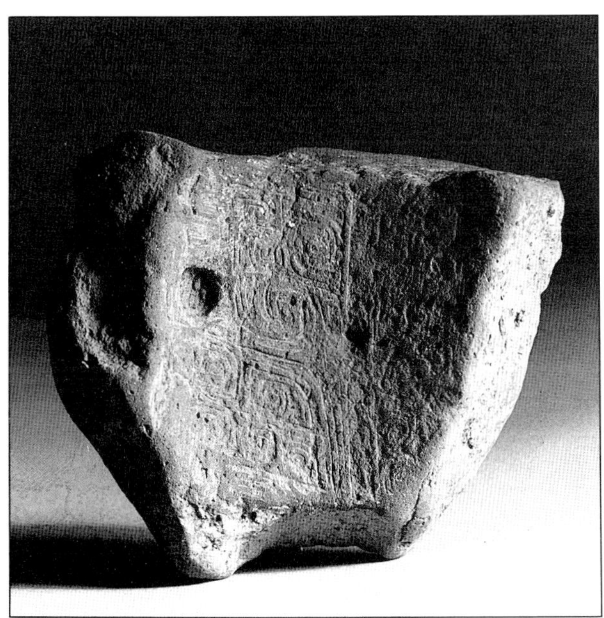

No. 40E

ceramic mold fragments is difficult to read. These fragments include:

A: an oblong eye and a complex spiral ground
B: a panel with a profile dragon
C: an eye among spirals
D: an eye, snout, and jaw alongside handle
E: an eye among spirals

After casting, the mold assembly was broken in order to remove the bronze. Molds were not reused, so that exactly identical bronze vessels do not occur in the Shang and early Western Zhou dynasties.

41
PIECE MOLD FOR A *JUE* VESSEL
Pottery fragment
Late Shang dynasty, Anyang period
13th-11th century B.C.
Length: 3-1/2 in. (8.9 cm)
The Seattle Art Museum, Eugene Fuller
Memorial Collection (38.16)

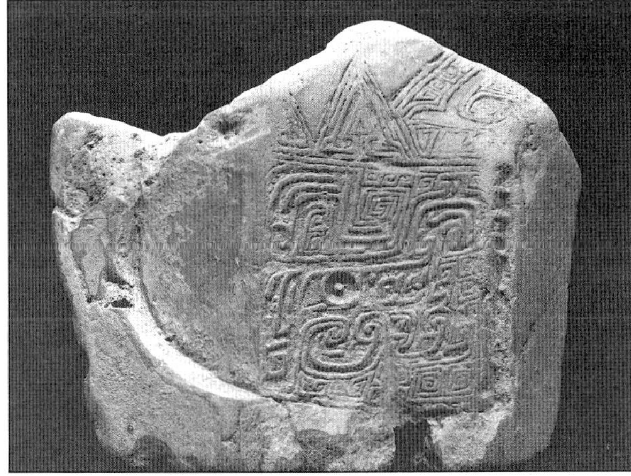

No. 41

This section, showing part of the flaring neck and the *taotie* mask frieze from handle to dividing flange, was used for casting one quadrant of a *jue* vessel.

42
MOLD STAMP
Ceramic
Eastern Zhou dynasty
5th century B.C.
Dimensions: 3-1/4 x 4-1/4 x 3/4 in.
(8.3 x 10.8 x 1.9 cm)
The Seattle Art Museum, Eugene Fuller
Memorial Collection (41.159)

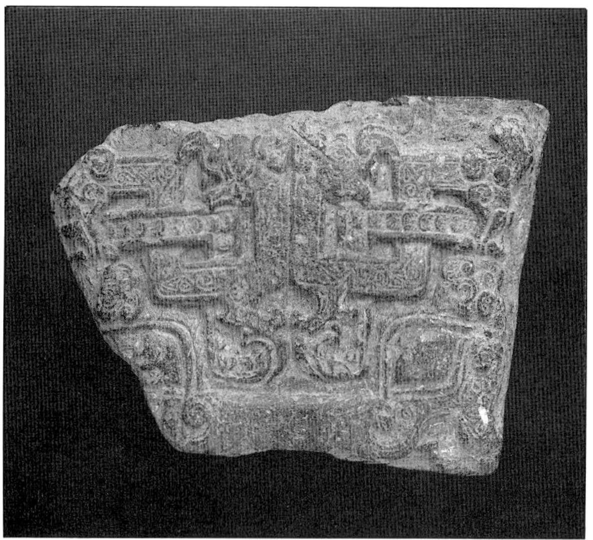

No. 42

This ceramic fragment is carved in relief with an image of an animal mask below a pair of profile dragons with flat, interlacing body bands. The reverse side has a protruding knob.

Blocks of clay were impressed with this stamp and fitted directly into the mold to become part of a larger, intricate design. Masks were often used as focal points for complex repeat patterns of interlacing dragons in Liyu-type bronzes.

43
COIN MOLD FRAGMENT
Red clay
Han dynasty (206 B.C.-A.D. 220)
Height: 3-3/8 in. (8.6 cm)
Lent by Dr. Paul Singer

Molds for bronze coins were usually stacked one above the other so that they could share a single pouring duct. Here the assembled layers are further packed in a coarse outer covering of clay. This fragment, which is illustrated bottom side up, contains the top third of a stack; the sprue hole is located on the top. Typically a stack would be about one foot high. The individual layers were probably made from a bronze "Mother mold," containing four coin models along with the sprue.

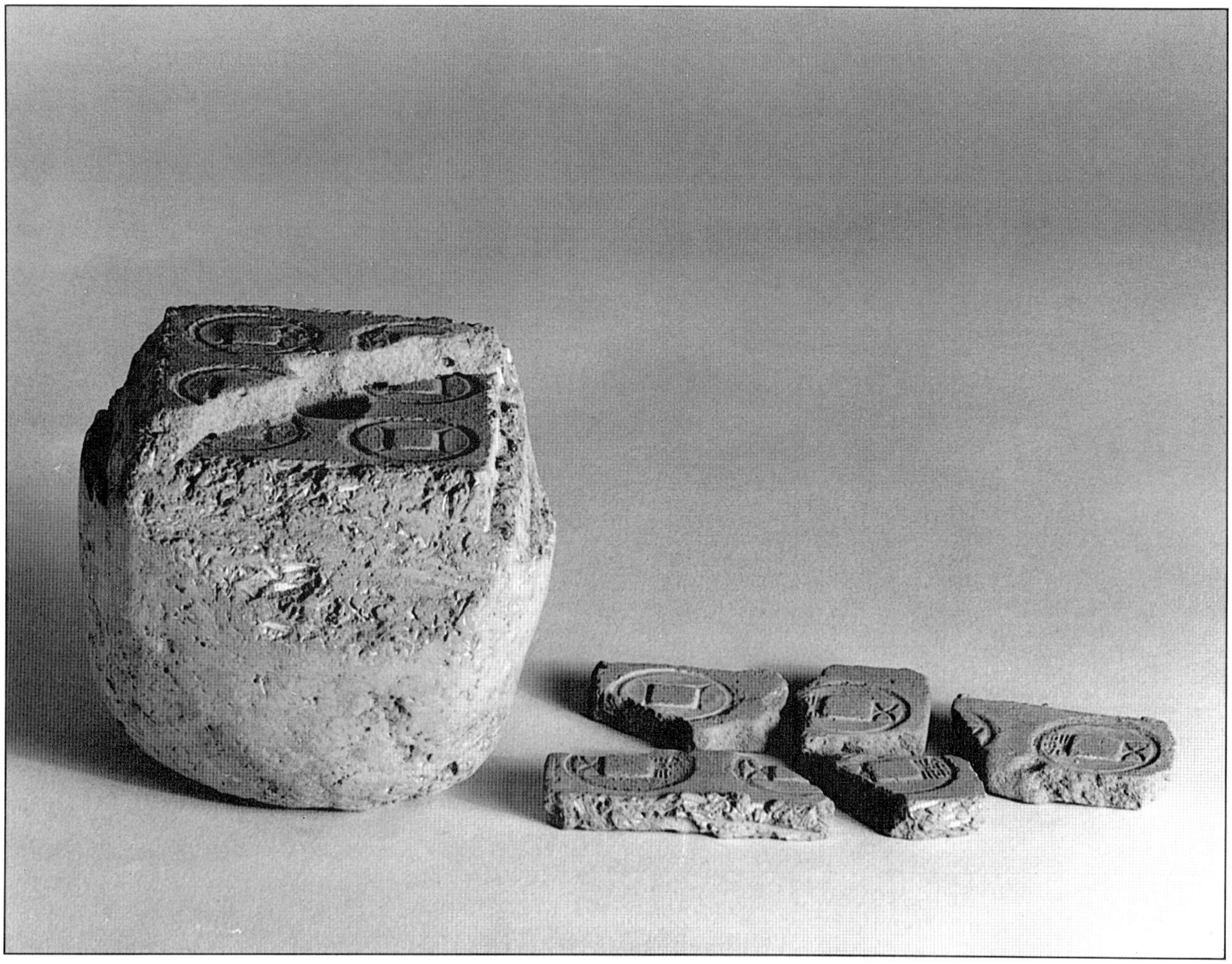

No. 43

44
COIN MOLD
Bronze
Han dynasty (206 B.C.-A.D. 220)
Length: 3-3/4 in. (9.5 cm)
Lent by Dr. Paul Singer

This rectangular piece is one layer of a stack-mold assembly. The pegs on the underside of one layer fit into the square holes on the upper surface of the next. A central channel branches into the circular depressions. The raised squares in the center of the circles create the perforations in coins for stringing them together in large numbers.

Clay and bronze molds for casting coins were equally common. Although it would have been easier to make clay molds, bronze molds had the greater advantage of durability and reusability. The surface was probably smoked to give it a fine carbon layer prior to casting. This common practice primarily aided the flow of the molten metal and, in this case, facilitated the removal of the coins from the metal mold after cooling.

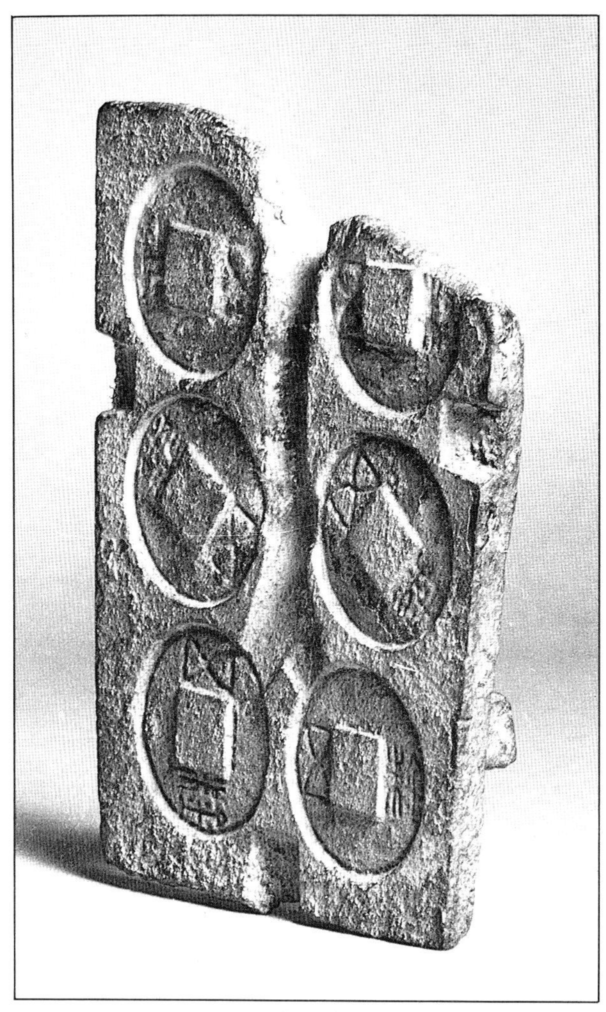

No. 44

45
MIRROR MOLD
Soapstone
Late or post-Han dynasty
2nd-3rd century
Dimensions: 9-1/2 x 8 x 7/8 in.
(24.1 x 20.3 x 2.2 cm)
The Seattle Art Museum, Eugene Fuller Memorial Collection (53.67)

This mold produced a mirror decorated in low relief with two figures of a seated immortal alternating with fantastic birds against a background of scrolls. The depressions in the mold created a large central knob and four nipples in the decorative frieze. An inscription and a sawtooth band border the rim.

The square holes in this mold piece were probably used for locking onto the pegs of another mold piece. The whole assembly would have sat on the wider end during pouring. Three ducts are visible at the narrow end of the mold. The center channel would have been the sprue and the other two the risers.

The use of soapstone molds are unusual. It is possible that this mold was used for casting multiple wax originals for later lost-wax casting.

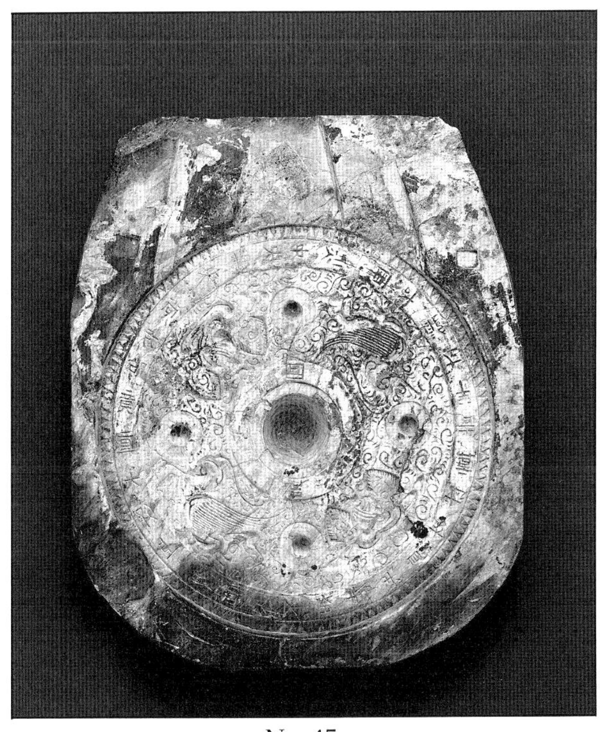

No. 45

THE LEAD RITUAL VESSELS

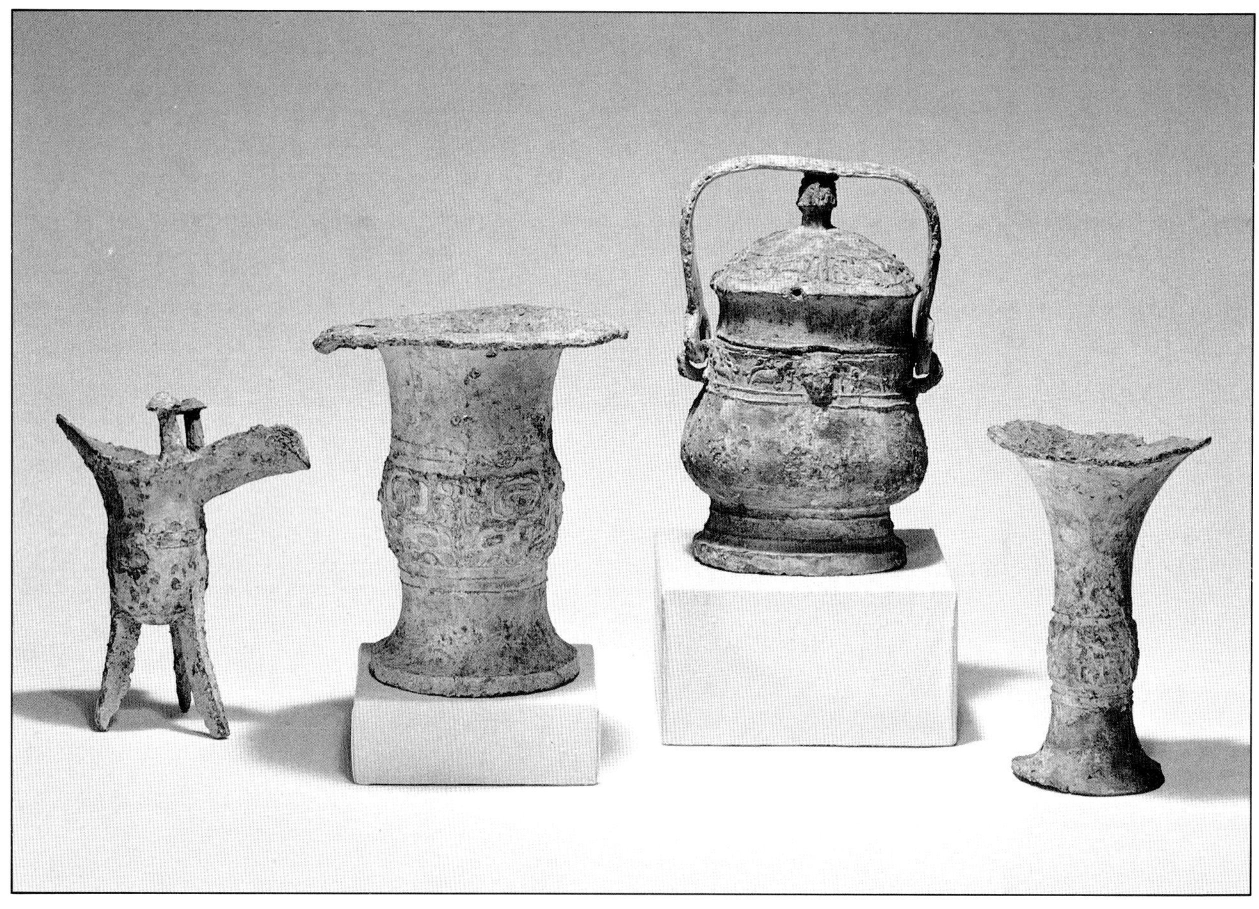

No. 46 (left to right: *jue*, *zun*, *you*, and *gu*)

46
SET OF VESSELS
Lead
Early Western Zhou dynasty
11th century B.C.
Heights: *gu*, 9-1/4 in. (23.5 cm); *you*, 10-1/2 in. (2.7 cm); *zun* 8-1/4 in. (21 cm); *jue* 8-1/2 in. (21. cm)
Hermitage Foundation Museum, Norfolk,Virginia (44.G.38c,d,e,f)

These four vessels come from a set of ten lead vessels formerly owned by Yamanaka and Company. The Hermitage Foundation Museum also has a *gui* and another *zun* from this set. Another two vessels from the set, a *jia* and *you*, are in the Rijksmuseum, Amsterdam (Fontein and Wu, nos. 11-12); and a *jue* obtained by the William Rockhill Nelson Gallery of Art, Kansas City, is now in the collection of the Freer Gallery of Art, Washington, D.C. (Cat. no. 47). The location of the last vessel of the set is not known. According to William Charles White, these vessels were obtained in Zhengzhou and their probable provenance was the Luoyang area (W. C. White, *Bronze Culture of Ancient China*, p. 176). Another set was excavated in a Western Zhou tomb at Luoyang (*Kaogu* [1956], no. 1: 27-28; Gettens, *The Freer Chinese Bronzes*, vol. 2, pp. 17-19).

An examination of the two vessels in the Rijksmuseum reveals the composition of the alloy to be 95 percent lead and 5 percent antimony. These vessels are evidence that lead was a casting medium in its own right. They show clearly the mold seams and the unfinished surface of the vessel after casting. This unfinished state seems to indicate that the lead vessels were intended for burial only. The softness of the metal has caused the vessels to bend out of shape readily. X-radiographic examination of the *you* shows the skeletal remains of birds that were offered as sacrifice. Some significance may be attached to the corresponding decoration of the narrow friezes with relief images of birds.

Former collection: Yamanaka & Co.

Published: W. C. White, *Bronze Culture of Ancient China* (Toronto: University of Toronto Press, 1956), pl. 97, 98 and 99; Gettens, *The Freer Chinese Bronzes*, vol. 2, pp. 17-19; p. 18, figs. 2 and 3.

47
JUE
Lead
Early Western Zhou dynasty
11th century B.C.
Height: 8-5/8 in. (21.9 cm)
Width: 6-3/8 in. (16.1 cm)
Freer Gallery of Art, Smithsonian Institution, Washington, D.C., Gift of William Rockhill Nelson Gallery of Art (SC-M-1)

This *jue* vessel, cast in a 99 percent lead alloy, is decorated with a single frieze consisting of two *taotie* masks in flat relief against a *leiwen* background. Vertical mold seams are clearly visible, running through the center of the spout, the tail, the handle, and the flange on the decorative frieze. They indicate the four-part division of the outer mold. The circular seam around the bottom marks the division between the outer mold and the interleg core piece. On a bronze vessel these seams would ordinarily be tooled off. The unfinished decoration also reveals ridges along the edges of the *taotie* mask (see detail). These ridges are the result of either preliminary outlining or redefinition of the decoration in the mold with a sharp tool prior to casting.

Former collections: Yamanaka & Co., Inc.; William Rockhill Nelson Gallery of Art, Kansas City

Published: W. C. White, *Bronze Culture of Ancient China* (Toronto: University of Toronto Press, 1956), p. 186, pl. 100; Gettens, *The Freer Chinese Bronzes*, vol. 2, p. 66, figs. 35-38.

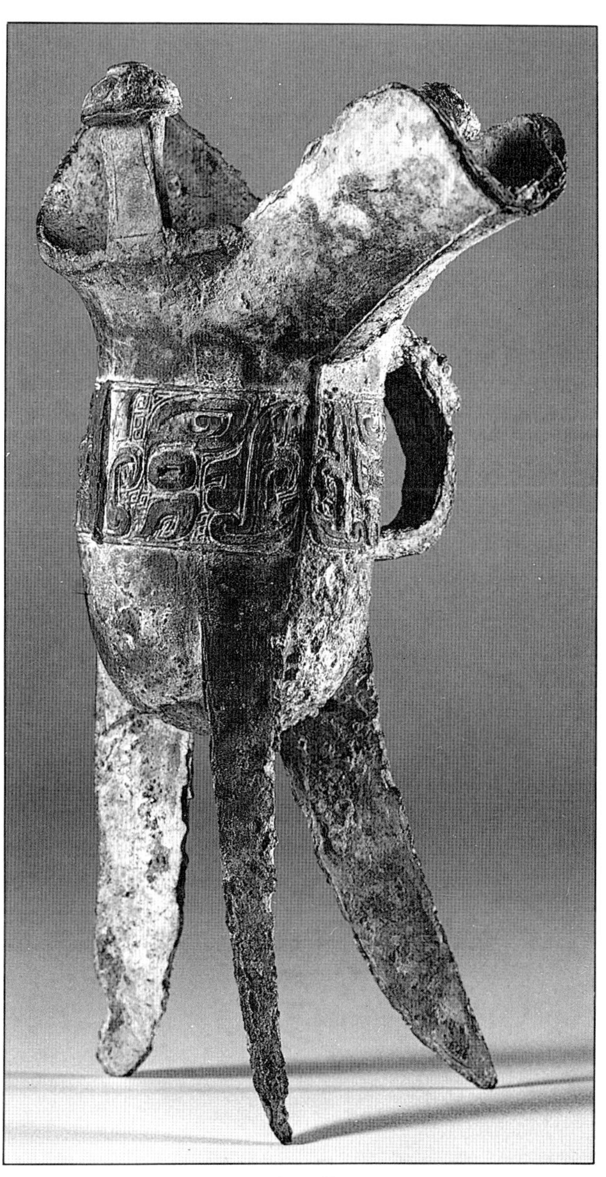

No. 47

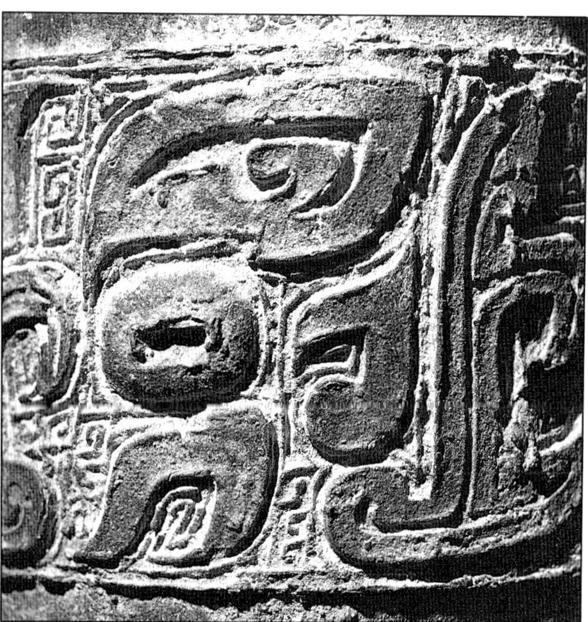

No. 47 (detail)

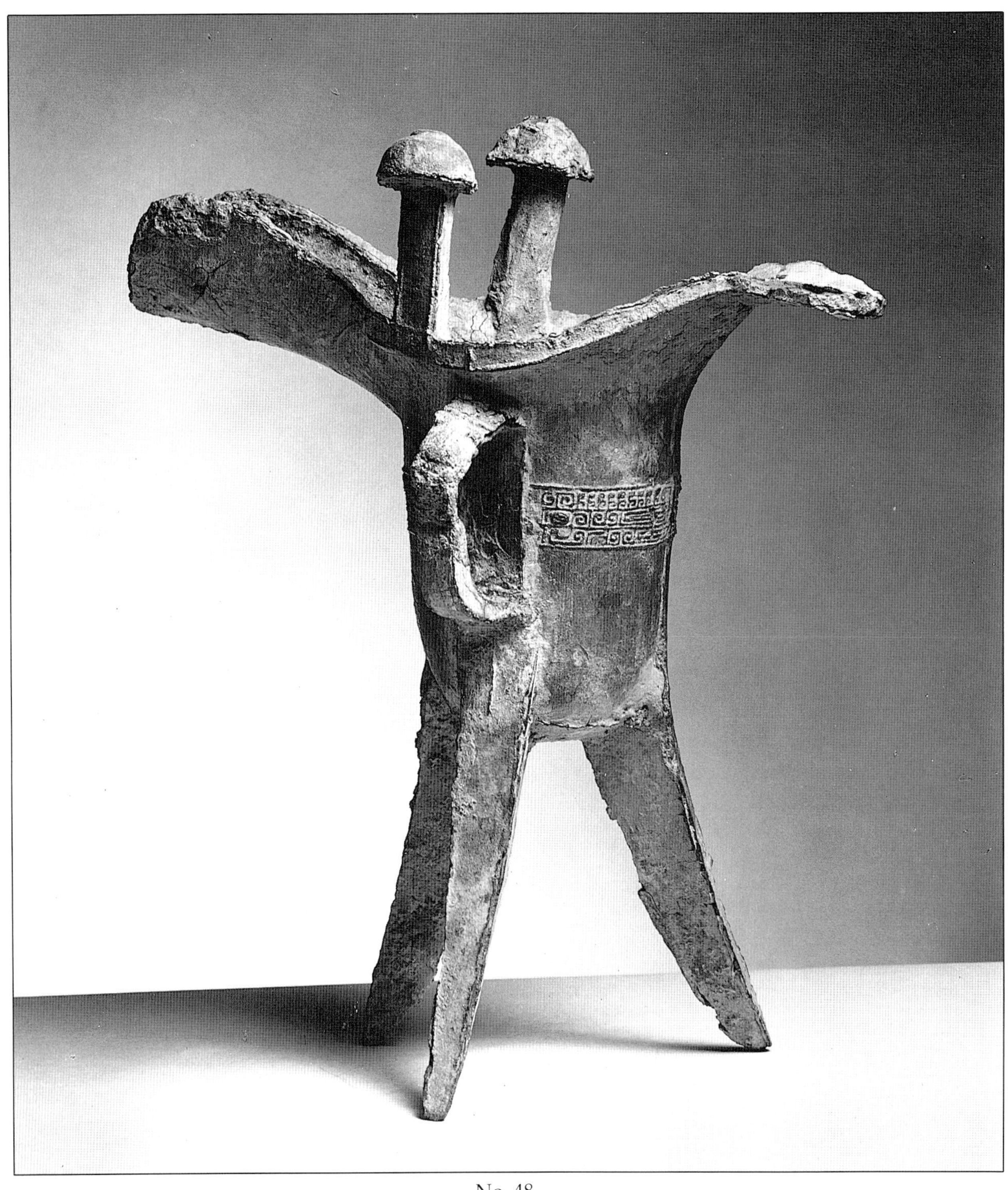

No. 48

48
JUE
Lead
Early Western Zhou dynasty
11th century B.C.
Height: 9 in. (22.9 cm)
Lent by Dr. Paul Singer

The decoration of this lead *jue*, a narrow frieze with two *taotie* masks rendered as three rows of raised scrolls, is a revival of Loehr's Style III found on Shang vessels of the Zhengzhou period. The pointed section of the rim has been bent out of shape. Mold seams reveal the same arrangement of mold pieces as in the previous *jue* (Cat. no. 47).

Published: Loehr, *Relics of Ancient China*, no. 42.

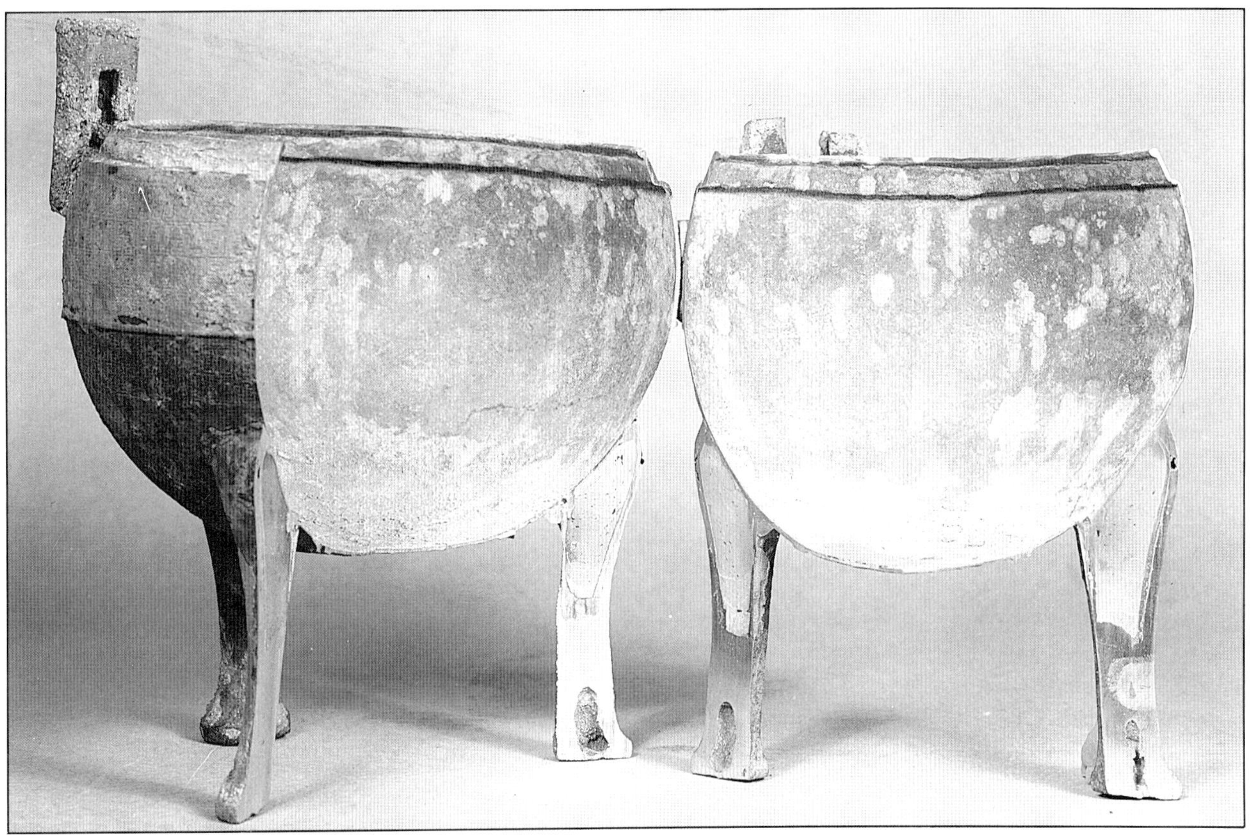

No. 49

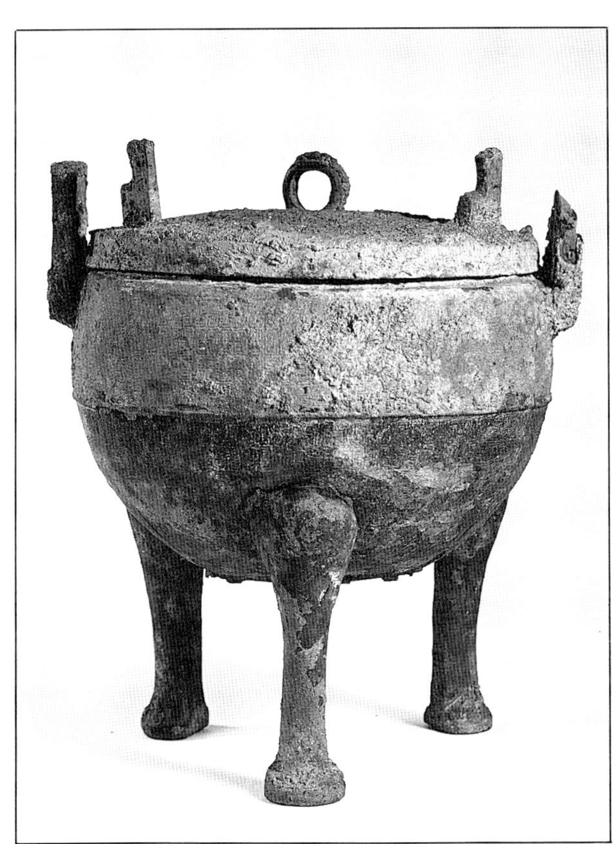

No. 49 (before sectioning)

49
SECTIONED *DING*
Bronze
Eastern Zhou dynasty
6th-5th century B.C.
Height of larger section, A: 10-1/16 in. (25.5 cm)
Width: 8-1/2 in. (21.5 cm)
Height of smaller section, B: 9-1/16 in. (23.0 cm)
Width: 7-1/8 in. (18.1 cm)
Freer Gallery of Art, Smithsonian Institution, Washington, D.C., Gift of Philadelphia Museum of Art (SC-B-58A and B)

This roughly corroded *ding* has been cut through, revealing the thickness of the walls and the original clay cores encased by the cabriole legs. Although its walls measure 1/64 in. (0.5 mm) at its thinnest, the vessel has the appearance of being heavier with the thickening of the rim to 3/32 in. (3.0 mm). The locked-on legs were cast separately, and the rest of the vessel was cast on afterward. It is apparent from the double layer of metal that the original legs were broken and then lengthened by overlay casting.

Since the legs were precast, they could not have been used as ducts for pouring the metal of the

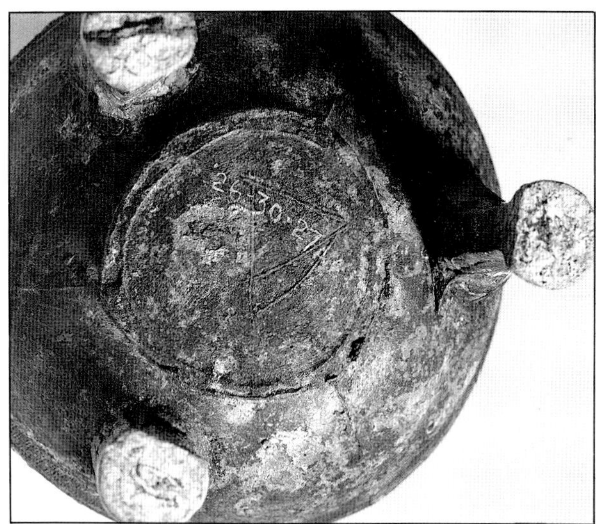

No. 49 (underside before sectioning)

vessel body. The double-ring seam around the bottom of the *ding* may indicate the location of the sprue and riser in the original mold assembly.

Published: Gettens, *The Freer Chinese Bronzes*, vol. 2, p. 81, figs. 67 and 68.

50
GU
Bronze, brass, and lead
Composite vessel
Late Shang dynasty fragments
with recent reconstruction
Height: 12-3/4 in. (32.3 cm)
Width: 6-3/4 in. (17.1 cm)
Freer Gallery of Art, Smithsonian Institution,
Washington, D.C.; Gallery Purchase (SC-B-14)

This *gu* has been partially stripped of its false patina to reveal that the entire top section of the vessel is new. Five authentic fragments dating from the late Shang dynasty are in the foot. They retain their original patina but are badly corroded. The worn edge of the rim reveals that the false patina was not an integral part of the metal surface and was easily peeled off. Other irregular characteristics of this *gu* include the lead eyes of the *taotie* mask on the restored neck and the soldered joints above and below the central bulb. The modern alloy is a brass containing 5 percent zinc. Since the decoration was cut into the surface, the protruding eyes were separately made in lead to reduce the total thickness of brass needed to make the vessel.

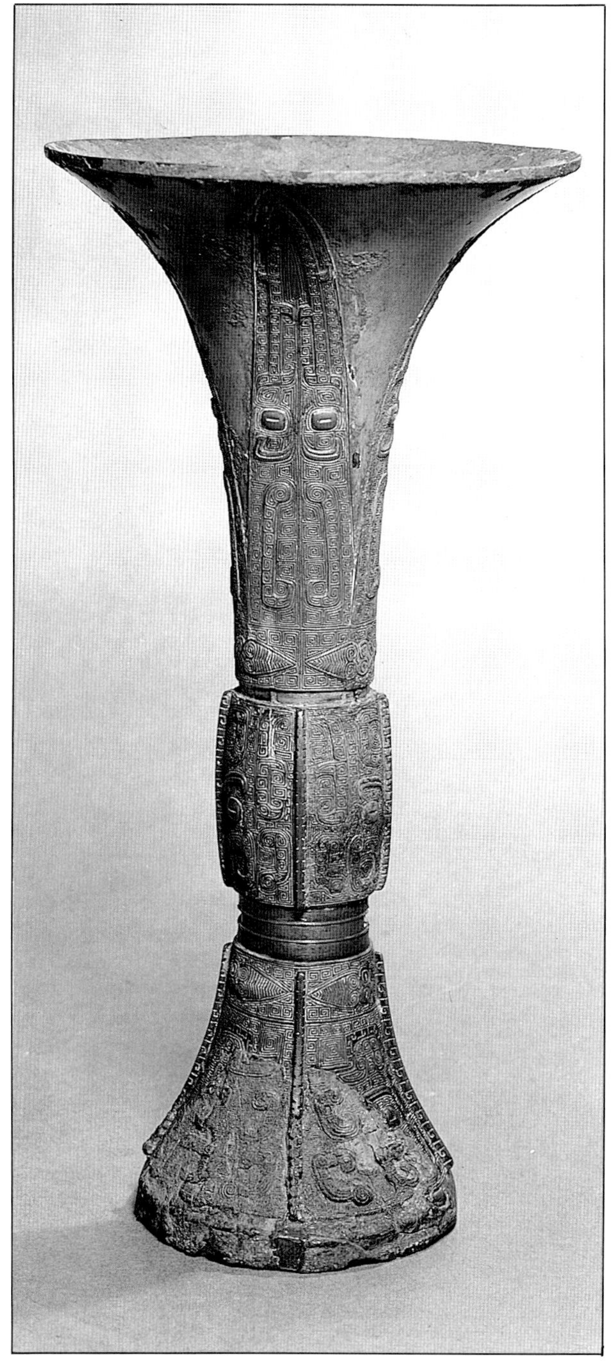

No. 50

The reconstruction, most certainly done in China, shows the extent to which the Chinese will restore an ancient bronze of which only a few fragments remain. The author saw a similar *gu* being repaired at the Palace Museum, Beijing, in 1973; soft solder and a low-zinc brass were the materials being used.

Published: Gettens, *The Freer Chinese Bronzes*, vol. 2, p. 215, fig. 291.

51
POU
Bronze
Late Shang dynasty, Anyang period
13th-11th century B.C.
Height: 14-3/8 in. (36.5 cm)
The Art Museum, Princeton University; Gift of Mr. and Mrs. Earl Morse (y1968-110)

This wide-mouthed vessel has a swelling body, sloping shoulders, and a high, conical foot. The restored sections display the original relief decoration of *taotie* masks on the belly beneath a narrow band of "eye-and-crescent" motifs and projecting whorl circles, profile dragons on the shoulder frieze, and *taotie* masks on the foot. Notched flanges subdivide the sides into quadrants, and projecting rams' heads are cast onto the shoulders.

Half the vessel has been stripped of its restorations to show its true corroded condition, as well as the skill of the restorer.

Published: Stephen Guglielmi, "Report on the Spurious Nature of a Shang Dynasty Bronze P'ou," *Record of the Art Museum, Princeton University*, 27 (1968), pp. 3-10.

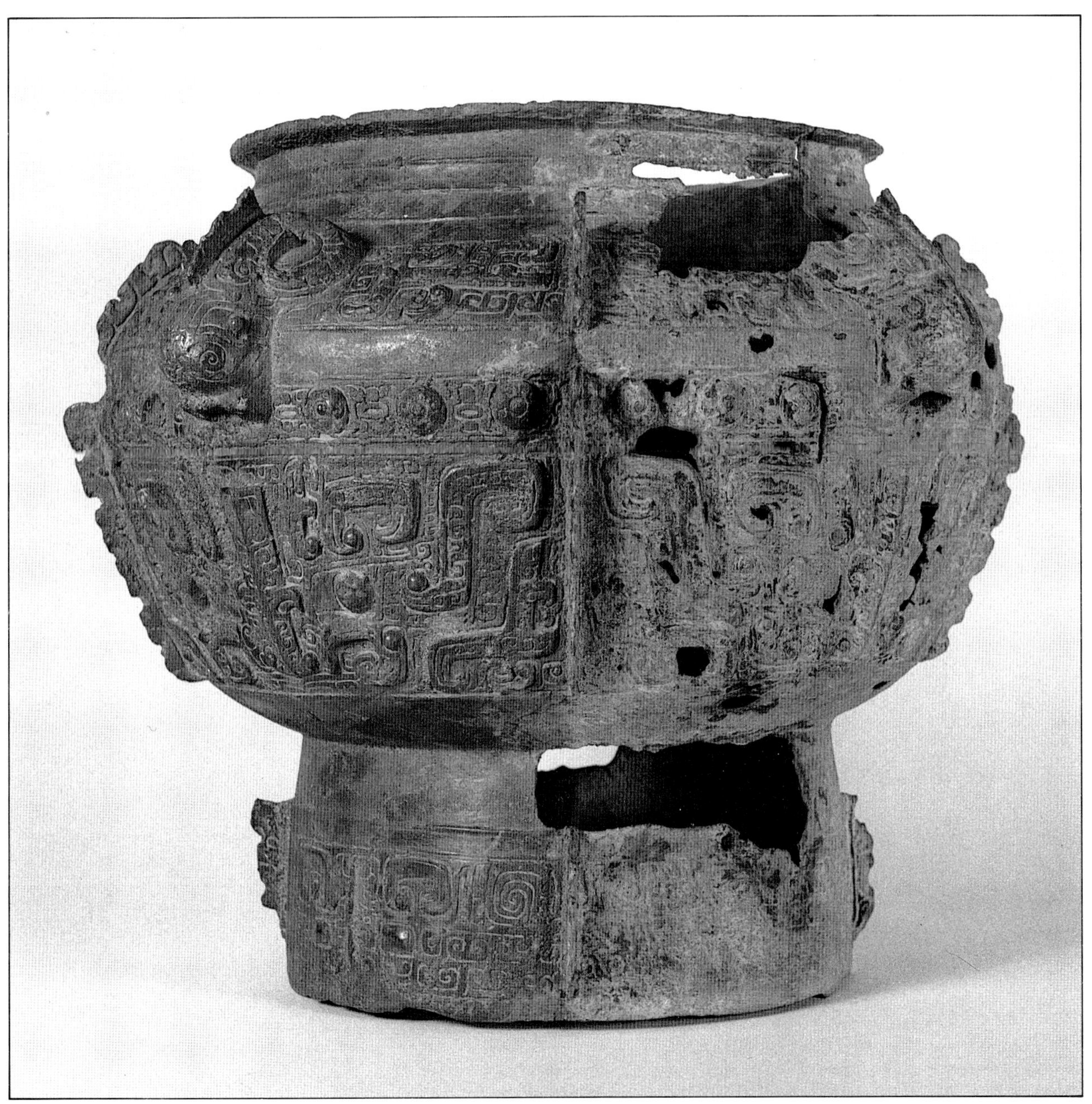

No. 51

THE MODERN REPRODUCTIONS

52
PLAQUE
Bronze (copper 96%, tin 0.2%, lead 0.2%, zinc 3.0%, iron 0.9%, selenium 0.4%)
Modern replica
Length: 6 in. (15.2 cm)
Width: 3-1/8 in. (7.9 cm)
On Loan to the Arthur M. Sackler Gallery, Smithsonian Institution, Washington, D.C.; Promised Gift

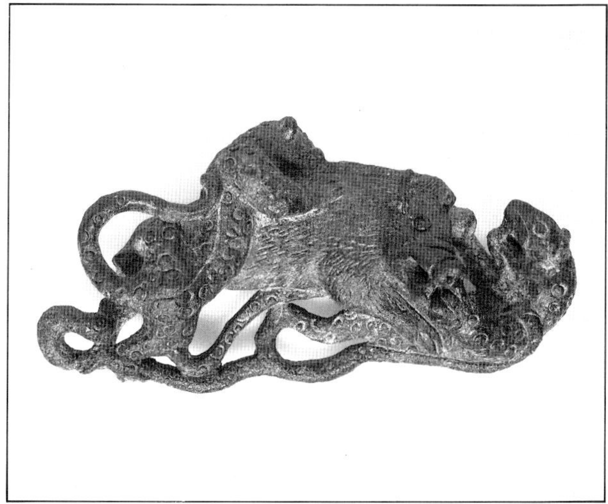

No. 52

This engraved bronze ornament realistically depicts in high relief a boar being attacked by two tigers or panthers. A serpent wraps around the shoulder of the tiger on the right, extends along the groundline, and bites the hind leg of the boar. The surface design is executed in cast, sunken lines. The ornament is cast as a shell and is open in the back. The legs, tails, and snake, cast in the round, extend in various directions from the main mass of the figures. This naturalism and the free abandon with shapes in the round are characteristic of lost-wax castings from the late Zhou and early Han periods from the Kingdom of Dian in Yunnan Province (southwestern China).

This plaque is nearly identical to one excavated at Shizhaishan in Yunnan Province (M10:4; Yunnan Provincial Museum, *Excavations of a Group of Tombs at Shizhaishan, Jinning, Yunnan Province* [in Chinese], [Beijing: Wenwu Press, 1959], vol. 2, pl. 75, no. 2). A close comparison reveals some differences, notably that the boar's snout connects with the tiger's left paw on our plaque, and that the flap of skin under the belly of the boar is missing. The detail on our plaque does not seem to be as fine as that on M10:4, although, where they can be seen, the sunken circles on our plaque appear to coincide with those on the excavated piece.

The plaque was examined technically at the Research Laboratory of the Museum of Fine Arts, Boston, by Dana Wang; and in the Technical Laboratory of the Arthur M. Sackler Gallery by the author. Energy-dispersive X-ray analysis at Boston revealed the alloy to be a leaded copper-zinc with traces of other metals. Tin was only detected at one spot. The analyses are shown in Table IV.

The analysis of our plaque is not consistent with excavated Dian material. Robert Murowchick has gathered together all of the analyses of Dian bronze material ("Yunnan and Its Environs: Development and Implications," Ph.D. diss., Harvard University, 1989). None of the analyses cited contains zinc in anywhere near the amount of this plaque. Generally zinc is below the detection limit of the analytical methods used. The Dian material consists of tin bronzes or leaded tin bronzes, with tin in the 5-15% range.

Metallographic study of a section removed by the Arthur M. Sackler Gallery Technical Laboratory revealed that the corrosion layers (probably cuprite and malachite) lie on top of the metal. There is no intergranular penetration. From the cross section we can tell that the plaque could not be as old as it is supposed to be. Some join traces are also visible on the edges of the plaque. This plaque may have been made as a surmoulage (reproduction casting),

TABLE IV

Site	Weight %						
	Copper	Zinc	Lead	Iron	Tin	Selenium	Arsenic
Leopard snout	97.7	1.4	0.1	0.4	0.2	0.2	-
Bottom vine	93.5	3.8	0.1	1.4	0.5	0.6	0.7
Boar snout	95.9	2.4	0.2	0.8	0.3	0.3	-
Leopard tail	95.4	2.4	0.3	0.8	0.4	0.6	-

using the Dian original as a model. A piece mold would have been pulled from the original, probably using plaster, and wax pulled from the piece mold. The joints in the piece mold left traces on the wax, which were smoothed down (but not perfectly). The boar's snout and tiger paw were not separated in the wax, and the flap under the boar's belly was removed along with the visible mold joints. The plaque was cast in the strange alloy, finished, and patinated; we would like to know the method of patination, and future electron microscope studies of the section might give us some clues.

An additional interesting point: selenium, present in this piece, is said to be characteristic of coppers from Yunnan. The selenium here points to this piece having been made in Yunnan, an aftercast from the original, now in the Yunnan Provincial Museum.

53 (not illustrated)
XI GONG (GUANG)
Bronze
Modern facsimile, after late Shang dynasty
Height: 5-1/2 in. (14 cm)
Length: 11-13/16 in. (19.9 cm)
Shanghai Museum

The *gong*, sometimes pronounced *guang*, is a wine vessel predominantly cast in the shape of an animal. This vessel, in the shape of a water buffalo, is unusual in having a base shaped like the animal's own four feet. Its head and back form the lid, while the neck forms the open spout. A small tiger sits on the back of the buffalo as a knob for the lid. The surface of the vessel is decorated with a vividly modeled long-crested phoenix on the sides and a dragon on the front.

54 (not illustrated)
FU GENG ZHI
Bronze
Modern facsimile, after early Western Zhou dynasty
Height: 5-13/16 in. (14.8 cm)
Diameter of the mouth: 2-15/16 in. (7.5 cm)
Shanghai Museum

The *zhi* is a drinking vessel with curving sides and a flaring mouth. It is decorated on the neck with a rising blade, or plantain leaf, pattern and a band of little birds underneath; the body is decorated with proudly standing phoenixes with long crests. This bird motif was very popular and was used throughout the Western Zhou period.

55 (not illustrated)
YI HOU SHI GUI
Bronze
Modern facsimile, after early WesternZhou dynasty
Height: 6-3/8 in. (16.2 cm)
Diameter of the mouth: 8-7/8 in. (22.5 cm)
Shanghai Museum

The *gui* container was used to serve staple foods like rice or corn. *Yi hou shi gui* was excavated in 1954, from Yandun Mountain, in Dantu County, Jiangsu Province. It has a shallow belly, high circular foot, and four large handles surmounted with animal heads. This object is decorated on the belly with raised whorl circles alternating with dragons; the foot is decorated with birds separated by four short flanges. The long inscription of 119 characters cast on the inside of the bottom is an important historical document. It relates the story of Zhou Kang Wang (King Kang of Zhou) conferring upon a certain Shi the marquisate of Yi (in present-day Jiangsu Province), as well as weapons, fields, and slaves.

56 (not illustrated)
LU HOU ZUN
Bronze
Modern facsimile, after early Western Zhou dynasty
Height: 8-3/4 in. (22.2 cm)
Diameter of the mouth: 8-1/8 in. (20.7 cm)
Shanghai Museum

This unusual *zun* is a type of wine container. It has an undulating eight-layered contour from its flared mouth to its five-tiered square base. The two heavy handles in the shape of animal heads have long taillike extensions that hang down along the tall base. Totally devoid of surface decoration, the object has a strange solemnity. Inside the bottom is an inscription of four lines (twenty-two characters), which records that the *zun* was made to commemorate Lu Hou's (Marquis Lu) punitive expedition to the East Country to help Ming Gong (Duke Ming).

57 (not illustrated)
YUE REN FANG DING
Bronze
Modern facsimile, after late Western Zhou dynasty
Height: 5-3/8 in. (13.6 cm)
Height to the rim: 3-5/8 in. (9.2 cm)
Length at the rim: 4-7/16 in. (11.4 cm)
Shanghai Museum

A *ding* is a cooking vessel generally having either three or four column-shaped feet. This piece is a rare oval shape with a flat bottom and without handles. It is decorated below the lip with a frieze of coiled animals above a wave pattern. A house-shaped square base has a hinged door and is used as a stove. Charcoal can be lit inside the base to heat the food. Two cross-shaped windows are set on each side of the base. An openwork interlocking animal-eye design decorates the back side of the base and acts as an air vent.

58 (not illustrated)
PAN LONG WEN ZHONG
Bronze
Modern facsimile, after Spring and Autumn period
Height: 12-1/8 in. (31.8 cm)
Shanghai Museum

The bell is an ancient Chinese percussion instrument. Its sides are decorated with three rows of six bosses. The space between the bosses is decorated with a wing-shaped pattern. An interlocking dragon design decorates the middle panel. Two different audio frequencies can be produced by striking the middle and the side panels of this specially designed bell. In ancient China, bells were arranged in graduated sizes in order to create a musical scale. These bells were called *bian zhong*.

59 (not illustrated)
GONG (GUANG)
Bronze
Modern forgery
Height: 5-1/4 in. (13.3 cm)
Length: 6-1/2 in. (16.5 cm)
Depth: 3-3/4 in. (9.5 cm)
Center for Conservation and Technical Studies, Harvard University Art Museums, Cambridge, Massachusetts (XVA 85)

This animal-shaped wine pouring vessel is a modern forgery after a late Shang original. It was made using the lost-wax process after an original in the Fogg Art Museum. An artificial patina was sprayed onto the bronze after an acid bath. Clay was applied to the handle to simulate remnants of core material and bombarded with radiation to see if it would pass a thermoluminescence test for authenticity. It did not.

The forgery was created and documented for a segment of the television series "Discover: The World of Science," produced by the Chedd-Angier Production Company.

THE MOLD ASSEMBLIES

60 (Color pl. VIIIA-G)
MOLD ASSEMBLY FOR A *ZHI* VESSEL
Modern reconstruction
Shanghai Museum

This set demonstrates the entire process of casting a bronze vessel, from the original clay model to the broken fragments of the mold after firing. A small and simple shape like this *zhi* would have required only two outer mold pieces with the addition of inner core and foot core pieces.

61 (not illustrated)
MOLD ASSEMBLY FOR A *DING* VESSEL
Modern reconstruction
Shanghai Museum

This reconstruction demonstrates one stage of the casting process for a *ding*. The complicated shape of the vessel requires additional outer mold pieces and an interleg core piece to form the inside of the legs. When assembled, the molten metal is poured into the empty casting space of one leg (the sprue) and the air from the space is pushed out through another leg (the riser).

62 (not illustrated)
MOLD ASSEMBLY FOR A *JUE* VESSEL
Modern reconstruction
Provided by Ho Shih-k'un
Institute of History and Philology
Academia Sinica, Taipei

COLOR PLATES

Pl. I (cat. no. 6) ▶

FANG JIA
Bronze
Shang dynasty, Anyang period
13th-11th century B.C.
Albright-Knox Art Gallery, Buffalo, New York,
Bequest of Arthur B. Michael, 1953 (53.2)

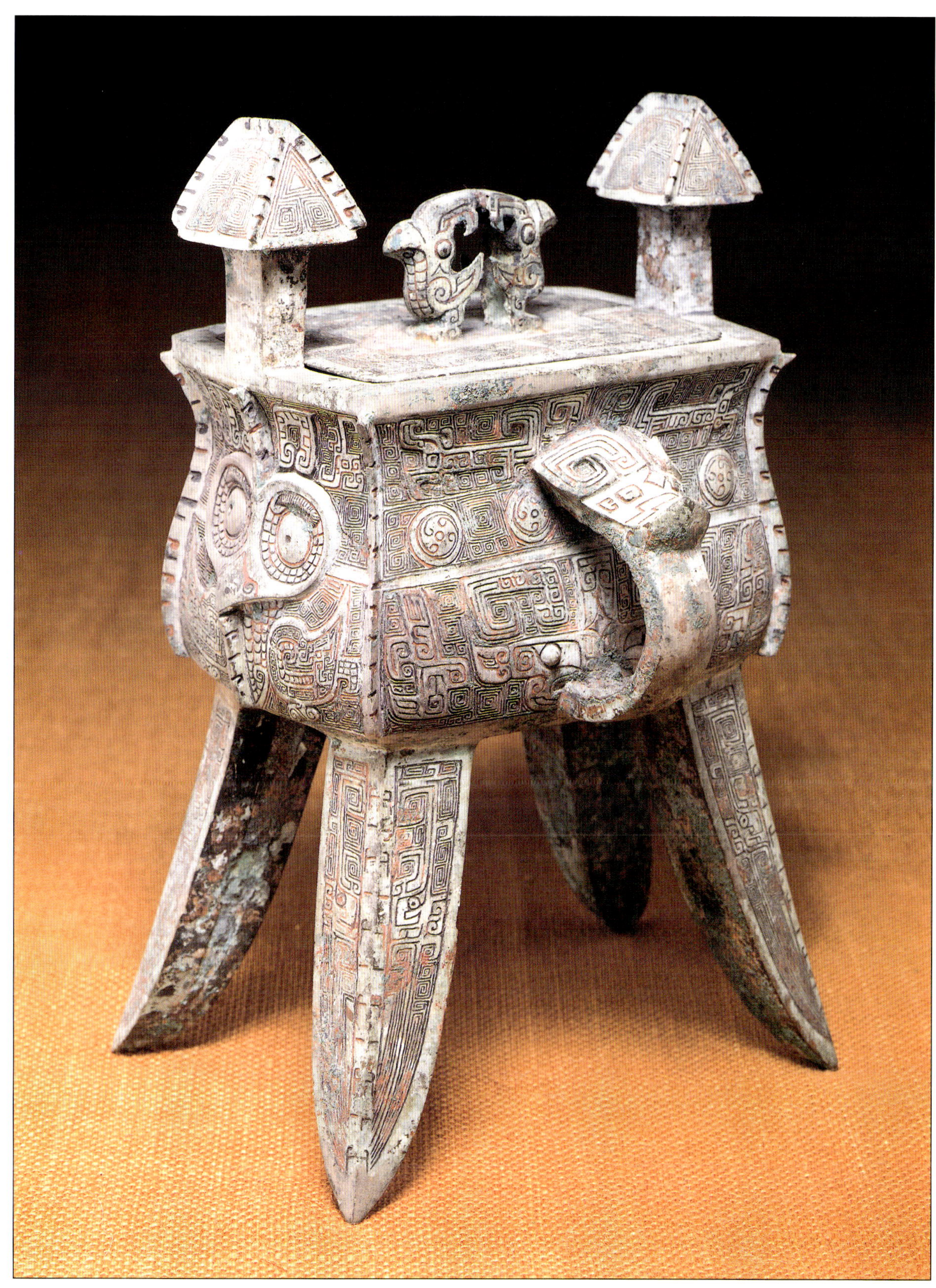

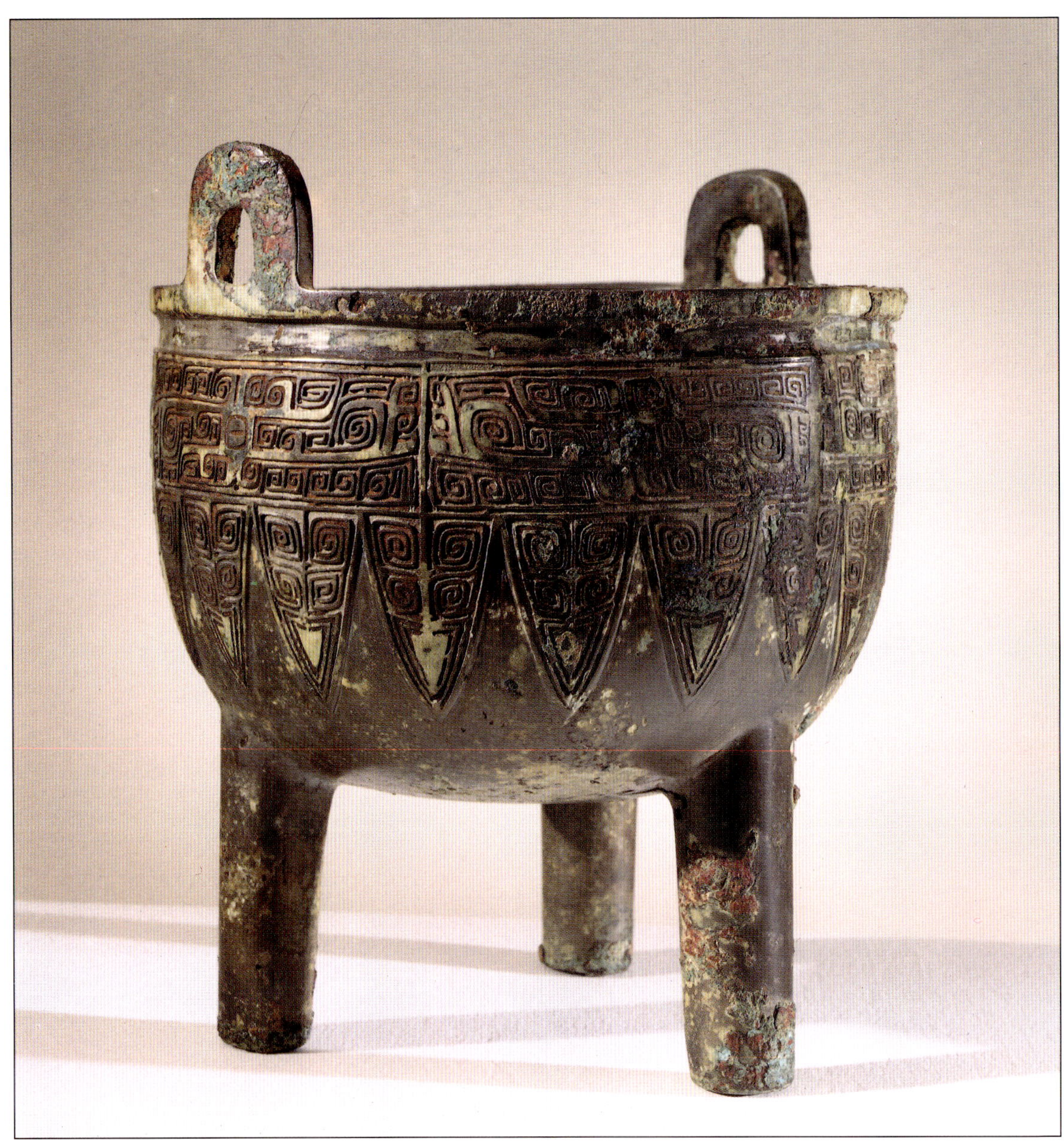

Pl. II (cat. no. 7)

DING
Bronze
Shang dynasty, Anyang period
13th-11th century B.C.
Three-character inscription
in the bottom of the bowl
Lent by Dr. Paul Singer

Pl. III (cat. no. 15) ▶

YOU
Bronze
Shang dynasty, Anyang period
11th century B.C.
Three-character inscription
in the lid and base
The Metropolitan Museum of Art,
Bequest of Addie W. Kahn,
1949 (49.135.5a,b)

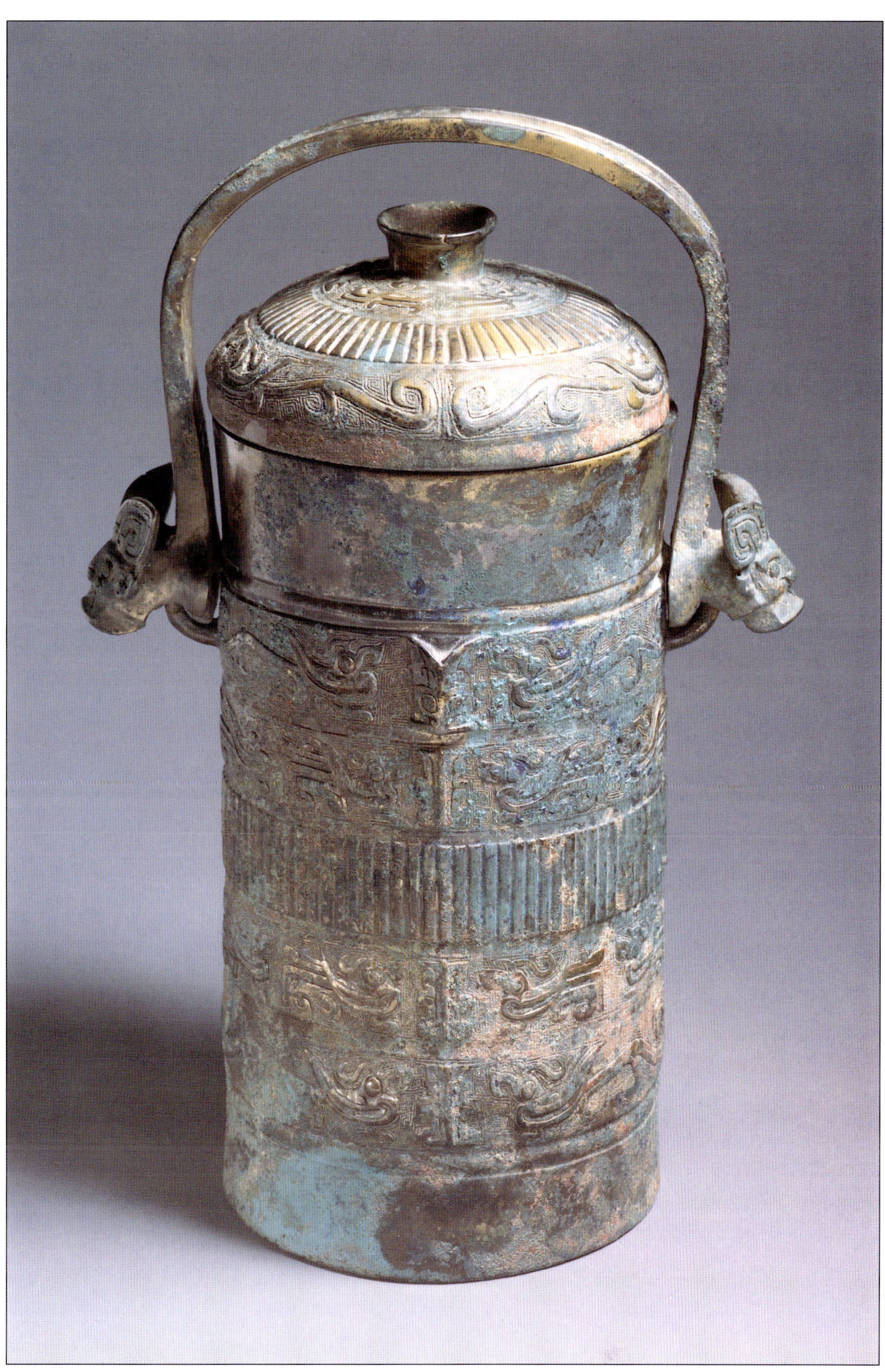

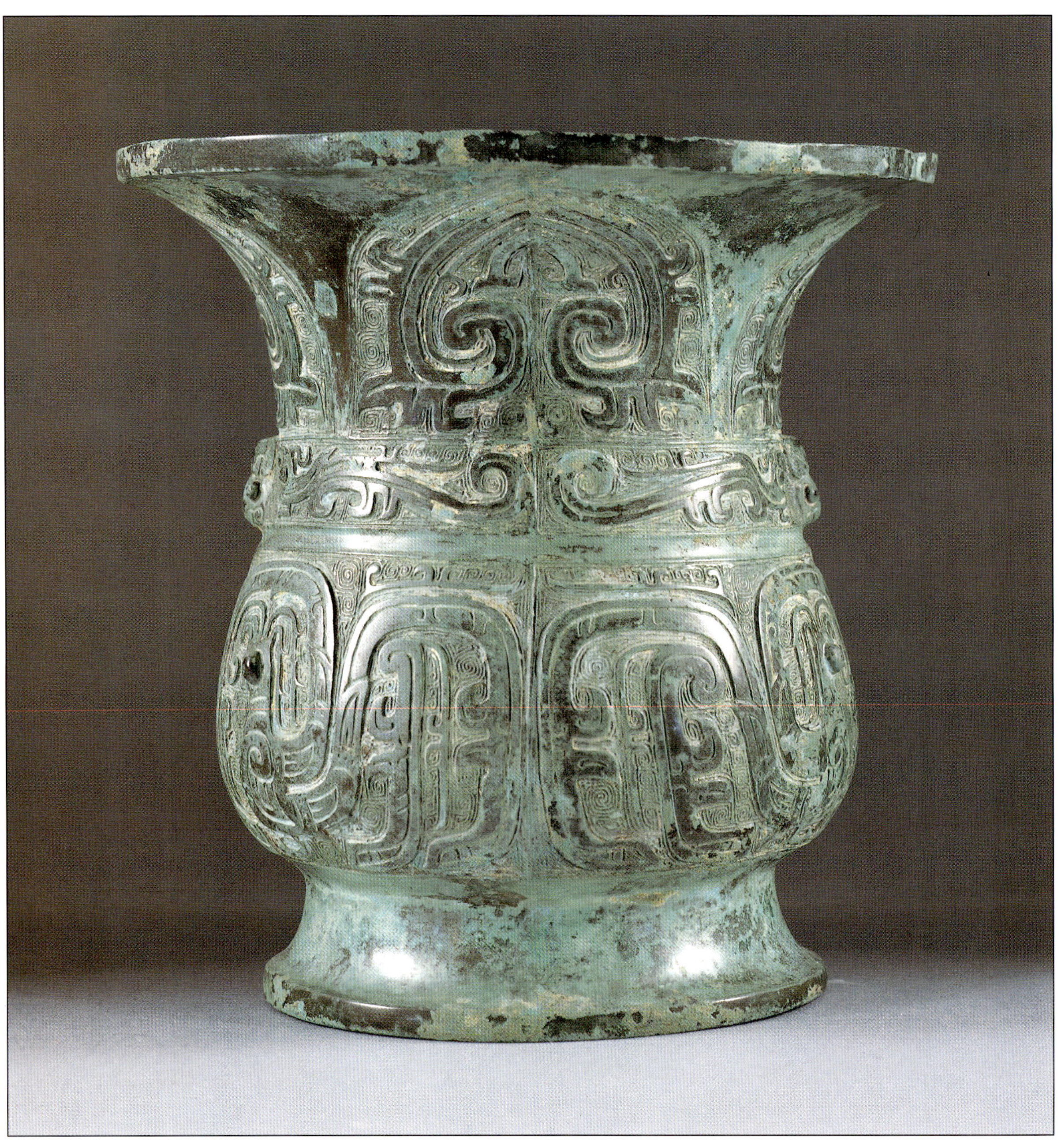

Pl. IV (cat. no. 16)

ZUN
Bronze
Early Western Zhou dynasty
11th-10th century B.C.
The Art Museum, Princeton University,
Museum Purchase, Carl Otto von Kienbusch, Jr.,
Memorial Collection (y1952-58)

Pl. V (cat. no. 24) ▶

HU
Bronze
Late Spring and Autumn/early Warring States period
6th-5th century B.C.
Dr. and Mrs. David Morowitz, Bethesda, Maryland

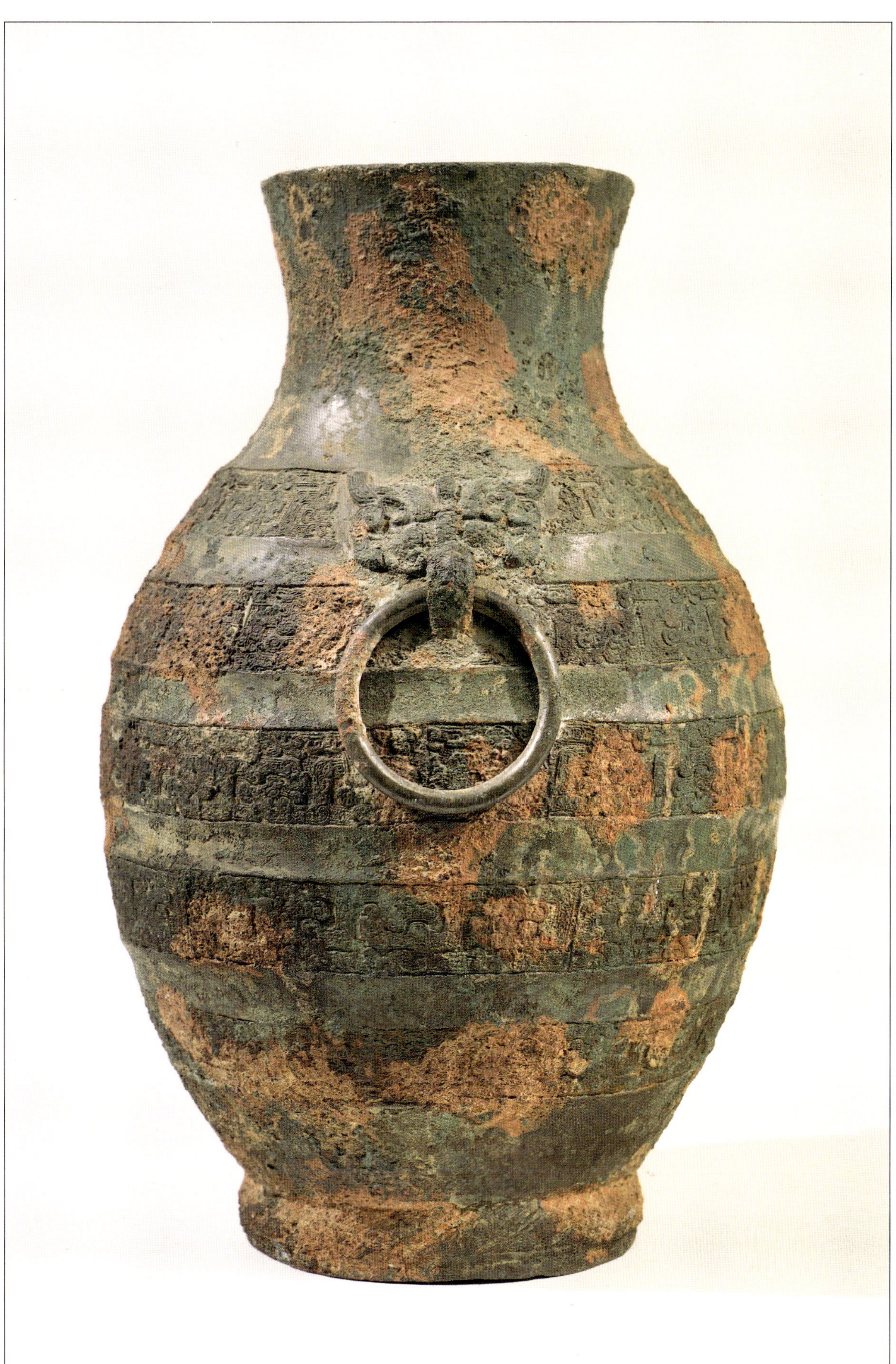

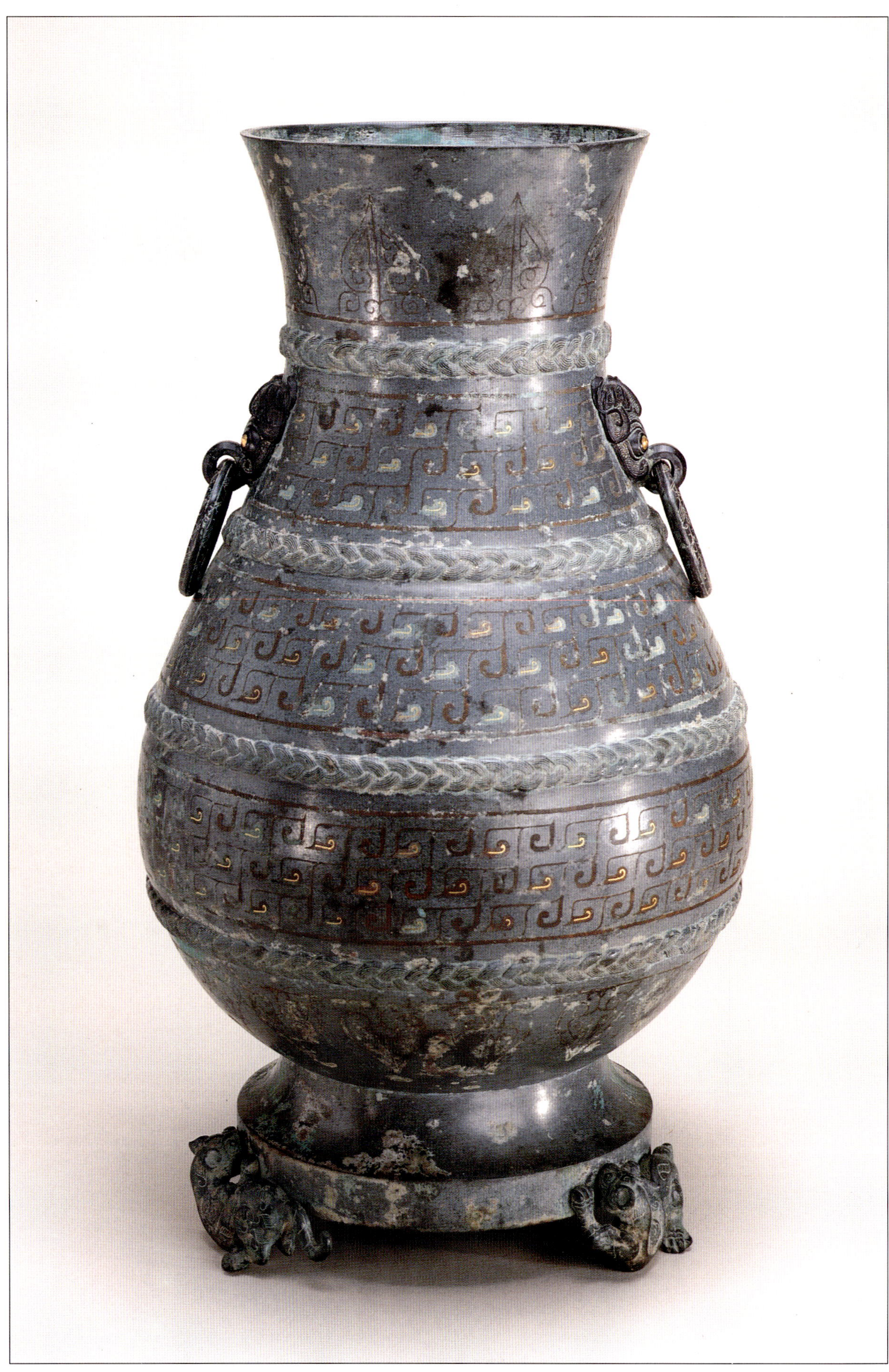

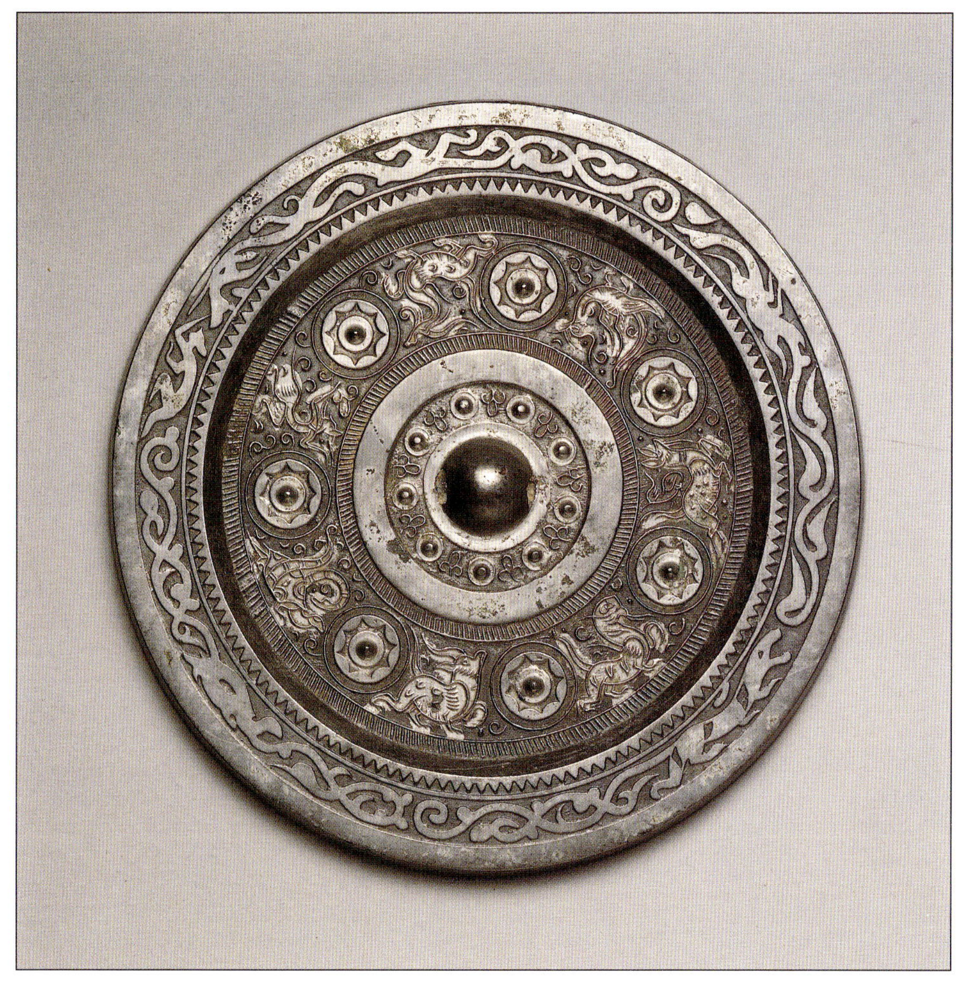

Pl. VII (cat. no. 37)

TWO-COLORED MIRROR
Bronze
Eastern Han dynasty
2nd-early 3rd century
Lent by D. H. Graham, Jr.

DETAIL ▼

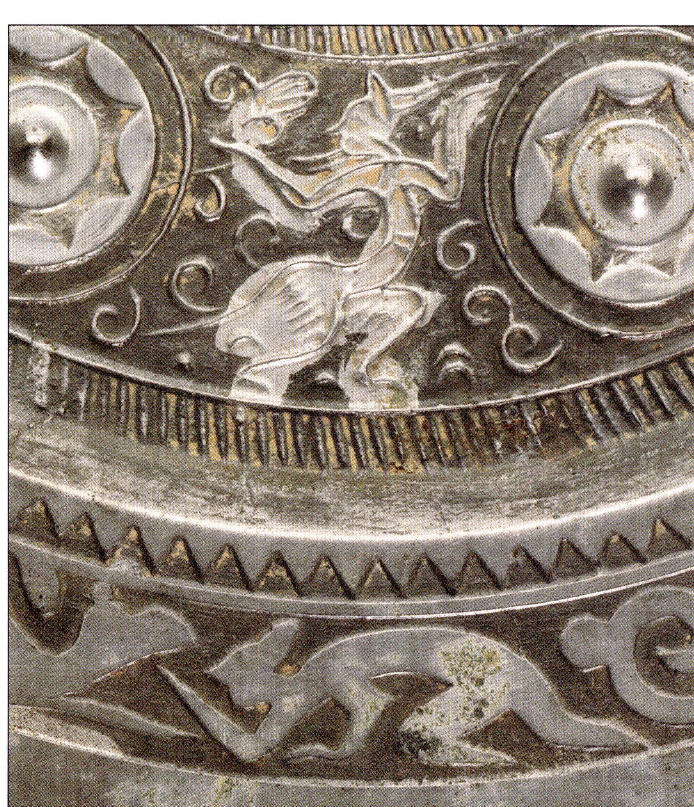

◀ Pl. VI (cat. no. 30)

HU
Bronze inlaid with gold and copper
Eastern Zhou dynasty
Late 6th or early 5th century B.C.
Arthur M. Sackler Gallery,
Smithsonian Institution,
Washington, D.C. (S1987.318)

Pl. VIII (cat. no. 60)

MOLD ASSEMBLY FOR A *ZHI* VESSEL
Modern reconstruction
The Shanghai Museum

A. The model together with the finished bronze.

B. The mold is made by taking a clay impression from the model. Keys are cut along the edges for refitting the pieces.

C. The outer mold pieces are separated, retouched, and fired.

D. The core pieces or inner molds are produced from the outer mold and shaved down to create the casting space. A pouring gate is cut into the top.

E. The reassembled mold.

F. Cross section of the mold assembly, showing the pouring gate and the casting space.

G. After firing, the outer mold is broken away.

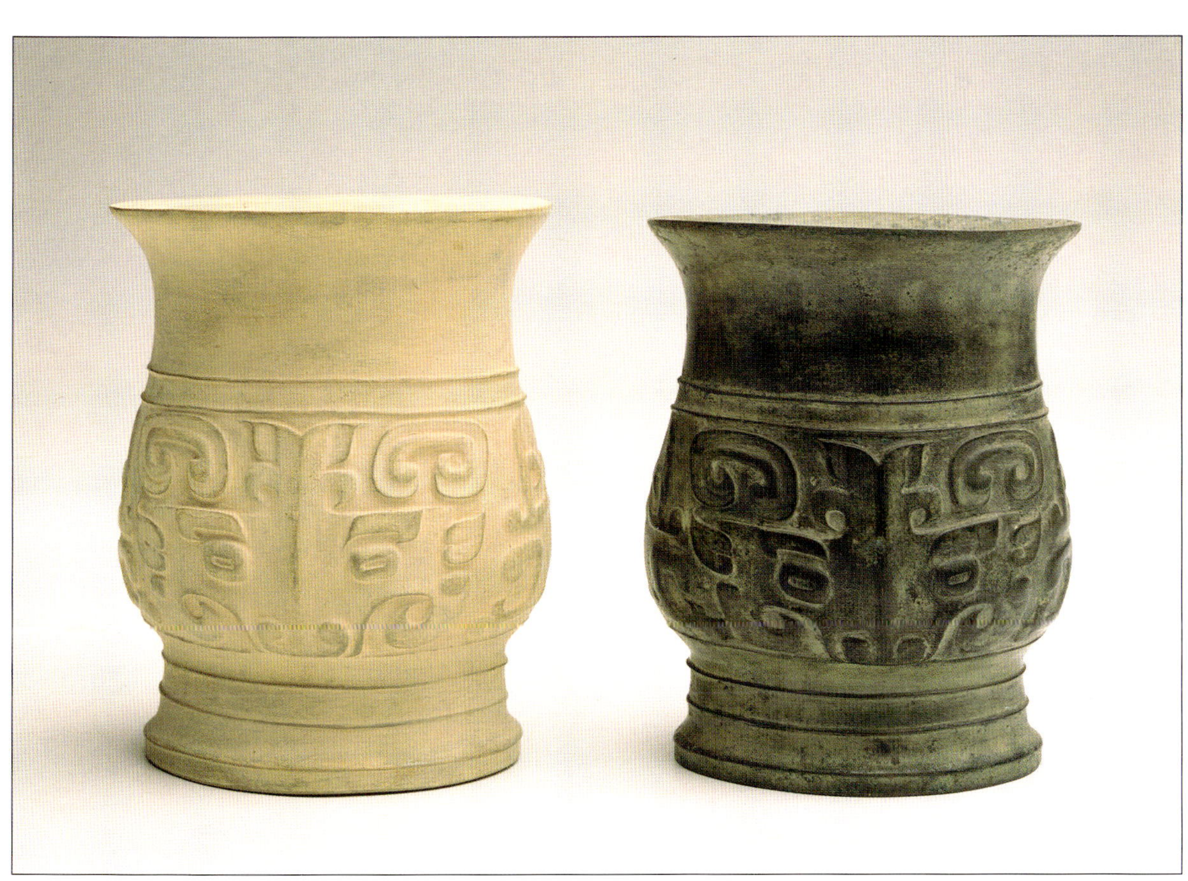

A

PICTURE CREDITS

TEXT FIGURES

1 & 2: Peter Lukic, after illustration in P. Knauth, *The Metalsmiths* (New York: Time-Life Books, 1974), pp. 116-117.

3a, 3b, 5: Courtesy of the Freer Gallery of Art, Smithsonian Institution, Washington, D.C.

4, 6, 7: Thomas Feist

8: Courtesy of the Department of Objects Conservation, The Metropolitan Museum of Art

CATALOGUE ILLUSTRATIONS

1, 4, 7, 18, 23, 44, 48: Otto E. Nelson

2, 25: Royal Ontario Museum

3, 10, 19, 26, 33, 34: Thomas Feist

5, 9, 13, 27, 46: Philip R. Morrison

6: Biff Henrich

8, 12: Courtesy of Yale University Art Gallery

11A & B, 15, 20, 22, 35, 36, 38, 39A & B: All rights reserved, The Metropolitan Museum of Art

16, 51: The Art Museum, Princeton University

17, 32: The University Museum, University of Pennsylvania (neg. no. S8-1052, S8-1785)

14, 21: Worcester Art Museum

24: David Morowitz

28: Shin Hada

28 (detail): Courtesy of W. Thomas Chase

29: The Art Institute of Chicago

30, 30 (detail), 31, 52: Arthur M. Sackler Gallery, Smithsonian Institution, Washington, D.C.

40A-E, 43: Courtesy of Dr. Paul Singer

41: Courtesy of the Seattle Art Museum

42, 45: Susan Dirk

47, 47 (detail), 49, 49 (details), 50: Courtesy of the Freer Gallery of Art, Smithsonian Institution, Washington, D.C.

53, 54, 55, 56, 57, 58, 60, 61: The Shanghai Museum

COLOR PLATES

I: Courtesy of Albright-Knox Art Gallery, Buffalo, New York

II: Thomas Feist

III: Copyright © 1991 By The Metropolitan Museum of Art, New York

IV: The Art Museum, Princeton University

V: Thomas Feist

VI: Arthur M. Sackler Gallery, Smithsonian Institution, Washington, D.C.

VII: Jerry Chong, Graphic Pictures Hawaii

VIII: The Shanghai Museum

BIBLIOGRAPHY

Chinese is romanized in the pinyin *system throughout the text and bibliography except for the names of Chinese authors writing in Western languages. Chinese terms cited in Western-language titles remain in their original form and have not been converted.*

Some of the highlights and a few of the primary sources on the subject of Chinese bronzes follow. A more technical bibliography can be found in my article "Bronze Casting in China: A Short Technical History." For a more complete bibliography on Chinese excavations, see Noel Barnard and Tamotsu Sato, *Metallurgical Remains of Ancient China*; Robert W. Bagley, "P'an-lung-ch'eng: A Shang City in Hupei"; and Jessica Rawson, *Western Zhou Bronzes from the Arthur M. Sackler Collections.* The forthcoming revision of Barnard & Sato's *Metallurgical Remains of Ancient China* is expected to have definitive answers or at least definitive reviews of various important questions. —W.T.C

An Zhimin. "Some Problems Concerning China's Early Copper and Bronze Artifacts." *Kaogu Xuebao* (1981) no. 3: 269-285. (An English version of this article appears in *Early China* 8 [1982]: 53-78.)

Andersson, Johann Gunnar. "The Goldsmith in Ancient China." *Bulletin of the Museum of Far Eastern Antiquities* 7 (1935): 1-38 with 21 plates.

Archaeometallurgy Group, Beijing University of Iron and Steel Technology. "A Preliminary Study of Early Bronze Artifacts," *Kaogu Xuebao* (1981) no. 3: 287-302.

Bagley, Robert W. "P'an-lung-ch'eng: A Shang City in Hupei." *Artibus Asiae* 39 (1977): 165-219.

_______. *Shang Ritual Bronzes in the Arthur M. Sackler Collections.* Washington, D.C. and Cambridge, MA: The Arthur M. Sackler Foundation and the Arthur M. Sackler Museum, 1987.

_______. "A Shang City in Sichuan Province." *Orientations* (November, 1990): 59-67.

Barnard, Noel. *Bronze Casting and Bronze Alloys in Ancient China.* Canberra: The Australian National University and Monumenta Serica, 1961.

_______. "Wrought Metal-working Prior to Middle Shang: A Problem in Archaeological and Art-historical Research Approaches." *Early China* 6 (1981): 4-30.

_______. "From Ore to Ingot — Mining, Ore-processing, and Smelting in Ancient China." *Proceedings of the Second International Conference on Sinology*, pp. 141-206. Taipei: Academia Sinica, 1989.

_______. "Thoughts on the Emergence of Metallurgy in Pre-Shang and Early Shang China, and a Technical Reappraisal of Relevant Bronze Artifacts of the Time." (Paper presented at The Hsia Culture Symposium, May 23-25, 1990, University of California at Los Angeles, 25 pp., 20 figures.)

_______. Review of Robert W. Bagley, *Shang Ritual Bronzes in the Arthur M. Sackler Collections. T'oung-pao* (1991): in press.

_______, and Tamotsu Sato. *Metallurgical Remains of Ancient China.* Tokyo: Nichiosha, 1975.

Barnes, I. Lynus, W. Thomas Chase, Laura Holmes, Emile C. Joel, Pieter Meyers, and Edward V. Sayre. "The Technical Examination, Lead Isotope Determination, and Elemental Analysis of Some Shang and Zhou Dynasty Bronze Vessels." In *The Beginning of the Use of Metals and Alloys*, edited by Robert Maddin, pp. 296-306. Papers delivered at the Second International Conference on the Beginning of the Use of Metals and Alloys, Zhengzhou, China, October 21-26, 1986. Cambridge, MA: MIT Press, 1986.

_______. "Lead Isotope Ratio Analysis of the Sackler Bronzes." (Paper presented at the Conference of the American Society for Mass Spectrometry, Denver, Colorado, May 24-29, 1987.)

Barnes, I. Lynus, Robert H. Brill, Emile C. Deal, and G. Venetia Piercy. "Lead Isotope Studies of Early Chinese Glasses." In *Research in Ancient Chinese Glasses*, edited by Gan Fuxi. Proceedings of the International Symposium on Glass. Beijing, 1986.

Becker, Marshall. "Sardinian Stone Moulds: An Interesting Means of Evaluating Bronze Age Metallurgical Technology." In vol. 1 of *Studies in Sardinian Archaeology*, edited by M. S. Balmuth and R. J. Rowlands, pp. 163-208. Ann Arbor: University of Michigan Press, 1984.

Biot, Edward, trans. *Le Tcheou-li ou Rites des Tcheou.* 2 vols. Paris: Imprimerie Nationale, 1851.

British Museum Research Laboratory Colloquium on Surface Colouring and Plating of Metals, June 14-16, 1990. Abstracts 25 pp. London: British Museum Research Laboratory, 1990.

Bunker, Emma. *Ancient Chinese Inlaid Bronzes.* London: Bluett and Sons Ltd., 1989.

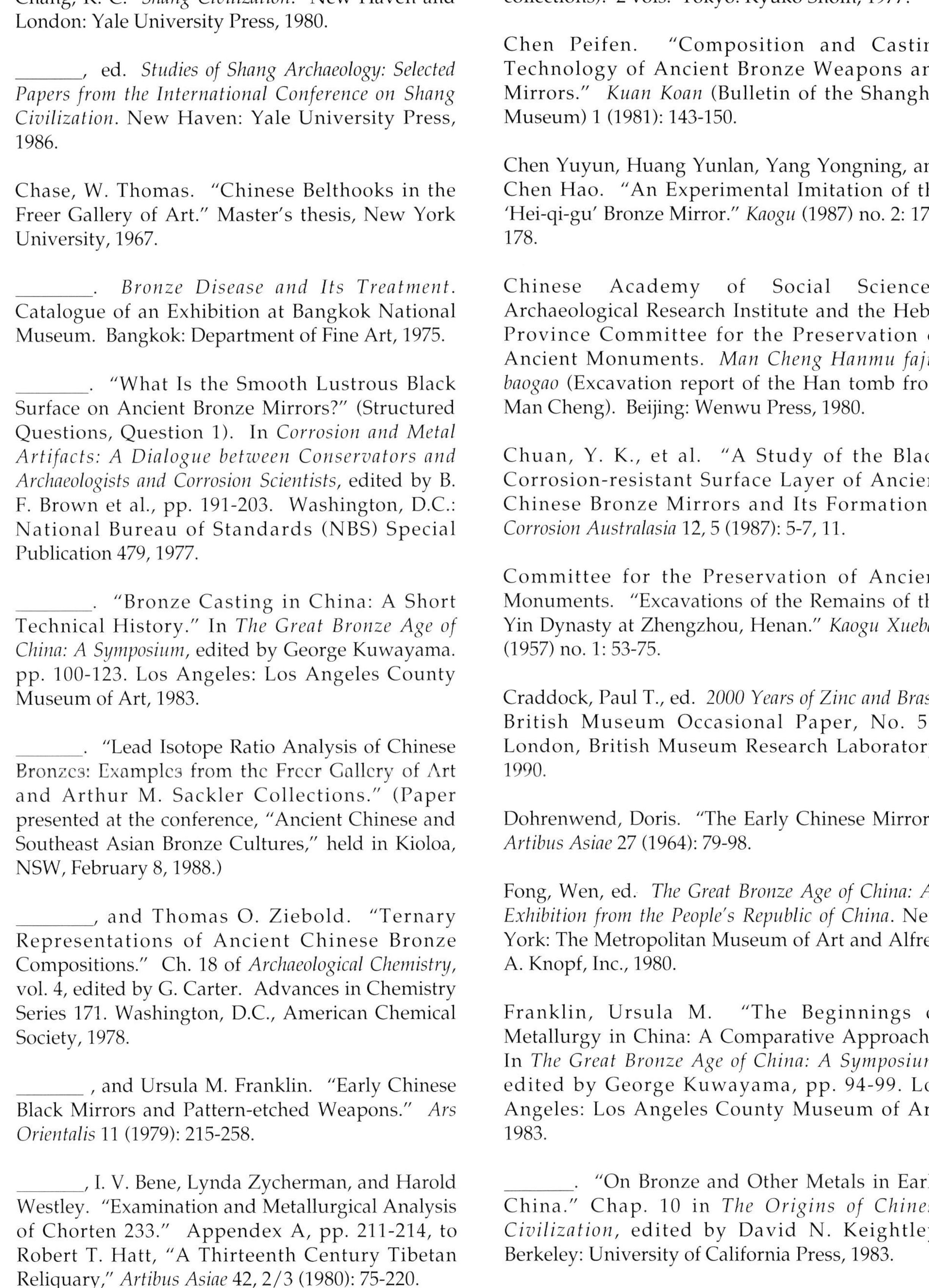

Chang, K. C. *Shang Civilization.* New Haven and London: Yale University Press, 1980.

_______, ed. *Studies of Shang Archaeology: Selected Papers from the International Conference on Shang Civilization.* New Haven: Yale University Press, 1986.

Chase, W. Thomas. "Chinese Belthooks in the Freer Gallery of Art." Master's thesis, New York University, 1967.

_______. *Bronze Disease and Its Treatment.* Catalogue of an Exhibition at Bangkok National Museum. Bangkok: Department of Fine Art, 1975.

_______. "What Is the Smooth Lustrous Black Surface on Ancient Bronze Mirrors?" (Structured Questions, Question 1). In *Corrosion and Metal Artifacts: A Dialogue between Conservators and Archaeologists and Corrosion Scientists*, edited by B. F. Brown et al., pp. 191-203. Washington, D.C.: National Bureau of Standards (NBS) Special Publication 479, 1977.

_______. "Bronze Casting in China: A Short Technical History." In *The Great Bronze Age of China: A Symposium*, edited by George Kuwayama. pp. 100-123. Los Angeles: Los Angeles County Museum of Art, 1983.

_______. "Lead Isotope Ratio Analysis of Chinese Bronzes: Examples from the Freer Gallery of Art and Arthur M. Sackler Collections." (Paper presented at the conference, "Ancient Chinese and Southeast Asian Bronze Cultures," held in Kioloa, NSW, February 8, 1988.)

_______, and Thomas O. Ziebold. "Ternary Representations of Ancient Chinese Bronze Compositions." Ch. 18 of *Archaeological Chemistry*, vol. 4, edited by G. Carter. Advances in Chemistry Series 171. Washington, D.C., American Chemical Society, 1978.

_______ , and Ursula M. Franklin. "Early Chinese Black Mirrors and Pattern-etched Weapons." *Ars Orientalis* 11 (1979): 215-258.

_______, I. V. Bene, Lynda Zycherman, and Harold Westley. "Examination and Metallurgical Analysis of Chorten 233." Appendex A, pp. 211-214, to Robert T. Hatt, "A Thirteenth Century Tibetan Reliquary," *Artibus Asiae* 42, 2/3 (1980): 75-220.

Chen Mengjia. *Yin Zhou qingtongqi fenlei tulu* (A corpus of Chinese bronzes in American collections). 2 vols. Tokyo: Kyūko Shoin, 1977.

Chen Peifen. "Composition and Casting Technology of Ancient Bronze Weapons and Mirrors." *Kuan Koan* (Bulletin of the Shanghai Museum) 1 (1981): 143-150.

Chen Yuyun, Huang Yunlan, Yang Yongning, and Chen Hao. "An Experimental Imitation of the 'Hei-qi-gu' Bronze Mirror." *Kaogu* (1987) no. 2: 175-178.

Chinese Academy of Social Sciences, Archaeological Research Institute and the Hebei Province Committee for the Preservation of Ancient Monuments. *Man Cheng Hanmu fajue baogao* (Excavation report of the Han tomb from Man Cheng). Beijing: Wenwu Press, 1980.

Chuan, Y. K., et al. "A Study of the Black Corrosion-resistant Surface Layer of Ancient Chinese Bronze Mirrors and Its Formation." *Corrosion Australasia* 12, 5 (1987): 5-7, 11.

Committee for the Preservation of Ancient Monuments. "Excavations of the Remains of the Yin Dynasty at Zhengzhou, Henan." *Kaogu Xuebao* (1957) no. 1: 53-75.

Craddock, Paul T., ed. *2000 Years of Zinc and Brass.* British Museum Occasional Paper, No. 50. London, British Museum Research Laboratory, 1990.

Dohrenwend, Doris. "The Early Chinese Mirror." *Artibus Asiae* 27 (1964): 79-98.

Fong, Wen, ed. *The Great Bronze Age of China: An Exhibition from the People's Republic of China.* New York: The Metropolitan Museum of Art and Alfred A. Knopf, Inc., 1980.

Franklin, Ursula M. "The Beginnings of Metallurgy in China: A Comparative Approach." In *The Great Bronze Age of China: A Symposium*, edited by George Kuwayama, pp. 94-99. Los Angeles: Los Angeles County Museum of Art, 1983.

_______. "On Bronze and Other Metals in Early China." Chap. 10 in *The Origins of Chinese Civilization*, edited by David N. Keightley. Berkeley: University of California Press, 1983.

Gettens, Rutherford John. *The Freer Chinese Bronzes.* Vol. 2, *Technical Studies.* Washington, D.C.: Smithsonian Institution, 1969.

Goodway, Martha, and Harold C. Conklin. "Quenched High-tin Bronzes from the Philippines." *Archaeomaterials* 2 (1987): 1-27.

Guo Baojun. *Shanbiaozhen yu Liulige*. Beijing: Kexue, 1959.

_______. *Shang Zhou tongqiqun zonghe yanjiu* (A comprehensive study of the Shang and Zhou bronze vessel group). Beijing: Wenwu Press, 1981.

Han Rubin. "Metalcasting in Ancient China." *Castings* (July-August 1986): 33-39.

_______. "Archaeometallurgy in China." *Materials Australasia* 18, no. 9 (1986): 4-6.

Henan Provincial Museum, Chinese Casting History Compilation Group. *Han dai die zhu* (Stack mold casting: the excavation and study of the Hong Fan kiln in Wen County). Beijing: Wenwu Press, 1978.

Hsu, Cho-yun. *Ancient China in Transition: An Analysis of Social Mobility, 722-222 B.C.* Stanford: Stanford University Press, 1965.

Hua Jueming. Introduction to *Shijie Yejin Fazhanshi* (A history of metallurgy) by R. F. Tylecote. Beijing: Kexue Jishu Wenxian Press, 1985.

Hubei Provincial Museum. *Suixian Zeng Hou Yi Mu* (The tomb of the Marquis of Zeng at Suixian). Beijing: Wenwu Press, 1980.

Institute of Archaeology, Chinese Academy of Social Sciences. *Yinxu Fu Hao Mu* (The tomb of Lady Hao at Yinxu in Anyang). Beijing: Wenwu Press, 1980.

Jacobsen, R. D. *Inlaid Bronzes of Pre-Imperial China: A Classic Tradition and Its Later Revivals.* Ann Arbor: University of Minnesota Press, 1986.

Kane, Virginia. "The Chronological Significance of the Inscribed Ancestor Dedication in the Production of Shang Dynasty Bronze Vessels." *Artibus Asiae* 25 (1973): 340-342.

_______. "The Independent Bronze Industries in the South of China Contemporary with the Shang and Western Zhou Dynasties." *Archives of Asian Art* 28 (1974-1975): 77-107.

Kerr, Rose. *Later Chinese Bronzes.* Victoria and Albert Museum, Far Eastern Series. London: Bamboo Publishing Company, Ltd., 1990.

Keyser, Barbara W. "Decor Replication in Two Late Chou Bronze *Chien*." *Ars Orientalis* 11 (1979): 127-162.

Knauth, Percy. *The Metalsmiths.* New York: Time-Life Books, 1974.

Lee, George J. *Selected Far Eastern Art in the Yale University Art Gallery.* New Haven: Yale University Press, 1970.

Li Chengguang, and Peng Qingye. "Excavations of Ancient Cemeteries in the Shahuqiao Region of Changsha." *Kaogu Xuebao* (1957) no. 4: 33-67.

Li Chi. *The Beginnings of Chinese Civilization.* Seattle: University of Washington Press, 1957.

Li Jinghua (Henan Bureau of Cultural Relics Archaeological Team). "The Casting Process of Han Dynasty Iron Ploughshares as Indicated by the Pottery Molds and Cores Unearthed from the Remains of Wancheng at Nanyang, Henan Province." *Wenwu* (1965) no. 7: 1-11.

Li Xueqin. *The Wonder of Chinese Bronzes.* Beijing: The Foreign Languages Press, 1980.

_______. *Eastern Zhou and Qin Civilizations*, trans. K. C. Chang. New Haven: Yale University Press, 1985.

Loehr, Max. "The Bronze Styles of the Anyang Period (1300-1028 B.C.)." *Archives of the Chinese Art Society of America* 7 (1953): 42-53.

_______. *Relics of Ancient China from the collection of Dr. Paul Singer.* New York: Asia Society, 1965.

_______. *Ritual Vessels of Bronze Age China.* New York: Asia Society, 1968.

Ma Chengyuan. *Ancient Chinese Bronzes.* Oxford: Oxford University Press, 1986.

Mabuchi, Hisao, and Yoshimitsu Hirao. "Lead Isotope Ratios of Lead Ores in East Asia in Relation to Bronze Artifacts." *Kōkogaku Zasshi* 73 (1987): 199-210, 245.

Mabuchi, Hisao, Yoshimitsu Hirao, and M. Nishida. "Lead Isotope Approach to the Understanding of Early Japanese Bronze Culture." *Archaeometry* 27 (1985): 131-159.

Meyers, Pieter, and Lore Holmes. "Technical Studies of Ancient Chinese Bronzes: Some Observations." In

The Great Bronze Age of China: A Symposium, edited by George Kuwayama, pp. 124-136. Los Angeles: Los Angeles County Museum of Art, 1983.

Needham, Joseph. *Science and Civilization in China*, vol. 4. Cambridge: Cambridge University Press, 1962.

Neill, Mary Gardner. *The Communion of Scholars: Chinese Art at Yale*. New York: China Institute in America, 1982.

Peng Zicheng, Deng Yanyao, and Liu Changfu. "The Application of the Lead Isotopes Ratio Method in Archaeological Research." *Kaogu* (1985) no. 11: 1032-1037.

Peng Zicheng, Wan Fubin, and Yao Shunan. "Tests on Ancient Bronze Drums of Beiliu Type by Lead Isotopes." *Kexue Tongbao* (1988), no. 11: 1027-1033.

Pope, John A., et al. *The Freer Chinese Bronzes*. Washington: Smithsonian Institution, 1967.

Rawson, Jessica. *The Chinese Bronzes of Yunnan*. London: Sidgwick and Jackson, 1983.

_______. *Chinese Bronzes: Art and Ritual*. London: The British Museum, 1987.

_______. *Western Zhou Bronzes from the Arthur M. Sackler Collections*. Cambridge, MA: Harvard University Press, 1990.

_______, and Emma Bunker. *Ancient Chinese and Ordos Bronzes*. Hong Kong: The Oriental Ceramic Society, 1990.

Rong Geng, *Shang Zhou yiqi tongkao* (The Bronzes of Shang and Zhou). 2 vols. Beijing: Harvard-Yenching Institute, 1941.

Selections of Chinese Art from Private Collections. New York: China Institute in America, 1986.

So, Jenny F. "*Hu* Vessels from Xinzheng: Toward a Definition of Chu Style." In *The Great Bronze Age of China: A Symposium*, edited by George Kuwayama, pp. 64-71. Los Angeles: Los Angeles County Museum of Art, 1983.

Soper, Alexander. "Early, Middle, and Late Shang: A Note." *Artibus Asiae* 28 (1966): 5-38.

Tan Derui. *The Splendid Craft of Lost Wax Casting in Ancient China*. Shanghai: Shanghai Scientific and Technical Literature Publishing House, 1989.

Thorp, Robert L. *The Son of Heaven: Imperial Arts of China*. Seattle: Son of Heaven Press, 1988.

_______, and Virginia Bower. *Spirit and Ritual*. New York: Metropolitan Museum of Art, 1982.

Tylecote, R. F. "Ancient Metallurgy in China." *The Metallurgist and Materials Technologist*, Sept. 1983, pp. 435-439.

Umehara, Sueji. *Seika = Ōbei shūcho Shina kodō seika* (Selected relics of ancient Chinese bronzes from collections in Europe and America). 7 vols. Kyoto, 1933.

_______. *Sengoku-shiki dōki no kenkyū* (*Etude des bronzes des royaumes combattants*). Kyoto, 1936.

_______. *Kodōki keitai no kōkogaku-teki kenkyū*. Kyoto, 1940.

Wan Jiabao. "Technical Studies of an Eastern Zhou Bronze *Ding*: Some Observations." *Zhugong* (Journal of the Chinese Foundrymen's Association) 57 (June 1988): 25-32.

Wang Zhangsui, Fan Chongzheng, Wang Shengjun, Zhang Maosen, Zhang Jingguo, and W. Thomas Chase. "Research on Powdery Corrosion of the Ancient Bell from Cai Hou Tomb." *Zhongguo Kexue* (1990) no. 6: 639-644.

Weber, Charles D. *Chinese Pictorial Bronze Vessels of the Late Chou Period*. Ascona: Artibus Asiae, 1968.

Weber, George W., Jr. *The Ornaments of Late Chou Bronzes*. New Brunswick: Rutgers University Press, 1973.

Wood, Nigel. "Ceramic Puzzles from China's Bronze Age." *New Scientist*, no. 1652 (18 February 1989): 50-53.

Wu Kunyi, and Li Xiuhui. "The Effect of Lead on the Properties of Bronze Drums." (Paper delivered at the International Conference on Bronze Drums, Kunming, Yunnan, China, September 1988.)

Zhu Qixin. "Bronze Vessels from a Spring and Autumn Period Tomb." *Orientations* (December, 1989): 54-57.

Zycherman, Lynda. "Technical Examination of Two Owl-Shaped *Tsun*." *Ars Orientalis* 13 (1982): 59-91.

CHINA INSTITUTE IN AMERICA

OFFICERS

Oscar L. Tang, Chairman
Clare Tweedy McMorris, Secretary
Frederick C. Chen, Treasurer

PRESIDENT

Charles P. Wang

BOARD OF TRUSTEES

Millie Chan
Morley L. Cho
Phyllis D. Collins
Herbert J. Coyne
JoAnn S. Delafield
Wen C. Fong
Houghton Freeman
John H.J. Guth
Robert L. Hoguet
Richard L. King
Marie Lee, Ex-officio
Anthony T. Limpe
William E. Little, Sr.
Henry Luce III
Elisabeth L. Moore
James A. Perkins
Eileen K.S. Pulling
Sophie Sa
Elizabeth Seitz
Phillips Talbot
Charlotte C. Weber
Marie-Hélène Weill
Wan-go H.C. Weng, President Emeritus
Mary deG. White
Von Sung Yang
Shyh-Jong Yue
Chi-ch'uan Wang, Emeritus

GALLERY COMMITTEE

Phyllis D. Collins, Chairperson
Wen C. Fong
Charlotte C. Weber
Marie-Hélène Weill
Wan-go H.C. Weng

ART COMMITTEE

Annette Juliano, Chairperson
Richard Barnhart
Myron S. Falk, Jr.
Vito Giacalone
Joan Hartman-Goldsmith
Jean Mailey
Mary Gardner Neill
Valrae Reynolds
Mary M. Tanenbaum
Suzanne Valenstein
James C. Y. Watt
Marie-Hélène Weill
Martie Young
Allen Wardwell

ART ADVISORY COMMITTEE

Theresa Tse Bartholomew
Claudia Brown
James Cahill
Betty Ecke
Wai-kam Ho
Donald Jenkins
Thomas Lawton
Lucy Lim
Yutaka Mino
Alfreda Murck
John Seto
Clarence F. Shangraw
Alexander C. Soper
Henry Trubner
Steven Weintraub
Marc F. Wilson
Wu Tung

CORPORATE CHAIRMAN'S COUNCIL

Asian Oceanic Capital Corporation
Bank Central Asia
The Bowery Savings Bank
BP America Inc.
Citibank, N.A.
Christie, Manson & Woods International, Inc.
Computer Associates International, Inc.
Corning Glass Works
The Equitable Financial Companies
Grumman International, Inc.
Hang Lung Development Company
The Hong Kong and Shanghai Banking Corporation
Johnson & Johnson International
George Little Management, Inc.
McCormick & Company
Merck Sharp & Dohme International
RJR Nabisco, Inc.
Pfizer International Inc.

Sotheby's
Starrett City-Grenadier Realty Corporation
Stemton Group, Inc.
Time-Warner, Inc.
Warner Communications Inc.
Wertheim Schroder & Co., Inc.

FOUNDATIONS

Asian Cultural Council
Chiang Ching-kuo Foundation for
International Scholarly Exchange
Corning Foundation
Herbert and Jeanine Coyne Foundation
Louise Crane Foundation
The Dillon Fund
Golden Family Foundation
Yu-Shan Han Irrevocable Trust
George Frederick Jewett Foundation
Albert Kunstadter Family Foundation
Lee Foundation, Singapore
The Henry Luce Foundation, Inc.
New York Community Trust
PepsiCo Foundation
The Shaw Foundation
The Starr Foundation
Taconic Foundation
Ho-Ching Yang Memorial Foundation
United Way of New York City

PATRONS

Marie-Hélène Weill, Chairperson,
Patrons and Sponsors
Frederick C. Chen
Mr. and Mrs. Thomas Tseng-tao Chen
John and Julia Curtis
Paul B. Day, Jr.
Mr. and Mrs. J. Dennis Delafield
John B. Elliott
Mr. and Mrs. John Exter
Mr. and Mrs. Myron S. Falk, Jr.
Mr. and Mrs. George J. Fan
Mr. and Mrs. Ivan Y.T. Feng
Constance Tang and Wen C. Fong
Houghton Freeman
Mr. and Mrs. John H.J. Guth
Mr. and Mrs. Robert L. Hoguet
Angela and Richard L. King
James J. Lally
Marie Lee
Sally Wong Leung
Mr. and Mrs. Anthony T. Limpe
Tracy Tang Limpe
William E. Little, Sr.
Henry Luce III
Mr. and Mrs. Howard McMorris II
Mrs. Maurice T. Moore
Mr. and Mrs. Thomas L. Pulling
Mr. and Mrs. Albert T. Quon
Mr. and Mrs. Richard J. Salisbury
Leslie Tang Schilling
Dr. and Mrs. Frederick Seitz
Mary M. and Charles J. Tanenbaum
Mr. and Mrs. Oscar L. Tang
Mrs. Gordon B. Tweedy
Mr. and Mrs. Chi-ch'uan Wang
Dr. and Mrs. John C. Weber
Leon J. Wender
Marie-Hélène and Guy A. Weill
James O. Welch, Jr.
Wan-go H.C. and Virginia D. Weng
Mary deG. White
Von Sung Yang

SPONSORS

Mr. and Mrs. Henry H. Arnhold
Millie Chan
Peter and Diana Chang
Pei-Yuan Chia
Roderick G.W. Chu
Catherine G. Curran
Eleanor T. Elliott
Gabriele Geier
Alice Shen and Baiyou Han
Mr. and Mrs. John N. Irwin, II
K.W. Liu
Liu Pi-Liang
Dr. Robert W. Lyons
Sally A. Miller
Mildred Mottahedeh
Martha B. Pickering
Ai-hua Qi
Mrs. Laurance S. Rockefeller
Mr. and Mrs. Peter L. Rosenberg
Hortense S. Sacks
Lillian S. Schloss
Mr. and Mrs. Michael B. Weisbrod
James S.L. Wu
Wellman H. Wu

VOLUNTEERS

Viola Baker
Mitchell Crespi
Rossi Fialla
Vertie Gibson
Jane Ho
Charles Johnson
Fong Y.H. Lee
Kathryn Lewis
Nancy Lu
Kaye Parlin
Janice Roland-Levy
Hortense S. Sacks
Nora Shih
Fania Stein
Suzanne Suba
Juanita Tabacman
Eulalia Tevriz
Louise Washington

EXHIBITION SPONSORS

This exhibition is made possible, in part, with public funds from the New York State Council on the Arts.

Additional funding for the exhibition and related programs were provided by:

Anonymous

Asian Cultural Council

Christie, Manson & Woods International, Inc.

Corning Foundation

Mr. and Mrs. Myron S. Falk, Jr.

Grumman International, Inc.

James J. Lally

The Henry Luce Foundation

Mr. and Mrs. Richard J. Salisbury

The Starr Foundation

and with the general support of the Patrons and Sponsors of China House Gallery.

Funding for this catalogue was generously provided by Charlotte C. and John C. Weber